catch on to
Cursive

A Whole Child Approach to Cursive Penmanship

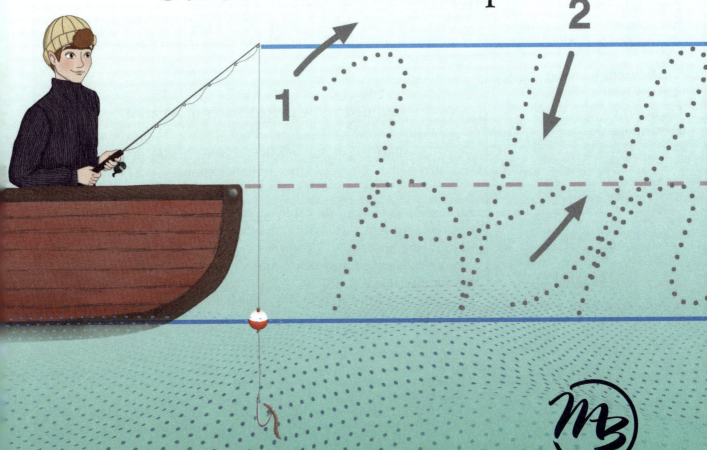

MasterBooks
CURRICULUM

Author:
Carrie Bailey

Illustrator:
Katie O'Dell

**Master Books
Creative Team:**

Editor: Craig Froman

Design: Jennifer Bauer

Cover Design:
Diana Bogardus

Copy Editors:
Judy Lewis
Willow Meek

Curriculum Review:
Kristen Pratt
Laura Welch
Diana Bogardus

First printing: October 2021

Copyright © 2021 by Carrie Bailey and Master Books®. All rights reserved. No part of this book may be reproduced, copied, broadcast, stored, or shared in any form whatsoever without written permission from the publisher, except in the case of brief quotations in articles and reviews. Permission for any other use of the material must be requested by email from the publisher at info@nlpg.com.

For information write:

    Master Books®, P.O. Box 726, Green Forest, AR 72638
Master Books® is a division of the New Leaf Publishing Group, Inc.

ISBN: 978-1-68344-244-8
ISBN: 978-1-61458-788-0 (digital)

Scripture quotations are from the ESV® Bible (The Holy Bible, English Standard Version®), copyright © 2001 by Crossway, a publishing ministry of Good News Publishers. Used by permission. All rights reserved.
NKJV — Scripture taken from the New King James Version. Copyright © 1982 by Thomas Nelson, Inc. Used by permission. All rights reserved.

Printed in the United States of America

Please visit our website for other great titles:
www.masterbooks.com

Permission is granted for copies of reproducible pages from this text to be made for use with immediate family members living in the same household. However, no part of this book may be reproduced, copied, broadcast, stored, or shared in any form beyond this use. Permission for any other use of the material must be requested by email from the publisher at info@nlpg.com.

Table of Contents

- Note to the Teacher 4
- Note from Skeeter 6
- Suggested Schedule 9
- Tackle Boxes 19
- Appendices
  - Activities for Older Students 451
  - Fishing Derby: Showcasing My Best Catch Worksheets 463
  - Course Badges 497
  - Gather Your Gear: Complete Supply List 505
  - Gather Your Gear Weekly List 506
  - Weigh-In Challenges 511
  - For Left-Handed Writers 525
  - Scope and Sequence 526
  - Cursive Letter Practice Chart 528

Please note that you can download the answer key to the puzzles included in this book at masterbooks.com/classroom-aids.

Note from the author: I like Charlotte Mason's philosophies, but I do not aspire to be her. I am an overall eclectic homeschool mom who happens to prefer a blend of several methodologies. I love learning that is developmentally based and that follows good instruction and modeling. This course is based on some of Charlotte Mason's ideas for teaching handwriting, as well as what I have personally learned in my training and teaching experience. Miss Mason would teach a slanted line and have her students practice it prior to having them write a letter A. This helped them learn the strokes needed before ever asking them to form a letter. I believe this method is effective in helping students learn penmanship. I also believe, as Miss Mason did, that subjects should not be separate, but rather intertwined. In this course, I have included exercises to help the students in developing their muscles to be successful with penmanship, Bible lessons, and a little science by using fishing as a subject. As someone who prefers to factor in a student's development, I did not want to cover children up with tons of practice or copying of letters without them having a good understanding of the strokes for the letters, as well the strength and stamina needed for penmanship. This course will help your students master the strokes needed for cursive penmanship while providing a fun theme with positive reinforcement. There is an alternate schedule with additional activities for older students or even for those who want to continue in practicing more.

Hello, teacher.

The Bible version used in this course is the ESV unless otherwise noted. Sometimes, I ask them to read from their Bibles or have used a version that was easier for them to read on their own or for copy work. Please choose the version your family prefers. It is very easy to adapt this course using your own version. Each week will have a prep page called "Tackle Box" with a corresponding number for each lesson which is for you and your student to prepare for the lesson.

I'd love to see your students' fishing derby showcases and artwork or activities they create. If you would, please share in the Master Books App using #ClubSkeeter.

In this course, the lessons have three main sections.

Gear Up!

You can't fish if you don't have the right gear and aren't prepared. Casting that pole and reeling in the big one takes strength. These exercises will build strength and warm up muscles for writing.

This section provides a how-to guide for making each letter, letter placement, spacing, and instruction and practice for students as they go through the course.

Every letter will be covered for three days. On the third day, there is a weigh-in section, and every few weeks, students will participate in a fishing derby where they review letters or Gear Up activities they have learned up to that point. This gives a fun way for built-in review and builds up their confidence. Watch for Weigh-In challenges throughout the course so they can complete the challenges.

Fishermen have contests, called fishing derbies, where they see who can catch the largest fish. Whoever catches the largest fish wins a prize. This is a time for students to review the letters and words they have learned and showcase their best work. They'll use the section in the back of the book labeled "Fishing Derby: Showcasing My Best Catch."

Evaluations for the Fishing Derby use colored weights to designate proficiency for students.

- **Green equals Proficient:** The student shows competency of the skills or movements and can apply them.
- **Yellow equals Basic:** The student has partial mastery and application of the skills and movements.
- **Red equals Below Basic:** The student has not mastered the skills needed and needs further practice and coaching.

They will have three guides throughout the course.

Skeeter helps with stories and encourages you, is your official guide to learning about fishing, but most importantly, guides you deeper in your walk with Christ.

Susie, Skeeter's sister, will help you know what supplies you need each week from the Gather Your Gear list as well as which day it is needed.

Susie's daughter, **Anna**, will be helping with reviewing and applying what you are learning through the weigh-in challenges.

The most important thing we can learn is God's Word. We'll be talking about:

- **Fishers of Men** — We'll talk about persevering, being patient, and applying effort like the disciples.

- **God's Creation** — When in nature, we can see the examples of God's handiwork. Students will see God's design in different fish.

- **Beatitudes/Sermon on the Mount** — Join me as we break down the Beatitudes into simpler terms and learn to apply them in our lives.

- **Parables** — Jesus told stories to help people understand spiritual things. We will look at His stories, or parables, so we can grow spiritually.

I hope you and your students have fun as you *Catch on to Cursive*.

Blessings,

Carrie

Carrie Bailey

Please read this note from your fishing guide, Skeeter, to your student(s).

Hello!

My name is Skeeter. I'm here to guide you in a nature adventure club called Club Skeeter. Writing in print or cursive neatly is called penmanship. This book is a guide to writing in cursive, or cursive penmanship. This book isn't only about cursive, but also about fishing, getting stronger, and learning more about God and His Word. You'll learn why writing in cursive is good for you, but for now, just know that this is a club full of adventure and fun. It's not all about pencil and paper, so get ready for the fun to begin.

In Club Skeeter, you'll earn badges as you complete weigh-in challenges from my niece, Anna. You can cut out the badges you earn and put them on an achievement board, if you like! Maybe on some poster board! I can't wait to see what badges you earn in Club Skeeter. Let's get this adventure going!

Your Guide,
Skeeter

Gear Up!

You will find Gear Up Activities throughout this cursive writing course. These activities go beyond the typical focus on hand-eye coordination when one is learning how to write. They are meant specifically for younger students taking the course as a fun way to help them with their overall growth, including balance, proper grip, focus, and more. You can mark off here as a student completes each activity. Note that the Bait & Tackle days are marked after each activity listed.

	Gear Up Activity	Focus Area
☐	**Making Waves:** Hold the pencil in one hand and make huge waves with your arm. Switch hands and do it with the other hand. Be sure to go back and forth, fast and slow, about 10 times each hand. (1.2, 5.5, 10.2, 14.1, 18.2, 23.2)	Crossing the mid-line; strengthening arm and back muscles for posture
☐	**Worm Squeezes:** Picking up worms is fun! Do worm squeezes by picking up the yarn worms with a pair of tweezers. (1.4, 6.2, 10.4, 14.3, 19.4, 29.2)	Strengthening fine motor skills
☐	**Anchor Up:** Stand with your feet about shoulder width apart. Bend over and pretend to pull up a heavy anchor. Give the anchor 10 good pulls all the way up. (2.3, 6.4, 14.4, 20.1, 24.2, 26.3, 29.3)	Core strength
☐	**Live Well Reaches:** Sit in a chair or side of a bathtub with your feet flat on the ground. Keep your feet spread apart. Bend over and touch the top of the ground between your feet as if you were touching the top of the live well in your boat. Do this 12 times. (2.5, 7.1, 11.1, 15.1, 25.2)	Core strength
☐	**Lighthouse Taps:** Lighthouses flash their lights, so we are going to tap for lighthouse flashes. Bring your pinky and thumb together to tap and open, tap and open, like a lighthouse flashes. Do this 12 times with both hands. (3.2, 7.3, 11.3, 15.3, 18.4, 26.5, 30.2, 34.3)	Strengthening fine motor skills
☐	**Paddle the Boat:** Sit in a chair or on the side of a bathtub with your feet flat on the ground. Pretend to paddle the boat. Make sure you swap sides so your boat doesn't get off course! Give a good 15 total strokes of the paddle for each side. (3.4, 7.5, 11.5, 15.5, 20.5, 23.5, 34.5)	Core strength; crossing the mid-line; upper arm strength
☐	**Don't Hit the Bridge:** The ships in the river need to get through. Place your hands flat on the ground with tips of toes on the ground and body lifted to be the bridge. Hold this for 10–15 seconds. (4.1, 8.2, 12.2, 16.2, 21.4, 27.4)	Core strength
☐	**Hook the Fish:** Also called Hook the Crawdads, Hook the Boot, and Hook the Fly. At the bottom of the page is a row of fish. Open paper clips and secure a paper clip to each fish. (4.2, 8.3, 12.3, 16.3, 21.1, 27.5, 31.2)	Strengthening fine motor skills

☐		**Hoist the Sails:** These are called side planks and are like a side pushup that holds your body up. Lay on your side, lift your body up with the arm closest to the ground. Your foot should be on its side on the ground. Your body makes a triangle shape like a sail. Hold the position for 8 seconds, relax, and repeat two times. Do both sides of your body. (4.3, 12.4, 18.3, 23.3, 28.1, 35.4)	Core strength
☐		**Aim and Cast:** Place a piece of paper or sticky note on a door or wall about eye level. You can make a target on it if you'd like. Take about 10 steps back and try to AIM and CAST the ball to hit the target. If you miss three times, you can step forward one step. Try to hit the paper/target in the middle at least three times in a row. (4.5, 8.4, 13.1, 16.4, 21.2, 24.5, 31.3, 36.2)	Eye-hand control, gross & fine motor control; arm strength
☐		**Lures in Mud:** Push the small objects into dough. Be sure to use your fingers to get them started and your thumb to get them all the way in. Push objects in with each hand at least 5 times. (5.1, 8.5, 13.2, 23.4, 35.5)	Strengthening fine motor skills (thumb opposition)
☐		**Walk the Plank:** Use painter's tape, a rope, or sidewalk chalk to make a long line, about 6 feet long. Walk the Plank by balancing on the line with one foot in front of the other. Do this three times. Don't fall in! There might be gators in that water! (5.2, 9.1, 13.3, 17.1, 22.2, 28.5, 36.1)	Core strength; crossing the midline; gross motor control
☐		**Don't Tip the Boat:** Balance on a bicycle, scooter, or skateboard for 15 seconds. (5.4, 9.3, 13.5, 17.3)	Core strength
☐		**The Eye of the Hook:** If you can, use a pushpin in the tip of an eraser or just a pencil with an eraser. Hold the pencil straight up and down in front of your nose. Bring it in slowly as you keep your eyes on the pin or eraser. Keep your focus. See how close you can bring it in before you see two of it. Hold this for 10 seconds, release, then do it two more times. (8.1, 16.1, 19.3, 24.1, 30.5)	Visual tracking
☐		**Marble in the Whirlpool:** Using a plastic lid with a lip or a round cake pan; place a marble inside. Have someone move the lid/pan so the marble rolls in the inside edge back and forth and eventually all the way around in a circle. Follow the marble with your eyes, but do not move your head. Move only your eyes as you follow the marble back and forth. Do this for one minute. (9.5, 17.5, 22.3, 26.1, 32.4)	Visual tracking
☐		**Crawdad Crawl.** You will use a tennis ball or a ball that size. You have two "pinchers" like the crawdad, which are your thumb and pointing finger. Start with the ball beside your foot, using only your two pinchers (thumb and pointer finger), roll the ball up the side of your leg to your hip, across your tummy, and back down the side of the other leg. This may be difficult at first, but it will get easier with practice. Do this three times. (20.3, 22.4, 27.1, 28.2, 32.2, 34.4, 36.5)	Fine motor control

Student Schedule

	Day	Assignment		Due Date	✓	Grade
		Younger Student Schedule	**Older Student Schedule**			
		First Semester–First Quarter				
Week 1	Day 1	Tackle Box 1 • Bait & Tackle 1.1 • pages 19–22	Tackle Box 1 • Bait & Tackle 1.1–2.2 pages 19–36			
	Day 2	Bait & Tackle 1.2 pages 23–24	Bait & Tackle 2.3–2.4 pages 37–40			
	Day 3	Bait & Tackle 1.3 pages 25–26	Bait & Tackle 2.5 • pages 41–42 Activity 1 • page 451			
	Day 4	Bait & Tackle 1.4 pages 27–28	Tackle Box 3 • Bait & Tackle 3.1–3.2 pages 43–48			
	Day 5	Bait & Tackle 1.5 pages 29–30	Bait & Tackle 3.3–3.4 pages 49–52			
Week 2	Day 6	Tackle Box 2 • Bait & Tackle 2.1 • pages 31–34	Bait & Tackle 3.5 • pages 53–54 Activity 2 • page 451			
	Day 7	Bait & Tackle 2.2 pages 35–36	Tackle Box 4 • Bait & Tackle 4.1–4.2 pages 55–60			
	Day 8	Bait & Tackle 2.3 pages 37–38	Bait & Tackle 4.3–4.4 pages 61–64			
	Day 9	Bait & Tackle 2.4 pages 39–40	Bait & Tackle 4.5 • pages 65–66 Activity 3 • page 451			
	Day 10	Bait & Tackle 2.5 pages 41–42	Tackle Box 5 • Bait & Tackle 5.1–5.2 pages 67–72			
Week 3	Day 11	Tackle Box 3 • Bait & Tackle 3.1 • pages 43–46	Bait & Tackle 5.3–5.4 pages 73–76			
	Day 12	Bait & Tackle 3.2 pages 47–48	Bait & Tackle 5.5 • pages 77–78 Activity 4 • page 451			
	Day 13	Bait & Tackle 3.3 pages 49–50	Tackle Box 6 • Bait & Tackle 6.1–6.2 pages 79–84			
	Day 14	Bait & Tackle 3.4 pages 51–52	Bait & Tackle 6.3–6.4 pages 85–88			
	Day 15	Bait & Tackle 3.5 pages 53–54	Bait & Tackle 6.5 • pages 89–90 Activity 5 • page 451			
Week 4	Day 16	Tackle Box 4 • Bait & Tackle 4.1 • pages 55–58	Tackle Box 7 • Bait & Tackle 7.1–7.2 pages 91–96			
	Day 17	Bait & Tackle 4.2 pages 59–60	Bait & Tackle 7.3–7.4 pages 97–100			
	Day 18	Bait & Tackle 4.3 pages 61–62	Bait & Tackle 7.5 • pages 101–102 Activity 6 • page 451			
	Day 19	Bait & Tackle 4.4 pages 63–64	Tackle Box 8 • Bait & Tackle 8.1–8.2 pages 103–108			
	Day 20	Bait & Tackle 4.5 pages 65–66	Bait & Tackle 8.3–8.4 pages 109–112			

	Day	Assignment		Due Date	✓	Grade
Week 5	Day 21	Tackle Box 5 • Bait & Tackle 5.1 • pages 67–70	Bait & Tackle 8.5 • pages 113–114 Activity 7 • page 451			
	Day 22	Bait & Tackle 5.2 pages 71–72	Tackle Box 9 • Bait & Tackle 9.1–9.2 pages 115–120			
	Day 23	Bait & Tackle 5.3 pages 73–74	Bait & Tackle 9.3–9.4 pages 121–124			
	Day 24	Bait & Tackle 5.4 pages 75–76	Bait & Tackle 9.5 • pages 125–126 Activity 8 • page 451			
	Day 25	Bait & Tackle 5.5 pages 77–78	Tackle Box 10 • Bait & Tackle 10.1–10.2 pages 127–132			
Week 6	Day 26	Tackle Box 6 • Bait & Tackle 6.1 • pages 79–82	Bait & Tackle 10.3–10.4 pages 133–136			
	Day 27	Bait & Tackle 6.2 pages 83–84	Bait & Tackle 10.5 • pages 137–138 Activity 9 • page 451			
	Day 28	Bait & Tackle 6.3 pages 85–86	Tackle Box 11 • Bait & Tackle 11.1–11.2 pages 139–144			
	Day 29	Bait & Tackle 6.4 pages 87–88	Bait & Tackle 11.3–11.4 pages 145–148			
	Day 30	Bait & Tackle 6.5 pages 89–90	Bait & Tackle 11.5 • pages 149–150 Activity 10 • page 452			
Week 7	Day 31	Tackle Box 7 • Bait & Tackle 7.1 • pages 91–94	Tackle Box 12 • Bait & Tackle 12.1–12.2 pages 151–156			
	Day 32	Bait & Tackle 7.2 pages 95–96	Bait & Tackle 12.3–12.4 pages 157–160			
	Day 33	Bait & Tackle 7.3 pages 97–98	Bait & Tackle 12.5 • pages 161–162 Activity 11 • page 452			
	Day 34	Bait & Tackle 7.4 pages 99–100	Tackle Box 13 • Bait & Tackle 13.1–13.2 pages 163–168			
	Day 35	Bait & Tackle 7.5 pages 101–102	Bait & Tackle 13.3–13.4 pages 169–172			
Week 8	Day 36	Tackle Box 8 • Bait & Tackle 8.1 • pages 103–106	Bait & Tackle 13.5 • pages 173–174 Activity 12 • page 452			
	Day 37	Bait & Tackle 8.2 pages 107–108	Tackle Box 14 • Bait & Tackle 14.1–14.2 pages 175–180			
	Day 38	Bait & Tackle 8.3 pages 109–110	Bait & Tackle 14.3–14.4 pages 181–184			
	Day 39	Bait & Tackle 8.4 pages 111–112	Bait & Tackle 14.5 • pages 185–186 Activity 13 • page 452			
	Day 40	Bait & Tackle 8.5 pages 113–114	Tackle Box 15 • Bait & Tackle 15.1–15.2 pages 187–192			

	Day	Assignment		Due Date	✓	Grade
Week 9	Day 41	Tackle Box 9 • Bait & Tackle 9.1 • pages 115–118	Bait & Tackle 15.3–15.4 pages 193–196			
	Day 42	Bait & Tackle 9.2 pages 119–120	Bait & Tackle 15.5 • pages 197–198 Activity 14 • page 452			
	Day 43	Bait & Tackle 9.3 pages 121–122	Tackle Box 16 • Bait & Tackle 16.1–16.2 pages 199–204			
	Day 44	Bait & Tackle 9.4 pages 123–124	Bait & Tackle 16.3–16.4 pages 205–208			
	Day 45	Bait & Tackle 9.5 pages 125–126	Bait & Tackle 16.5 • pages 209–210 Activity 15 • page 452			

First Semester–Second Quarter

	Day	Assignment		Due Date	✓	Grade
Week 1	Day 46	Tackle Box 10 • Bait & Tackle 10.1 • pages 127–130	Tackle Box 17 • Bait & Tackle 17.1–17.2 pages 211–216			
	Day 47	Bait & Tackle 10.2 pages 131–132	Bait & Tackle 17.3–17.4 pages 217–220			
	Day 48	Bait & Tackle 10.3 pages 133–134	Bait & Tackle 17.5 • pages 221–222 Activity 16 • page 452			
	Day 49	Bait & Tackle 10.4 pages 135–136	Tackle Box 18 • Bait & Tackle 18.1–18.2 pages 223–228			
	Day 50	Bait & Tackle 10.5 pages 137–138	Bait & Tackle 18.3–18.4 pages 229–232			
Week 2	Day 51	Tackle Box 11 • Bait & Tackle 11.1 • pages 139–142	Bait & Tackle 18.5 • pages 233–234 Activity 17 • page 453			
	Day 52	Bait & Tackle 11.2 pages 143–144	Tackle Box 19 • Bait & Tackle 19.1–19.2 pages 235–240			
	Day 53	Bait & Tackle 11.3 pages 145–146	Bait & Tackle 19.3–19.4 pages 241–244			
	Day 54	Bait & Tackle 11.4 pages 147–148	Bait & Tackle 19.5 • pages 245–246 Activity 18 • page 453			
	Day 55	Bait & Tackle 11.5 pages 149–150	Tackle Box 20 • Bait & Tackle 20.1–20.2 pages 247–252			
Week 3	Day 56	Tackle Box 12 • Bait & Tackle 12.1 • pages 151–154	Bait & Tackle 20.3–20.4 pages 253–256			
	Day 57	Bait & Tackle 12.2 pages 155–156	Bait & Tackle 20.5 • pages 257–258 Activity 19 • page 453			
	Day 58	Bait & Tackle 12.3 pages 157–158	Tackle Box 21 • Bait & Tackle 21.1–21.2 pages 259–264			
	Day 59	Bait & Tackle 12.4 pages 159–160	Bait & Tackle 21.3–21.4 pages 265–268			
	Day 60	Bait & Tackle 12.5 pages 161–162	Bait & Tackle 21.5 • pages 269–270 Activity 20 • page 453			

	Day	Assignment		Due Date	✓	Grade
Week 4	Day 61	Tackle Box 13 • Bait & Tackle 13.1 • pages 163–166	Tackle Box 22 • Bait & Tackle 22.1–22.2 pages 271–276			
	Day 62	Bait & Tackle 13.2 pages 167–168	Bait & Tackle 22.3–22.4 pages 277–280			
	Day 63	Bait & Tackle 13.3 pages 169–170	Bait & Tackle 22.5 • pages 281–282 Activity 21 • page 453			
	Day 64	Bait & Tackle 13.4 pages 171–172	Tackle Box 23 • Bait & Tackle 23.1–23.2 pages 283–288			
	Day 65	Bait & Tackle 13.5 pages 173–174	Bait & Tackle 23.3–23.4 pages 289–292			
Week 5	Day 66	Tackle Box 14 • Bait & Tackle 14.1 • pages 175–178	Bait & Tackle 23.5 • pages 293–294 Activity 22 • page 453			
	Day 67	Bait & Tackle 14.2 pages 179–180	Tackle Box 24 • Bait & Tackle 24.1–24.2 pages 295–300			
	Day 68	Bait & Tackle 14.3 pages 181–182	Bait & Tackle 24.3–24.4 pages 301–304			
	Day 69	Bait & Tackle 14.4 pages 183–184	Bait & Tackle 24.5 • pages 305–306 Activity 23 • page 453			
	Day 70	Bait & Tackle 14.5 pages 185–186	Tackle Box 25 • Bait & Tackle 25.1–25.2 pages 307–312			
Week 6	Day 71	Tackle Box 15 • Bait & Tackle 15.1 • pages 187–190	Tackle Box 25 • Bait & Tackle 25.3–25.4 pages 313–316			
	Day 72	Bait & Tackle 15.2 pages 191–192	Bait & Tackle 25.5 • pages 317–318 Activity 24 • page 453			
	Day 73	Bait & Tackle 15.3 pages 193–194	Tackle Box 26 • Bait & Tackle 26.1–26.2 pages 319–324			
	Day 74	Bait & Tackle 15.4 pages 195–196	Bait & Tackle 26.3–26.4 pages 325–328			
	Day 75	Bait & Tackle 15.5 pages 197–198	Bait & Tackle 26.5 • pages 329–330 Activity 25 • page 453			
Week 7	Day 76	Tackle Box 16 • Bait & Tackle 16.1 • pages 199–202	Tackle Box 27 • Bait & Tackle 27.1–27.2 pages 331–336			
	Day 77	Bait & Tackle 16.2 pages 203–204	Bait & Tackle 27.3–27.4 pages 337–340			
	Day 78	Bait & Tackle 16.3 pages 205–206	Bait & Tackle 27.5 • pages 341–342 Activity 26 • page 453			
	Day 79	Bait & Tackle 16.4 pages 207–208	Tackle Box 28 • Bait & Tackle 28.1–28.2 pages 343–348			
	Day 80	Bait & Tackle 16.5 pages 209–210	Bait & Tackle 28.3–28.4 pages 349–352			

	Day	Assignment		Due Date	✓	Grade
Week 8	Day 81	Tackle Box 17 • Bait & Tackle 17.1 • pages 211–214	Bait & Tackle 28.5 • pages 353–354 Activity 27 • page 453			
	Day 82	Bait & Tackle 17.2 pages 215–216	Tackle Box 29 • Bait & Tackle 29.1–29.2 pages 355–360			
	Day 83	Bait & Tackle 17.3 pages 217–218	Bait & Tackle 29.3–29.4 pages 361–364			
	Day 84	Bait & Tackle 17.4 pages 219–220	Bait & Tackle 29.5 • pages 365–366 Activity 28 • page 454			
	Day 85	Bait & Tackle 17.5 pages 221–222	Tackle Box 30 • Bait & Tackle 30.1–30.2 pages 367–372			
Week 9	Day 86	Tackle Box 18 • Bait & Tackle 18.1 • pages 223–226	Bait & Tackle 30.3–30.4 pages 373–376			
	Day 87	Bait & Tackle 18.2 pages 227–228	Bait & Tackle 30.5 • pages 377–378 Activity 29 • page 454			
	Day 88	Bait & Tackle 18.3 pages 229–230	Tackle Box 31 • Bait & Tackle 31.1–31.2 pages 379–384			
	Day 89	Bait & Tackle 18.4 pages 231–232	Bait & Tackle 31.3–31.4 pages 385–388			
	Day 90	Bait & Tackle 18.5 pages 233–234	Bait & Tackle 31.5 • pages 389–390 Activity 30 • page 454			
		Mid–Term Grade				

Please note that you can download the answer key to the puzzles included in this book at masterbooks.com/classroom-aids.

Student Schedule

	Day	Assignment		Due Date	✓	Grade
		Younger Student Schedule	**Older Student Schedule**			
		Second Semester–First Quarter				
Week 1	Day 91	Tackle Box 19 • Bait & Tackle 19.1 • pages 235–238	Tackle Box 32 • Bait & Tackle 32.1–32.2 pages 391–396			
	Day 92	Bait & Tackle 19.2 pages 239–240	Bait & Tackle 32.3–32.4 pages 397–400			
	Day 93	Bait & Tackle 19.3 pages 241–242	Bait & Tackle 32.5 • pages 401–402 Activity 31 • page 454			
	Day 94	Bait & Tackle 19.4 pages 243–244	Tackle Box 33 • Bait & Tackle 33.1–33.2 pages 403–408			
	Day 95	Bait & Tackle 19.5 pages 245–246	Bait & Tackle 33.3–33.4 pages 409–412			
Week 2	Day 96	Tackle Box 20 • Bait & Tackle 20.1 • pages 247–250	Bait & Tackle 33.5 • pages 413–414 Activity 32 • page 454			
	Day 97	Bait & Tackle 20.2 pages 251–252	Tackle Box 34 • Bait & Tackle 34.1–34.2 pages 415–420			
	Day 98	Bait & Tackle 20.3 pages 253–254	Bait & Tackle 34.3–34.4 pages 421–424			
	Day 99	Bait & Tackle 20.4 pages 255–256	Bait & Tackle 34.5 • pages 425–426 Activity 33 • page 454			
	Day 100	Bait & Tackle 20.5 pages 257–258	Tackle Box 35 • Bait & Tackle 35.1–35.2 pages 427–432			
Week 3	Day 101	Tackle Box 21 • Bait & Tackle 21.1 • pages 259–262	Bait & Tackle 35.3–35.4 pages 433–436			
	Day 102	Bait & Tackle 21.2 pages 263–264	Bait & Tackle 35.5 • pages 437–438 Activity 34 • page 454			
	Day 103	Bait & Tackle 21.3 pages 265–266	Tackle Box 36 • Bait & Tackle 36.1–36.2 pages 439–444			
	Day 104	Bait & Tackle 21.4 pages 267–268	Bait & Tackle 36.3–36.4 pages 445–448			
	Day 105	Bait & Tackle 21.5 pages 269–270	Bait & Tackle 36.5 • pages 449–450 Activity 35 • page 454			
Week 4	Day 106	Tackle Box 22 • Bait & Tackle 22.1 • pages 271–274	Activity 36 • page 454			
	Day 107	Bait & Tackle 22.2 pages 275–276	Activity 37 • page 455			
	Day 108	Bait & Tackle 22.3 pages 277–278	Activity 38 • page 455			
	Day 109	Bait & Tackle 22.4 pages 279–280	Activity 39 • page 455			
	Day 110	Bait & Tackle 22.5 pages 281–282	Activity 40 • page 455			

	Day	Assignment		Due Date	✓	Grade
Week 5	Day 111	Tackle Box 23 • Bait & Tackle 23.1 • pages 283–286	Activity 41 • page 455			
	Day 112	Bait & Tackle 23.2 pages 287–288	Activity 42 • page 455			
	Day 113	Bait & Tackle 23.3 pages 289–290	Activity 43 • page 455			
	Day 114	Bait & Tackle 23.4 pages 291–292	Activity 44 • page 455			
	Day 115	Bait & Tackle 23.5 pages 293–294	Activity 45 • page 455			
Week 6	Day 116	Tackle Box 24 • Bait & Tackle 24.1 • pages 295–298	Activity 46 • page 455			
	Day 117	Bait & Tackle 24.2 pages 299–300	Activity 47 • page 455			
	Day 118	Bait & Tackle 24.3 pages 301–302	Activity 48 • page 455			
	Day 119	Bait & Tackle 24.4 pages 303–304	Activity 49 • page 455			
	Day 120	Bait & Tackle 24.5 pages 305–306	Activity 50 • page 455			
Week 7	Day 121	Tackle Box 25 • Bait & Tackle 25.1 • pages 307–310	Activity 51 • page 455			
	Day 122	Bait & Tackle 25.2 pages 311–312	Activity 52 • page 456			
	Day 123	Bait & Tackle 25.3 pages 313–314	Activity 53 • page 456			
	Day 124	Bait & Tackle 25.4 pages 315–316	Activity 54 • page 456			
	Day 125	Bait & Tackle 25.5 pages 317–318	Activity 55 • page 456			
Week 8	Day 126	Tackle Box 26 • Bait & Tackle 26.1 • pages 319–322	Activity 56 • page 456			
	Day 127	Bait & Tackle 26.2 pages 323–324	Activity 57 • page 456			
	Day 128	Bait & Tackle 26.3 pages 325–326	Activity 58 • page 456			
	Day 129	Bait & Tackle 26.4 pages 327–328	Activity 59 • page 456			
	Day 130	Bait & Tackle 26.5 pages 329–330	Activity 60 • page 456			

	Day	Assignment		Due Date	✓	Grade
Week 9	Day 131	Tackle Box 27 • Bait & Tackle 27.1 • pages 331–334	Activity 61 • page 456			
	Day 132	Bait & Tackle 27.2 pages 335–336	Activity 62 • page 456			
	Day 133	Bait & Tackle 27.3 pages 337–338	Activity 63 • page 456			
	Day 134	Bait & Tackle 27.4 pages 339–340	Activity 64 • page 457			
	Day 135	Bait & Tackle 27.5 pages 341–342	Activity 65 • page 457			
		Second Semester–Second Quarter				
Week 1	Day 136	Tackle Box 28 • Bait & Tackle 28.1 • pages 343–346	Activity 66 • page 457			
	Day 137	Bait & Tackle 28.2 pages 347–348	Activity 67 • page 457			
	Day 138	Bait & Tackle 28.3 pages 349–350	Activity 68 • page 457			
	Day 139	Bait & Tackle 28.4 pages 351–352	Activity 69 • page 457			
	Day 140	Bait & Tackle 28.5 pages 353–354	Activity 70 • page 457			
Week 2	Day 141	Tackle Box 29 • Bait & Tackle 29.1 • pages 355–358	Activity 71 • page 457			
	Day 142	Bait & Tackle 29.2 pages 359–360	Activity 72 • page 457			
	Day 143	Bait & Tackle 29.3 pages 361–362	Activity 73 • page 457			
	Day 144	Bait & Tackle 29.4 pages 363–364	Activity 74 • page 457			
	Day 145	Bait & Tackle 29.5 pages 365–366	Activity 75 • page 457			
Week 3	Day 146	Tackle Box 30 • Bait & Tackle 30.1 • pages 367–370	Activity 76 • page 458			
	Day 147	Bait & Tackle 30.2 pages 371–372	Activity 77 • page 458			
	Day 148	Bait & Tackle 30.3 pages 373–374	Activity 78 • page 458			
	Day 149	Bait & Tackle 30.4 pages 375–376	Activity 79 • page 458			
	Day 150	Bait & Tackle 30.5 pages 377–378	Activity 80 • page 458			

	Day	Assignment		Due Date	✓	Grade
Week 4	Day 151	Tackle Box 31 • Bait & Tackle 31.1 • pages 379–382	Activity 81 • page 458			
	Day 152	Bait & Tackle 31.2 pages 383–384	Activity 82 • page 458			
	Day 153	Bait & Tackle 31.3 pages 385–386	Activity 83 • page 458			
	Day 154	Bait & Tackle 31.4 pages 387–388	Activity 84 • page 458			
	Day 155	Bait & Tackle 31.5 pages 389–390	Activity 85 • page 458			
Week 5	Day 156	Tackle Box 32 • Bait & Tackle 32.1 • pages 391–394	Activity 86 • page 458			
	Day 157	Bait & Tackle 32.2 pages 395–396	Activity 87 • page 458			
	Day 158	Bait & Tackle 32.3 pages 397–398	Activity 88 • page 458			
	Day 159	Bait & Tackle 32.4 pages 399–400	Activity 89 • page 459			
	Day 160	Bait & Tackle 32.5 pages 401–402	Activity 90 • page 459			
Week 6	Day 161	Tackle Box 33 • Bait & Tackle 33.1 • pages 403–406	Activity 91 • page 459			
	Day 162	Bait & Tackle 33.2 pages 407–408	Activity 92 • page 459			
	Day 163	Bait & Tackle 33.3 pages 409–410	Activity 93 • page 459			
	Day 164	Bait & Tackle 33.4 pages 411–412	Activity 94 • page 459			
	Day 165	Bait & Tackle 33.5 pages 413–414	Activity 95 • page 459			
Week 7	Day 166	Tackle Box 34 • Bait & Tackle 34.1 • pages 415–418	Activity 96 • page 460			
	Day 167	Bait & Tackle 34.2 pages 419–420	Activity 97 • page 460			
	Day 168	Bait & Tackle 34.3 pages 421–422	Activity 98 • page 460			
	Day 169	Bait & Tackle 34.4 pages 423–424	Activity 99 • page 460			
	Day 170	Bait & Tackle 34.5 pages 425–426	Activity 100 • page 460			

	Day	Assignment		Due Date	✓	Grade
Week 8	Day 171	Tackle Box 35 • Bait & Tackle 35.1 • pages 427–430	Activity 101 • page 460			
	Day 172	Bait & Tackle 35.2 pages 431–432	Activity 102 • page 460			
	Day 173	Bait & Tackle 35.3 pages 433–434	Activity 103 • page 460			
	Day 174	Bait & Tackle 35.4 pages 435–436	Activity 104 • page 460			
	Day 175	Bait & Tackle 35.5 pages 437–438	Activity 105 • page 461			
Week 9	Day 176	Tackle Box 36 • Bait & Tackle 36.1 • pages 439–442	Activity 106 • page 461			
	Day 177	Bait & Tackle 36.2 pages 443–444	Activity 107 • page 461			
	Day 178	Bait & Tackle 36.3 pages 445–446	Activity 108 • page 461			
	Day 179	Bait & Tackle 36.4 pages 447–448	Activity 109 • page 461			
	Day 180	Bait & Tackle 36.5 pages 449–450	Activity 110 • page 461			
		Final Grade				

Name _____

TACKLE BOX 1

> Hi, I'm Susie, and this is my daughter Anna. You already met my little brother, Skeeter. This page is to help you prepare for each lesson. A tackle box holds extra fishing gear much like this page has supplies and information for the lessons. I am here to host the fishing derbies and help you navigate the following:
>
> - Learn new fishing terms and supplies
> - Gather Your Gear — list your supplies
> - Weigh-in for each challenge

> My mom's helping me earn my fishing badge for my Nature & Character Club at my church. Our club helps me learn about all things nature-related as well as helps us build character. We've created a club just for the kids using *Catch on to Cursive* called Club Skeeter. You'll be earning badges by completing weigh-in challenges just like me!

> Check out the supplies for each day under Gather Your Gear. Many of the supplies in the course are used more than once, so be sure to keep them in a safe place. You will always want a Bible and a pencil for each day. Today you're learning the parts of a fishing pole.

Day 2:
☐ 18-inch piece of ribbon
☐ An unsharpened pencil (keep for the remainder of the course)

Day 5:
☐ Tweezers
☐ Yarn cut into 4-inch pieces (picking up worms)

Tackle Box 1   19

Today you're learning the parts of a fishing pole.

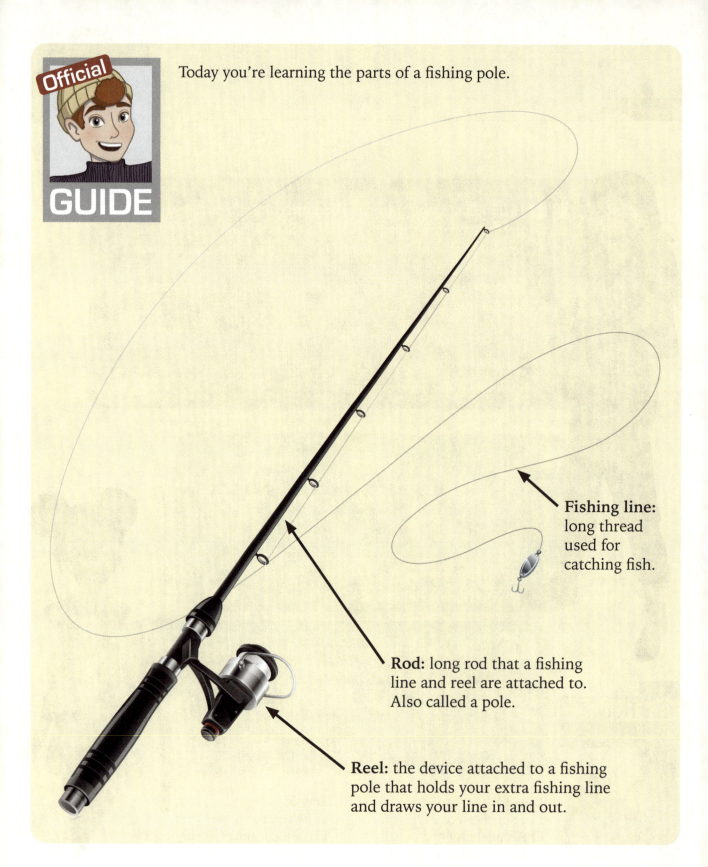

Fishing line: long thread used for catching fish.

Rod: long rod that a fishing line and reel are attached to. Also called a pole.

Reel: the device attached to a fishing pole that holds your extra fishing line and draws your line in and out.

Name _____

Bait & Tackle 1.1

" Hi! I'm ready to help guide you on your fishing expedition. Each day, you will have 3–4 sections to complete. This first week, we will just be getting your feet wet — that means introducing you to all the new things. Check out this first section called Gear Up. Writing is a lot like fishing. You need to be strong, so Gear Up will help you build your muscles. "

Gear Up!

Read Luke 5:4–6. The disciple's jobs were fishermen. They had worked hard all night but caught nothing. Notice when they followed the instructions given, and trusted the Lord to help them, they received the reward. Effort and perseverance pay off. Put the effort in and do your best, pray and ask God to help you, and the reward will come. Let's get started!

Keep the Water Flowing: Try connecting the dots without lifting your pencil. Keep smooth fluid lines like water.

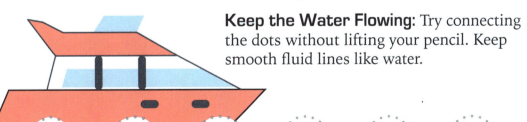

Bait & Tackle 1.1 21

Trace the fishing lines to help the fishermen find their fish.

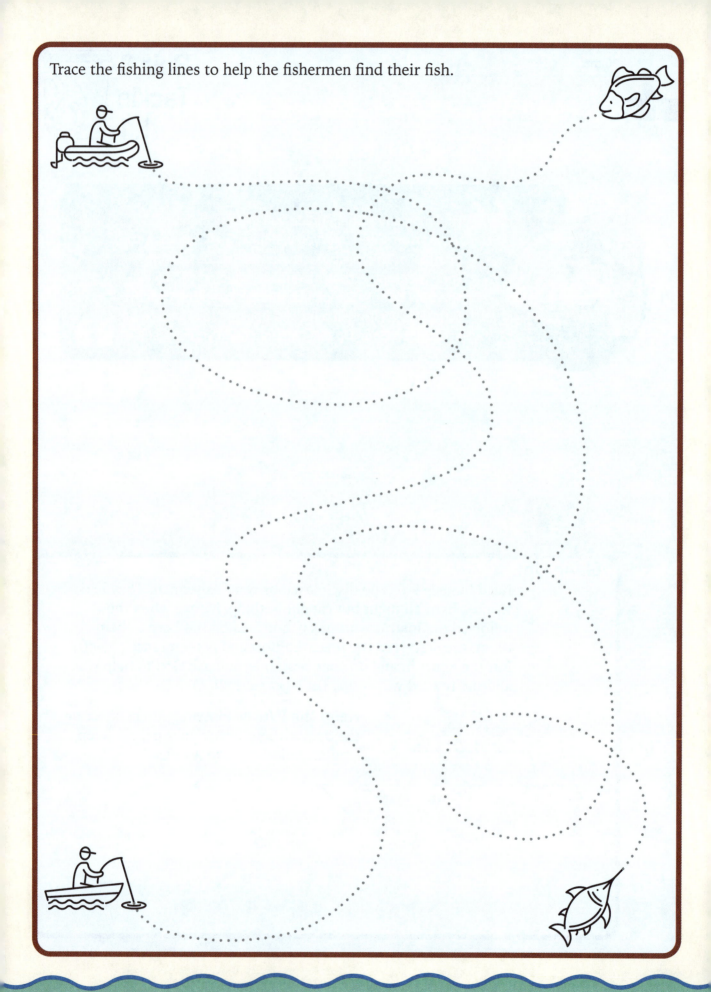

Name

Bait & Tackle 1.2

> Whew whee! You are going to be so strong! The Gear Up section will work those muscles. Remember, becoming a skilled fisherman takes time and effort much like handwriting takes time and effort. It also takes a lot of patience. Get ready to persevere into a patient person. After you do your Gear Up activity, check out the awesome fishing guide that will help you learn how to make each letter, where to put the letters, and more!

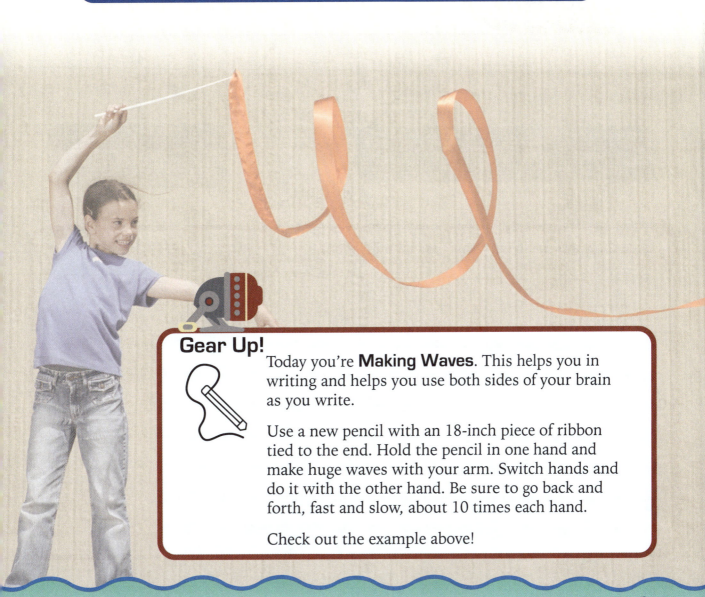

Gear Up!

Today you're **Making Waves**. This helps you in writing and helps you use both sides of your brain as you write.

Use a new pencil with an 18-inch piece of ribbon tied to the end. Hold the pencil in one hand and make huge waves with your arm. Switch hands and do it with the other hand. Be sure to go back and forth, fast and slow, about 10 times each hand.

Check out the example above!

Take a look at the fisherman, his pole, and his boat below. You'll be seeing this image through the entire course and writing your cursive letters on the lines, so read carefully through the descriptions of each special line or area.

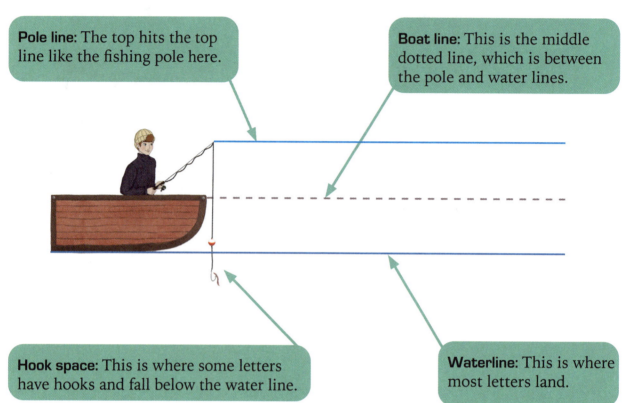

Pole line: The top hits the top line like the fishing pole here.

Boat line: This is the middle dotted line, which is between the pole and water lines.

Hook space: This is where some letters have hooks and fall below the water line.

Waterline: This is where most letters land.

Trace the wave made with this pencil and ribbon.

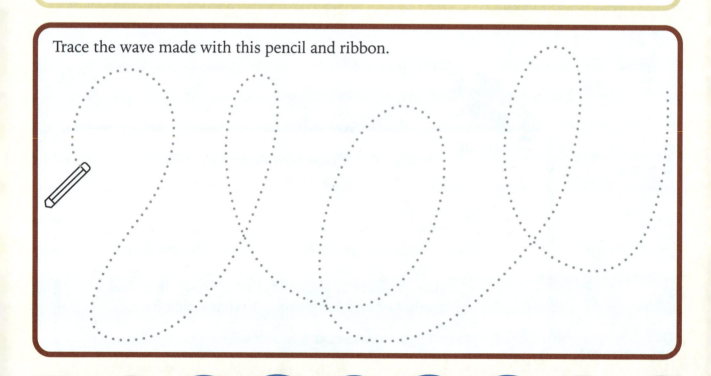

24 Hooked on Cursive

Name _____

Bait & Tackle 1.3

> "Well, what did you think of the boat guide? I think it will really help you know how to write in cursive. Did you know fishing is an art? There are many moving parts, but it's a beauty and technique all its own. Cursive is also an art. In the next section, called Go Fish, you will get to apply what you learn from the Guide. Just like a good fisherman, it will take practice, patience, and technique. Let's get started with your Gear Up, then follow your Guide before you check out the Go Fish section."

Gear Up!

Don't Rock the Boat! Trace without lifting your pencil. Keep smooth, fluid lines like water.

Draw a line to match the guide with the correct terms for each position.

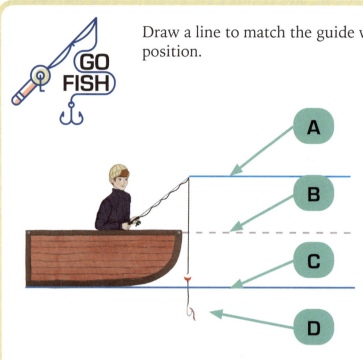

Waterline: This is where most letters land.

Hook space: This is where some letters have hooks and fall below the water line.

Pole line: The top hits the top line like the fishing pole here.

Boat line: This is the middle dotted line, which is between the pole and water lines.

Trace the different waves.

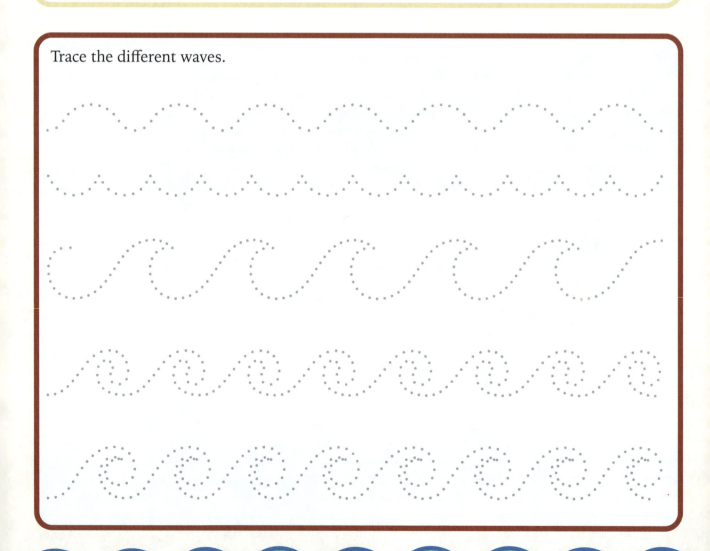

26 Hooked on Cursive

Name _____

Bait & Tackle 1.4

> " You know every fisherman wants to be able to say he or she caught the biggest fish. Catching the biggest fish is a good feeling, just like doing your best is a good feeling. We use a fish scale to weigh and measure our fish. My niece, Anna, will be helping you weigh in every few days. All fishermen must measure their catch. Right now, you have a job! We have to have bait! Most fish like worms, so you better find us some. "

Gear Up!

Worm Squeezes: Picking up worms is fun! Do worm squeezes by picking up the yarn worms with a pair of tweezers.

Make sure you get 5–10 worms with each hand.

Bait & Tackle 1.4   27

Find and circle the waterline on your guide.

Place an X on the hook space.

Draw a line on the entire boat line without lifting your pencil.

Put a large dot on the pole line.

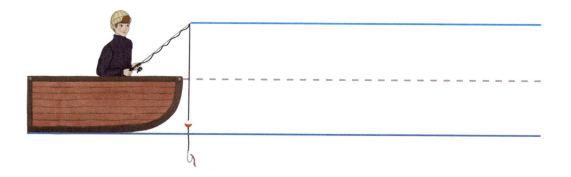

Go fish by tracing the fishing line. Remain slow and steady and don't lift your pencil.

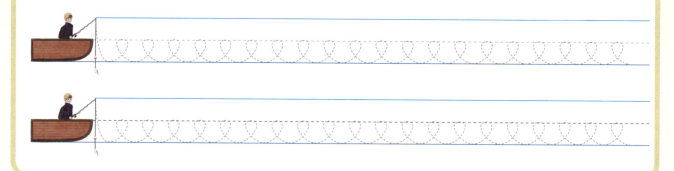

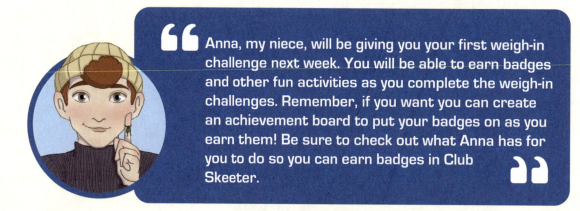

"Anna, my niece, will be giving you your first weigh-in challenge next week. You will be able to earn badges and other fun activities as you complete the weigh-in challenges. Remember, if you want you can create an achievement board to put your badges on as you earn them! Be sure to check out what Anna has for you to do so you can earn badges in Club Skeeter."

Name

Bait & Tackle 1.5

"Well, it looks like you are getting stronger and are ready to try out what you have learned. Remember, just like it took the disciples following Jesus' teachings for a long time before they were ready to go out and spread the Gospel, it will also take you a while to learn how to write in cursive. Patience is a virtue, or a good thing to have."

Gear Up!

Fishing Line Frenzy: Trace the loopy fishing line, but do not lift your pencil. Keep your motion smooth like water.

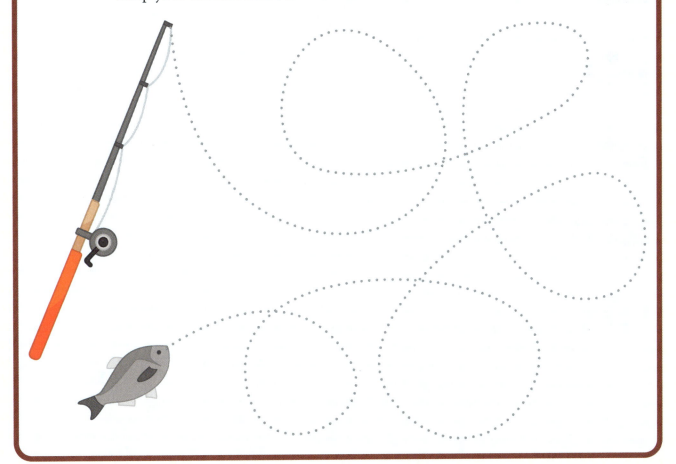

Bait & Tackle 1.5   29

Draw a line from the term to the position for each one.

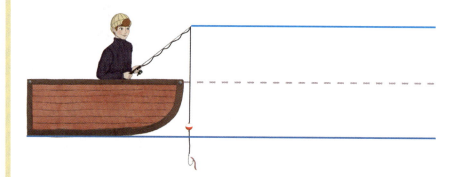

Waterline

Hook Space

Pole Line

Boat Line

Go fish by tracing the fishing line. Remain slow and steady and don't lift your pencil.

Hooked on Cursive

Name

"I'm going to help you with the weigh-in section and introducing your Gear Up exercises. Each letter you learn, there will be a challenge for you to complete in the weigh-in sections. This week your challenge for weighing in is to practice making waves from the Gear Up section on day 2 last week."

"Hey there! Remember to gather your gear before you begin. You will learn some new terms that are used on a boat."

Gather Your Gear

Day 1:
- ☐ Pushpins (thumb tacks)
- ☐ One of the following: cutting board, cork board, or foam sheet (Poking holes in paper — be sure to place either a cutting board, cork board, or foam sheet behind your page.)

Official GUIDE

Live well: a tank on a fishing boat, usually in the floor of the boat, that holds fish to keep them alive while you continue fishing. Water is pulled in as the boat moves and is pumped inside the tank to keep oxygen in the water.

Anchor: a heavy object with curved sides and hooks on the ends that will hook in the bottom of a body of water to hold a boat from drifting away.

Hook: curved piece of metal with a sharp edge called a barb which hooks fish as it tries to eat it.

DID YOU KNOW?

Weather affects fishing. In summer, the sun warms the waters. If a just-right temperature is at the top of the water, like a morning in the warm summer, the fish will be close to the top and looking for a good meal. If it is too cool at the top, like in fall or winter, they will go deeper to get warm. If the sun makes the surface of the water too hot, the fish will go deeper to cooler water. It's interesting how God created their environment to help them keep a good temperature.

Name _____

Bait & Tackle 2.1

> "Hey, Skeeter here. I just wanted to tell you to relax and take your time today. Persevere and show patience. Hebrews 6:12 says "so that you may not be sluggish, but imitators of those who through faith and patience inherit the promises." I know you can show patience in your effort and get the reward. If you rush when trying to put a worm on your hook, you will get poked by the hook. OUCH! So slow down and take your time. Remember, cursive letters connect, so you don't need to lift your pencil when making the letters."

Gear Up!

Poke the fish! Place either a cutting board, cork board, or sheet of foam behind your paper. Using pushpins (thumb tacks), make a hole in each dot. Make sure you swap hands after 10 pokes. Use your thumbs to help give you strength and stability.

> "Oh fun! You get to poke the fish!"

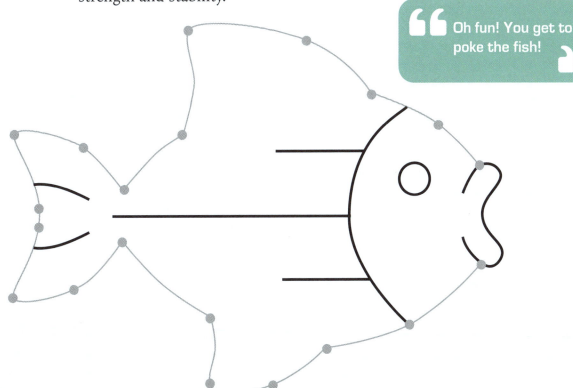

Lowercase c: Start at the **waterline**, swim up and over to the **boat line**. Swim backward and down to the **waterline** and flow with current out to connect to another c.

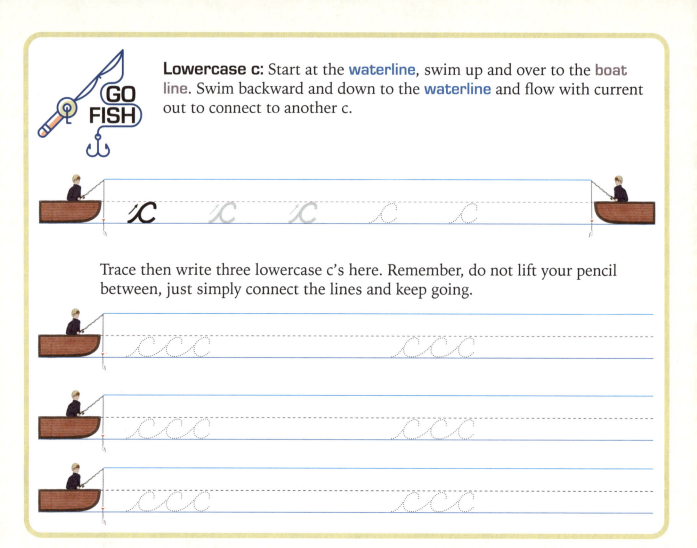

Trace then write three lowercase c's here. Remember, do not lift your pencil between, just simply connect the lines and keep going.

☐ **REMINDER:** Take some time to work on your weigh-in challenge.

Name

Bait & Tackle 2.2

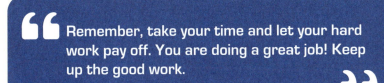
" Remember, take your time and let your hard work pay off. You are doing a great job! Keep up the good work. "

Gear Up!

Help the fish escape through the maze of hooks, then color the page in.

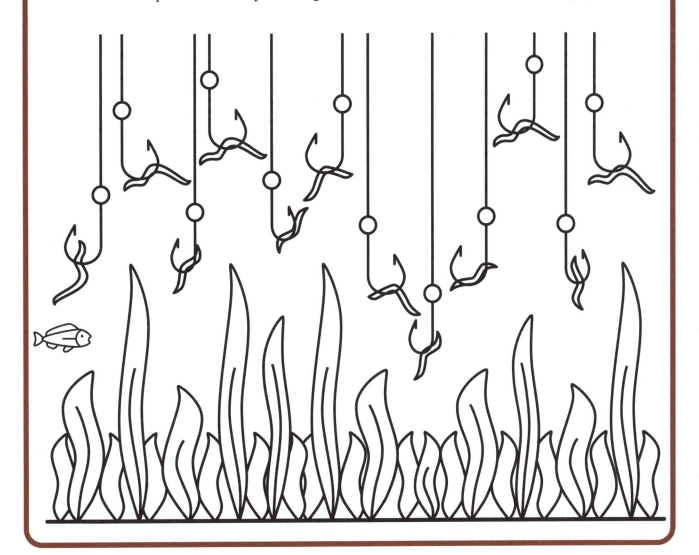

Lowercase c: Start at the **waterline**, swim up and over to the **boat line**. Swim backward and down to the **waterline** and flow with current out to connect to another c.

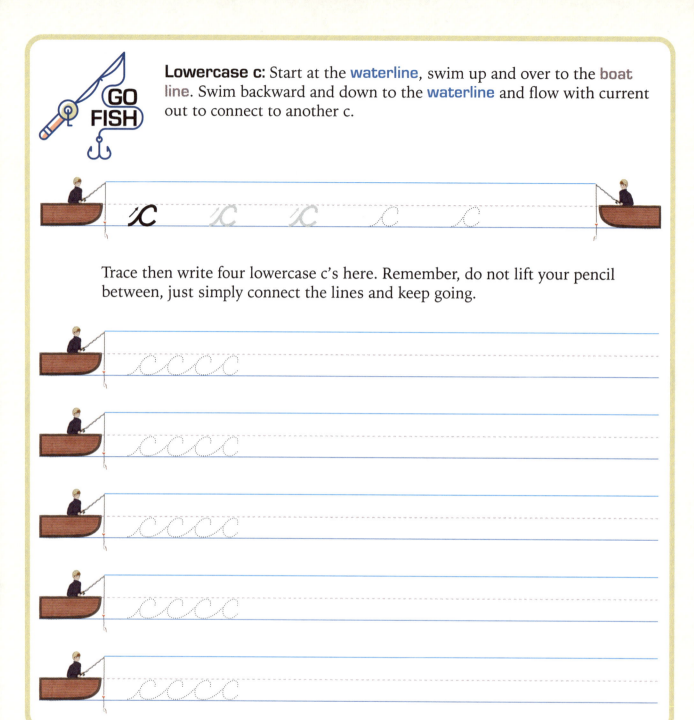

Trace then write four lowercase c's here. Remember, do not lift your pencil between, just simply connect the lines and keep going.

REMINDER: Take some time to work on your weigh-in challenge.

Hooked on Cursive

Name _____

Bait & Tackle 2.3

"Did you know that the disciples were common people with ordinary jobs? Yet God used them to share the good news of the Gospel. You don't have to have a following or be considered famous in our world for God to use you. As a matter of fact, He uses those who are humble and have the heart of a servant. Galatians 6:9 says, "And let us not grow weary of doing good, for in due season we will reap, if we do not give up." Don't give up! Keep on persevering!"

"Hey, let's do anchor up exercises to build up muscles. Believe it or not, these exercises help your posture which helps you write more neatly."

Gear Up!

Anchor Up: Stand with your feet about shoulder width apart. Bend over and pretend to pull up a heavy anchor. Give the anchor 10 good pulls all the way up.

Lowercase c: Start at the waterline, swim up and over to the boat line. Swim backward and down to the waterline and flow with current out to connect to another c.

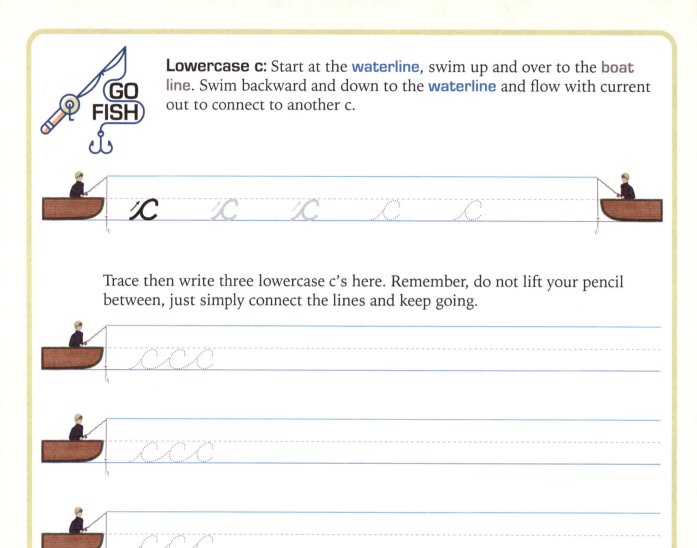

Trace then write three lowercase c's here. Remember, do not lift your pencil between, just simply connect the lines and keep going.

> Hey, it's time to weigh in. Remember, fishermen weigh the fish they catch to see who has the largest catch. Did you make the big catch this week as you made waves with the wave wands? If so, color in the 10 on the fishing scale.
>
> Your next challenge is to do the anchor up activity from today for two more days.

Name _____

Bait & Tackle 2.4

"Remember, keep your pencil moving and don't lift between letters. That would be a bad habit you would have to break later. You've got this! Keep on persevering as you show me how you can navigate through the tangled rope."

Gear Up!

All Tangled Up! Trace the tangled rope without lifting your pencil off the paper.

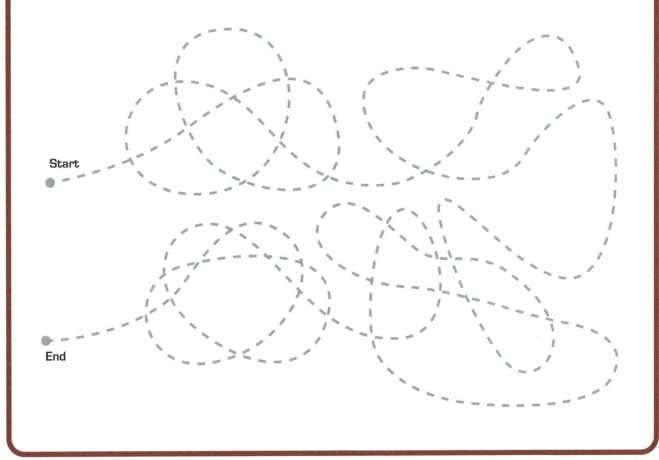

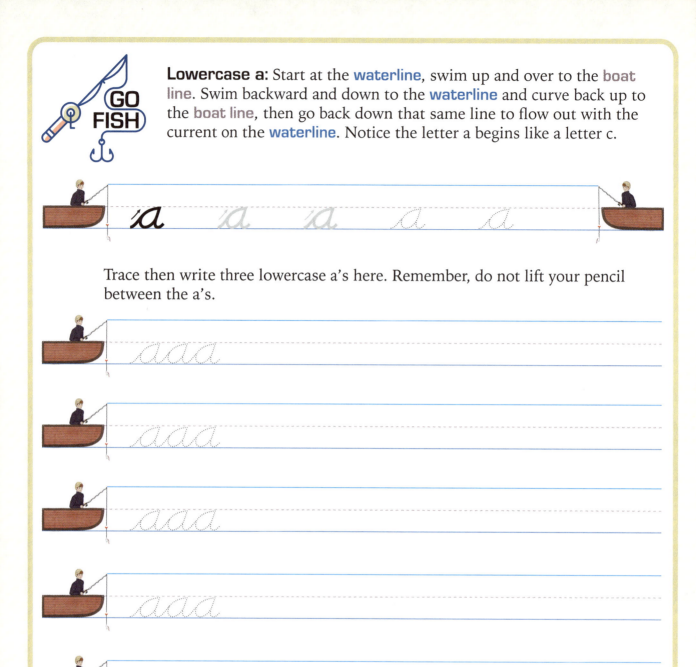

Lowercase a: Start at the waterline, swim up and over to the boat line. Swim backward and down to the waterline and curve back up to the boat line, then go back down that same line to flow out with the current on the waterline. Notice the letter a begins like a letter c.

Trace then write three lowercase a's here. Remember, do not lift your pencil between the a's.

☐ **REMINDER:** Take some time to work on your weigh-in challenge.

Name _____

Bait & Tackle 2.5

> Let's practice saying that verse out loud. "And let us not grow weary of doing good, for in due season we will reap, if we do not give up." Don't give up! Galatians 6:9. Great job! Did you know in fishing boats there is a built-in box in the floor that holds water for you to keep the fish you catch alive? That box is called a live well. It usually has a lid that lifts on one side, like a cooler would. Check out your Gear Up section today.

> Hey, today we are still working on building muscles. Check it out.

Gear Up!

Live Well Reaches: Sit in a chair or side of a bathtub with your feet flat on the ground. Keep your feet spread apart. Bend over and touch the top of the ground between your feet as if you were touching the top of the live well in your boat. Do this 12 times.

Bait & Tackle 2.5

Lowercase a: Start at the **waterline**, swim up and over to the **boat line**. Swim backward and down to the **waterline** and curve back up to the **boat line**, then go back down that same line to flow out with the current on the **waterline**. Notice the letter a begins like a letter c.

Trace then write four lowercase a's here. Remember, do not lift your pencil between the a's.

☐ **REMINDER:** Take some time to work on your weigh-in challenge.

Name _____

TACKLE BOX 3

" You have two challenges this week. One — I told you last week about doing two days of the anchor up activity and you will weigh in today. You will get another challenge in the weigh-in section, so be sure to check it out. "

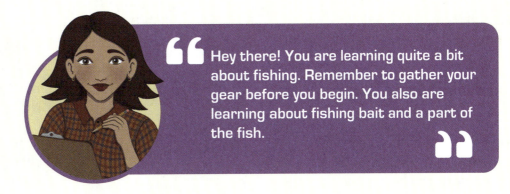

" Hey there! You are learning quite a bit about fishing. Remember to gather your gear before you begin. You also are learning about fishing bait and a part of the fish. "

Gather Your Gear

Day 3:
☐ Cotton swabs
☐ Sidewalk chalk (rubbing cotton swabs on chalk to use them as a paint brush to put scales on a fish)

Lure: artificial (not real) bait designed to get the attention of fish. The movement, bright colors, and often metal shining lures, or entices, the fish in. Lures have hooks, and when the fish try to eat the bait, they are caught.

Bait: the lure, hook, and/or live animal, such as worms and crickets, used for fishing.

Scales: small ridged plate that is on the skin of a fish.

Fishing Derby: when fishermen compete in a tournament to see who can win with the best catch.

Name _____

Bait & Tackle 3.1

"Hey, do you know why it is important to learn cursive? It is important because cursive will help you in life. What if you couldn't read the letters from famous people before you? Or what if you couldn't read an important document like the Constitution of the United States? Those documents and letters are important for our freedom and history. If you can't read them, then it limits you to where you must depend on someone else to read and tell you the truth. We will be talking each day about why you should learn cursive. Let's get more practice in and learn more letters!"

Gear Up!

Hooks and Lures: Trace the hooks and connect them to the lures. Do not lift your pencil. Before using your pencil, use your eyes to follow the path from the hook to the lure.

Lowercase a: Start at the **waterline**, swim up and over to the **boat line**. Swim backward and down to the **waterline** and curve back up to the **boat line**, then back down that same line to flow out with the current on the **waterline**.

Write three lowercase a's here. Remember, do not lift your pencil between the a's.

" Hey, it's time to weigh in. Did you strengthen your muscles by doing two days of the anchor up activity? If so, color in the fish on the trophy.

Your next challenge is to do live well reaches from Bait and Tackle 2.5. Do 5 each day until your next weigh-in. "

46 Hooked on Cursive

Name _____

Bait & Tackle 3.2

"Hey there! Another reason it is important to learn cursive is because learning something new is good for our brains. Our brains can become bored by going over the same things all the time. If we learn something new, it helps us to exercise our brains. God created our brains so that activities, like writing, help relieve stress. It is a soothing technique for us. Do you know what else is soothing to me? The light on a lighthouse. Today, you will be learning to tap your fingers like a light on a lighthouse flashes."

"Oh! I just love lighthouses! They are so pretty. Be sure to touch your pinky to your thumb on each hand."

Gear Up!

Lighthouse Taps: Lighthouses flash their lights, so we are going to tap for lighthouse flashes. Bring your pinky and thumb together to tap and open, tap and open, like a lighthouse flashes. Do this 12 times with both hands.

Lowercase d: Start at the waterline, swim up and over to the boat line. Swim backward and down to the waterline and curve back up to the pole line, then back down that same line to flow out with the current on the waterline. That is very close to the lowercase a you just learned.

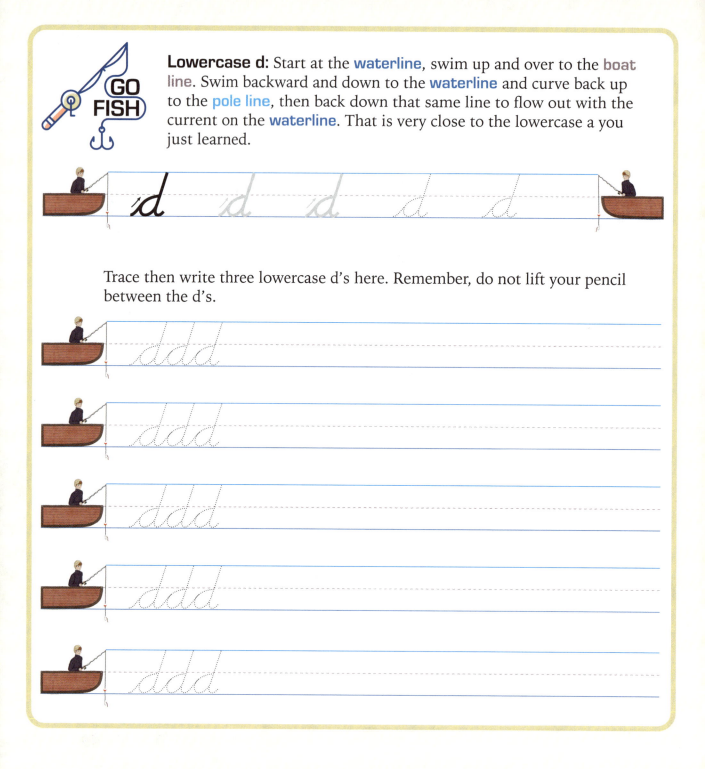

Trace then write three lowercase d's here. Remember, do not lift your pencil between the d's.

☐ **REMINDER:** Take some time to work on your weigh-in challenge.

Name

Bait & Tackle 3.3

> One of the biggest reasons cursive is important is because it helps us grow in character. The Bible tells us in 2 Peter 1:5–8 (NIRV) "So you should try very hard to add goodness to your faith. To goodness, add knowledge. To knowledge, add the ability to control yourselves. To the ability to control yourselves, add the strength to keep going. To the strength to keep going, add godliness. To godliness, add kindness for one another. And to kindness for one another, add love. All these things should describe you more and more. They will make you useful and fruitful as you know our Lord Jesus Christ better." Wow! Knowledge, strength to keep going, perseverance, patience . . . all these traits listed are traits we are building by learning cursive. Let's keep applying these traits as we put in the effort to learn cursive.

Gear Up!

Oh, what fun! You get to use a cotton swab as a paint brush! Rub your cotton swab on the sidewalk chalk to get enough chalk on it to use it to paint the scales on the fish by rubbing.

Lowercase d: Start at the **waterline**, swim up and over to the **boat line**. Then swim backwards and down to the **waterline** and curve back up to the **pole line**, then back down that same line to flow out with the current on the **waterline**.

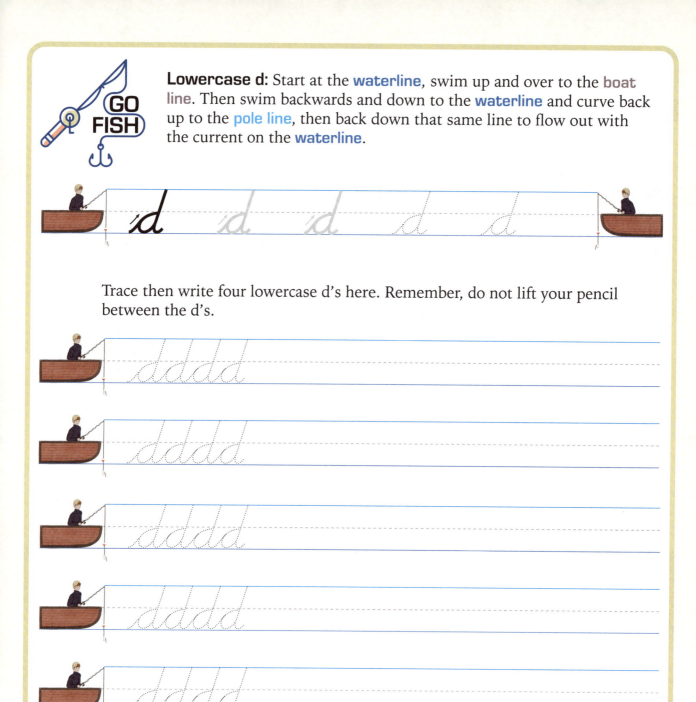

Trace then write four lowercase d's here. Remember, do not lift your pencil between the d's.

☐ **REMINDER:** Take some time to work on your weigh-in challenge.

Name _____

Bait & Tackle 3.4

> Reason number four for learning cursive is that you can write faster in cursive than in print. Writing is a way to communicate with others. If your writing isn't neat, then others won't be able to understand what you write. It's important to practice so you can write neat and quickly. When you get older and are taking notes or need to quickly write something, cursive will really help you get it all down quickly. It's kind of like which boat will help you get to the best fishing hole the quickest! I know I want mine to get there first. Keep practicing in your other subjects so you can become a master at writing in cursive.

> Uncle Skeeter has let me paddle his fishing boat on the pond. Now it's your turn to pretend to paddle the boat.

Gear Up!

Paddle the Boat: Sit in a chair or on the side of a bathtub with your feet flat on the ground. Pretend to paddle the boat. Make sure you swap sides so your boat doesn't get off course! Give a good 15 total strokes of the paddle for each side.

Lowercase d: Start at the waterline, swim up and over to the boat line. Then swim backwards and down to the waterline and curve back up to the pole line, then back down that same line to flow out with the current on the waterline.

Trace then write three lowercase d's here. Remember, do not lift your pencil between the d's.

> Hey, it's time to weigh in. How did the live well reaches go? If you did the extra days of live well reaches, then you earn a live well badge and may color the badge. This is your first badge for you to cut out and add it to your achievement board. You'll find them in the back starting on page 497!

Name

Bait & Tackle 3.5

" The last reason it is important to learn cursive is to develop many skills that will help you in all areas of your life. Here is a list of a few ways that cursive can help you:

- focus
- spelling
- reading
- self-confidence

These are all great skills for you to have. I hope you see the value in learning cursive, just like I see the value in learning to fish! "

Gear Up!

Dot-to-Dot Fish: Trace the dots without lifting your pencil to make a fish. Try to find the path with your eyes before you begin with your pencil.

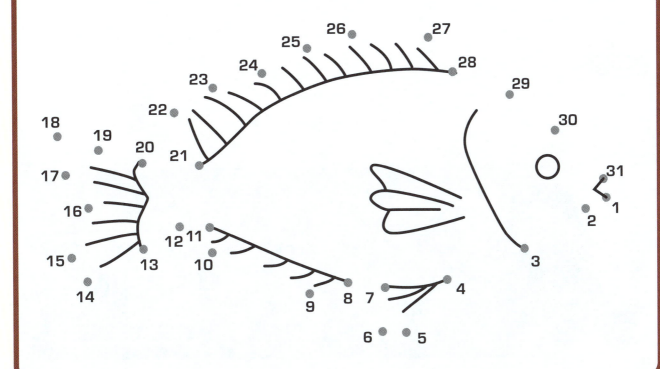

Review your letters: letters c, a, and d

Lowercase c: Start at the waterline, swim up and over to the boat line. Swim backward and down to the waterline and flow with the current out to connect to another c.

Lowercase a: Start at the waterline, swim up and over to the boat line. Swim backward and down to the waterline and curve back up to the boat line, then back down that same line to flow out with the current on the waterline.

Lowercase d: Start at the waterline, swim up and over to the boat line. Then swim backwards and down to the waterline and curve back up to the pole line, then back down that same line to flow out with the current on the waterline.

Trace the letters c, a, and d. Connect the letters and don't lift your pencil until all are written. Trace them three times, and then write them once on your own. Be sure to leave a pinky space between each set.

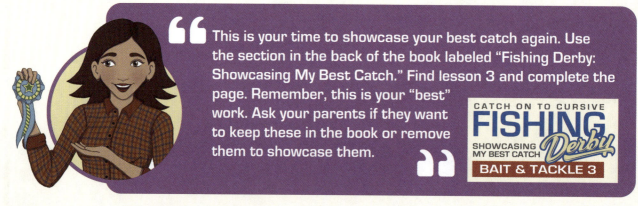

"This is your time to showcase your best catch again. Use the section in the back of the book labeled "Fishing Derby: Showcasing My Best Catch." Find lesson 3 and complete the page. Remember, this is your "best" work. Ask your parents if they want to keep these in the book or remove them to showcase them."

CATCH ON TO CURSIVE
FISHING Derby
SHOWCASING MY BEST CATCH
BAIT & TACKLE 3

Name

 TACKLE BOX 4

"Are you ready for another challenge? This week you are to keep a pinky space between words as you write in your schoolwork."

"Gather your gear before you begin each week. Be sure to get your parents' approval to do the activity for Bait and Tackle 4.5. You have some neat fishing terms this week. Check them out on the next page."

 Gather Your Gear

Day 2:
☐ Paper clips

Day 4:
☐ Pushpins (thumb tacks)
☐ One of the following: cutting board, cork board, or foam sheet

Day 5:
☐ Sticky notes or paper
☐ Ball (tennis or approx. size)

Sails: the cloth or material that is used to catch wind on a boat. Sail shapes can vary.

Hoist: means to raise or lift; a device that lifts.

Cast: throw something in a specific direction. To cast your line means to throw it out using your fishing pole.

Dock: a structure near the water's edge that is on the ground and extends out into the water. This provides a place for you to get out over the water to fish.

Name _____

Bait & Tackle 4.1

Read or have a parent read Luke 5:1–11

" Can you imagine what fishing all night long and catching nothing would feel like? In Luke, we see Simon Peter telling the Lord how they had been working all night, but he would do what the Lord said. Because of the obedience of Peter, they caught enough fish that their nets broke. They even called to their fishing partners in another boat to come help them, and they filled both ships! That is a lot of fish! Everyone was amazed. Peter fell at the feet of Jesus. Jesus told him that he now would be a fisher of men. A fisher of men is someone who shares the Gospel message with others. I know this is a cursive course, but what if we had a great catch of souls for Jesus because your family shared Jesus with someone? Your family can be fishers of men just like Peter. "

" Have you ever seen a ship or boat go under a bridge? I always hold my breath until it is under because I am scared it will hit the bridge! Some bridges even lift to allow boats through. Isn't that neat? "

Gear Up!

Don't Hit the Bridge: The ships in the river need to get through. Place your hands flat on the ground with tips of toes on the ground and body lifted to be the bridge. Hold this for 10–15 seconds.

Lowercase o: Start at the waterline, swim up and over to the boat line. Then swim backwards and down to the waterline and curve back up to the boat line. Swim out across the boat line.

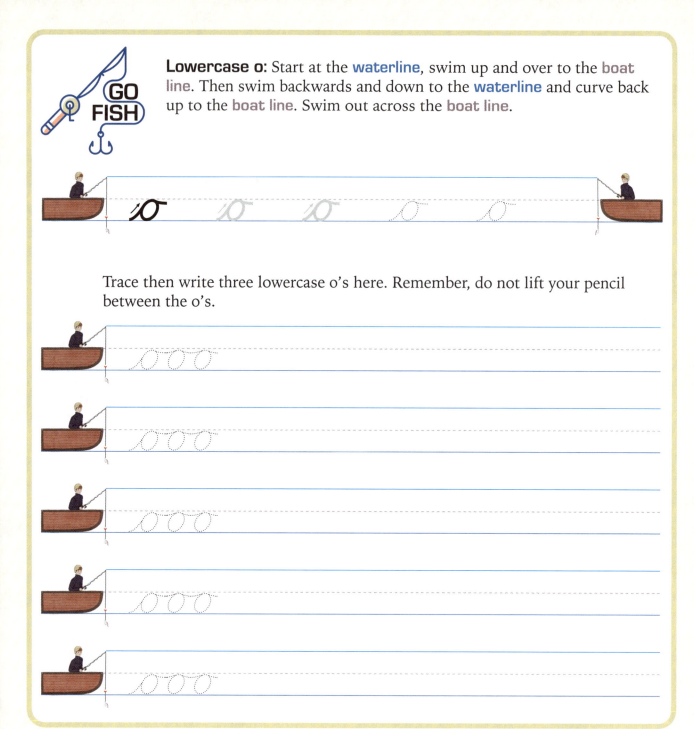

Trace then write three lowercase o's here. Remember, do not lift your pencil between the o's.

☐ **REMINDER:** Take some time to work on your weigh-in challenge.

Name

Bait & Tackle 4.2

> "Perseverance is defined as persistence in doing something despite difficulty or delay in achieving success. Sometimes you go fishing and catch nothing. You might not even get a little bite or nibble. Just like the disciples' fishing trip . . . everything in life doesn't come quickly. We must put in the effort, even if something is difficult, and later get the reward for it. Penmanship is exactly like this. It is a slow process of working without instant reward. Keep up the good effort and before you know it, you'll be writing in cursive like me!"

> "Wow, you get to hook fish! Don't worry, they aren't real hooks."

Gear Up!

Hook the Fish: At the bottom of the page is a row of fish. Open paper clips and secure a paper clip to each fish.

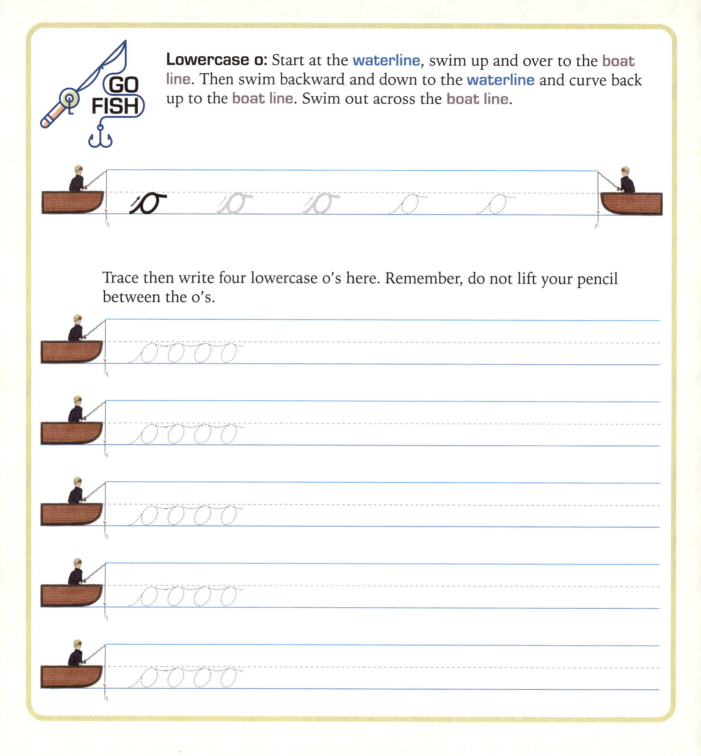

Lowercase o: Start at the waterline, swim up and over to the boat line. Then swim backward and down to the waterline and curve back up to the boat line. Swim out across the boat line.

Trace then write four lowercase o's here. Remember, do not lift your pencil between the o's.

☐ **REMINDER:** Take some time to work on your weigh-in challenge.

Name _____

Bait & Tackle 4.3

 "Check this move out! Lift your body off the ground... it's like a sideways pushup! I wonder if the disciples did these to help build strong muscles. Whew! This requires strength. Remember, you don't lift your pencil when writing in cursive."

"Remember on this week's Tackle Box, you learned the terms *hoist* and *sail*. Well, now you get to hoist the sails, which is a fancy way to say lift the sails."

Gear Up!

Hoist the Sails: These are called side planks and are like a side pushup that holds your body up. Lay on your side, lift your body up with the arm closest to the ground. Your foot should be on its side on the ground. Your body makes a triangle shape like a sail. Hold the position for 8 seconds, relax, and repeat two times. Do both sides of your body.

 **Lowercase o:** Start at the **waterline**, swim up and over to the **boat line**. Then swim backward and down to the **waterline** and curve back up to the **boat line**. Swim out across the **boat line**.

Trace then write three lowercase o's here. Remember, do not lift your pencil between the o's.

 "Hey, it's time to weigh in. Were you able to keep a pinky space between words as you wrote? If you completed this challenge, color in the hand with the pinky held up.

Your next challenge is to hoist the sails once a day (see page 61)."

Name _____

Bait & Tackle 4.4

"Remember earlier in Luke's gospel how the disciples' nets broke from all the fish, and God told Peter he would be a fisher of men? God used another example of them fishing all night in John 21. Jesus was on the shore and He, again, gave specific instructions to catch fish. This time, they caught 153 fish, but the nets didn't break. This is symbolic of the disciples being fishers of men and catching souls."

"Today you are going to be poking a fish again! That will be fun. I also noticed that a lowercase c, a, d, o, and the lowercase g you will learn today, all start out the with the same motion! That makes it easier to remember as you write."

Gear Up!

Poke the fish! Place either a cutting board, cork board, or sheet of foam behind your paper. Using pushpins (thumb tacks) to make a hole in each dot. Make sure you swap hands after 10 pokes. Use your thumbs to help give you strength and stability.

Lowercase g: Start at the waterline, swim up and over to the boat line. Then swim backward and down to the waterline and curve back up to the boat line (this is just like the letter a so far), then go back down that same line, but this letter has a hook! Keep going down to the hook space and curve down and back to make a loop as you swim back up to flow out the waterline.

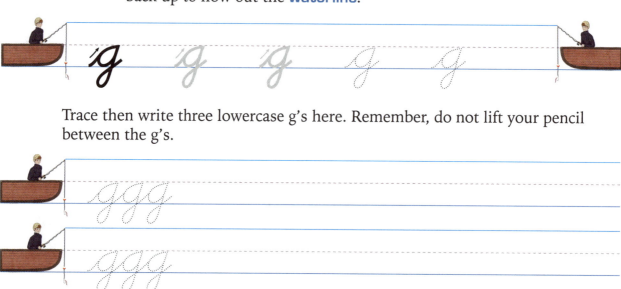

Trace then write three lowercase g's here. Remember, do not lift your pencil between the g's.

☐ **REMINDER:** Take some time to work on your weigh-in challenge.

Name _____

Bait & Tackle 4.5

> "Today's Gear Up activity is so fun! Sometimes when you are fishing off a dock or in a small pond, you must aim to get your cast to just the right spot. If you miss, you might get all tangled up and break your line. In Gear Up today, you are aiming and casting . . . check it out!"

> "I know you will be throwing a ball today, but be sure to get your parents' permission and don't throw the ball too hard. The point is to hit the center of the target."

Gear Up!

Aim and Cast: Please get the approval of your parent before doing this activity.

Place a piece of paper or sticky note on a door or wall about eye level. You can make a target on it if you'd like. Take about 10 steps back and try to AIM and CAST the ball to hit the target. If you miss three times, you can step forward one step. Try to hit the paper/target in the middle at least three times in a row.

Lowercase g: Start at the waterline, swim up and over to the boat line. Then swim backward and down to the waterline and curve back up to the boat line (this is just like the letter a so far), then go back down that same line, but this letter has a hook! Keep going down to the hook space and curve down and back to make a loop as you swim back up to flow out the waterline.

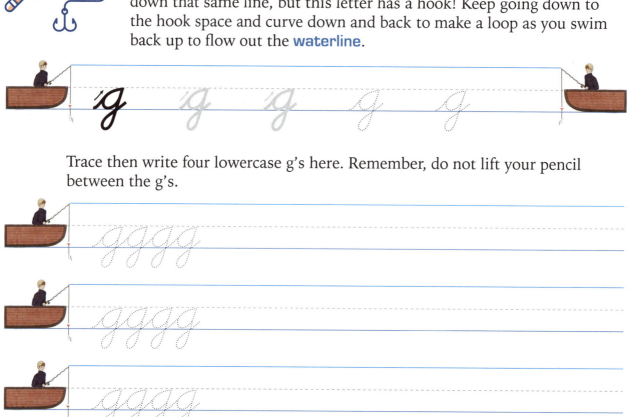

Trace then write four lowercase g's here. Remember, do not lift your pencil between the g's.

☐ **REMINDER:** Take some time to work on your weigh-in challenge.

Name _____

TACKLE BOX 5

" You had a challenge from last week to hoist the sails, and that weigh in is today. Be sure to check out the weigh-in section for your next challenge. "

" Be sure to gather your gear before you begin. We don't have many fishing terms this week, but we have one that will help you understand the Bible message this week. "

Gather Your Gear

Day 1:
☐ Small objects such as beads, small buttons, or sunflower seeds
☐ Play-Doh or other dough

Day 2:
☐ Painter's tape or rope or sidewalk chalk or 2x4

Day 3:
☐ Pushpins from lesson 2

Day 4:
☐ Bicycle or scooter or skateboard. Any item to help you balance

Day 5:
☐ Wave wand from Bait and Tackle 1.1

Tackle Box 5   67

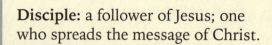
Official GUIDE

Disciple: a follower of Jesus; one who spreads the message of Christ.

DID YOU KNOW?

In warmer weather, we want to use a bait that floats up closer to the top to catch fish that have come up to the warmer temperature. If the top waters become too warm, then you'll want to use a bait that sinks down lower in the water.

Name _____

Bait & Tackle 5.1

> "One of the most special relationships in the Bible to me is the relationship the disciples had with Jesus. Can you imagine walking and talking with Jesus daily? In Mark 1:14–20 the Bible tells us that Jesus was beginning His ministry. It says,
>
> Now after John was arrested, Jesus came into Galilee, proclaiming the gospel of God, and saying, "The time is fulfilled, and the kingdom of God is at hand; repent and believe in the gospel." Passing alongside the Sea of Galilee, he saw Simon and Andrew the brother of Simon casting a net into the sea, for they were fishermen. And Jesus said to them, "Follow me, and I will make you become fishers of men." And immediately they left their nets and followed him. And going on a little farther, he saw James the son of Zebedee and John his brother, who were in their boat mending the nets. And immediately he called them, and they left their father Zebedee in the boat with the hired servants and followed him.
>
> I sure would have loved to have been there when Jesus' earthly ministry was started. I think being a disciple was super special, but the best part is that we are also called to be His disciples! How cool is that? Several of the disciples were fishermen just like me."

> "Grab some dough and small objects, such as beads, buttons, or sunflower seeds for this activity. Be sure to clean up when you're done. We sure wouldn't want your dough to dry out."

Gear Up!

Lures in Mud: Push the small objects into dough. Be sure to use your fingers to get them started and your thumb to get them all the way in. Push objects in with each hand at least 5 times.

Lowercase g: Start at the **waterline**, swim up and over to the **boat line**. Then swim backward and down to the **waterline** and curve back up to the **boat line** (this is just like the letter a so far), then back down that same line, but this letter has a hook! Keep going down to the hook space and curve down and back to make a loop as you swim back up to flow out the **waterline**.

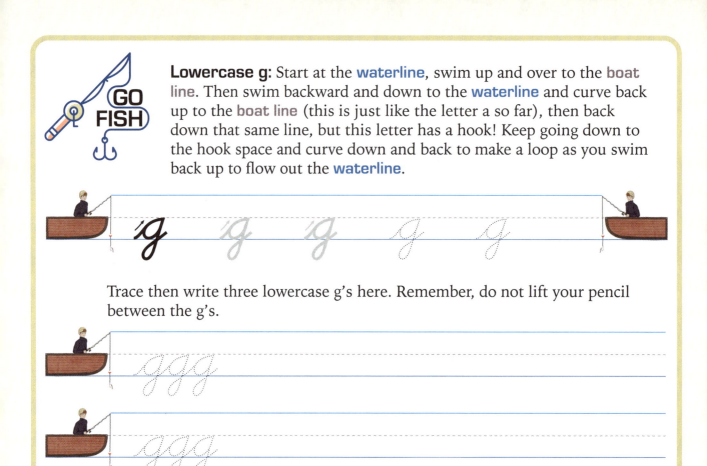

Trace then write three lowercase g's here. Remember, do not lift your pencil between the g's.

" Did you hoist the sails each day? If so, trace the sails on the sailboat.

Your next challenge is to use a capital letter in regular print when you begin a new sentence in your writing this week. "

70 Hooked on Cursive

Name _____

Bait & Tackle 5.2

> " What are some ways you can be a disciple? Tell a parent. Wow! Check it out! We have another letter that begins just like the lowercase letters you have learned so far! "

 Gear Up!

Walk the Plank: Use painter's tape, a rope, or sidewalk chalk to make a long line, about 6 feet long. Walk the Plank by balancing on the line with one foot in front of the other. Do this three times. Don't fall in! There might be gators in that water!

(You can also use a 2x4 or balance beam.)

Lowercase q: Start at the waterline, swim up and over to the boat line. Then swim backward and down to the waterline and curve back up to the boat line (this is just like the letter a so far), then back down that same line, but this letter also has a hook! Keep going down to the hook space, but this time curve down and forward to make a loop that touches your line at the base of the waterline. Swim out to the waterline.

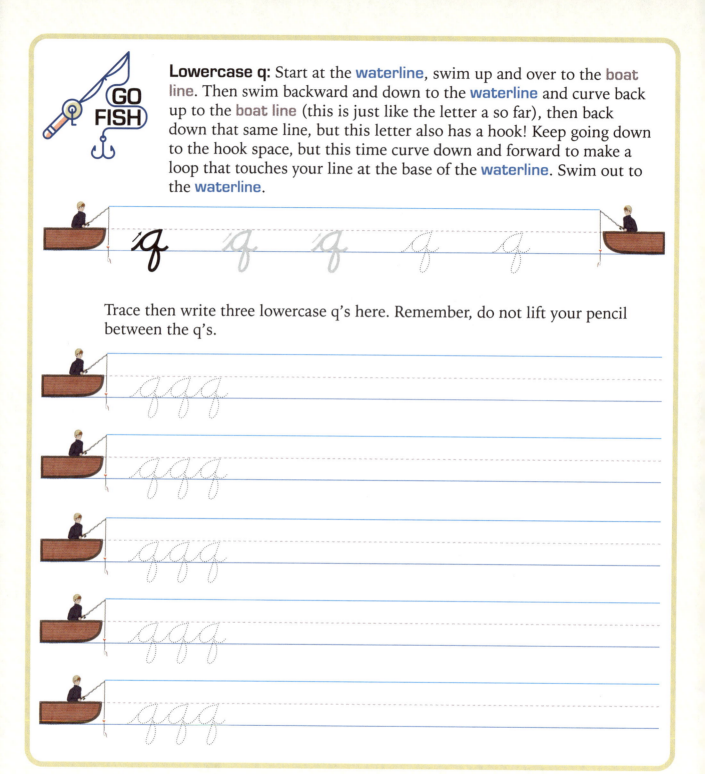

Trace then write three lowercase q's here. Remember, do not lift your pencil between the q's.

☐ **REMINDER:** Take some time to work on your weigh-in challenge.

Name _____

Bait & Tackle 5.3

"Jesus told His first disciples that He would make them fishers of men. That means that they were going to win people to Jesus. We are also fishers of men. Each time your family shares the good news of the Gospel with someone, they are helping grow the Kingdom of God. Keep up the good effort with your family and *catch souls!*"

Gear Up!

Sting like a Stingray: Place either a cutting board, cork board, or sheet of foam behind your paper. Using pushpins (thumb tacks), make a hole in each dot. Make sure you swap hands after 10 pokes. Use your thumbs to help give you strength and stability.

Use pushpins to poke the edges of the sting ray.

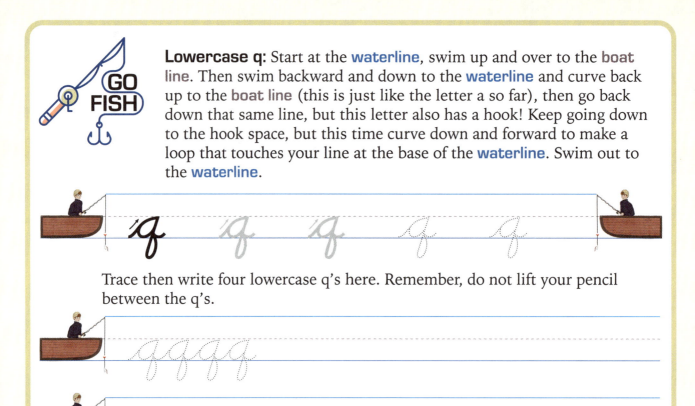

Lowercase q: Start at the **waterline**, swim up and over to the **boat line**. Then swim backward and down to the **waterline** and curve back up to the **boat line** (this is just like the letter a so far), then go back down that same line, but this letter also has a hook! Keep going down to the hook space, but this time curve down and forward to make a loop that touches your line at the base of the **waterline**. Swim out to the **waterline**.

Trace then write four lowercase q's here. Remember, do not lift your pencil between the q's.

☐ **REMINDER:** Take some time to work on your weigh-in challenge.

Name _____

Bait & Tackle 5.4

> "One time, I was in a canoe fishing with Anna, and I leaned a bit too far. Wouldn't you know that my boat tipped over and all my gear went into the river! I wonder if the disciples tipped their boat. I know the big catch they had pulled their boat lower to the water. Be sure not to tip the boat today, and remember not to lift your pencil when writing."

> "I sure hope your balance is better than Uncle Skeeter's or you're going to be wet!"

Gear Up!

Don't Tip the Boat: Balance on a bicycle, scooter, or skateboard for 15 seconds.

Bait & Tackle 5.4   75

Lowercase q: Start at the waterline, swim up and over to the boat line. Then swim backward and down to the waterline and curve back up to the boat line (this is just like the letter a so far), go back down that same line, but this letter also has a hook! Keep going down to the hook space, but this time curve down and forward to make a loop that touches your line at the base of the waterline. Swim out to the waterline.

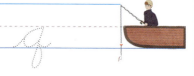

Trace then write three lowercase q's here. Remember, do not lift your pencil between the q's.

Did you use a capital letter when beginning a sentence this week? If you completed this challenge, complete the dot-to-dot capital letter picture below.

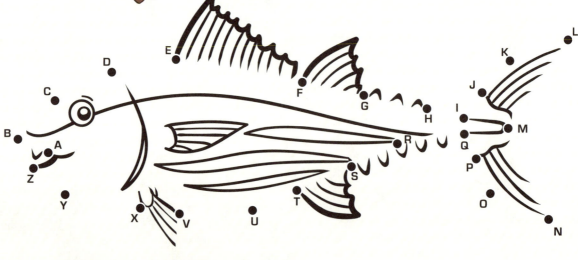

Hooked on Cursive

Name _____

Bait & Tackle 5.5

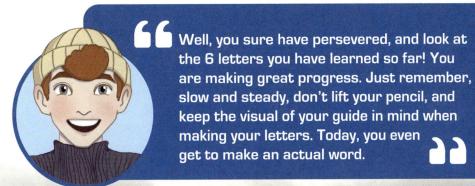

"Well, you sure have persevered, and look at the 6 letters you have learned so far! You are making great progress. Just remember, slow and steady, don't lift your pencil, and keep the visual of your guide in mind when making your letters. Today, you even get to make an actual word."

Gear Up!

Making Waves: Use your wave wands from week 1 to make more waves! Be sure to make 8's sideways and upright with both hands.

Bait & Tackle 5.5 77

Review your letters: letters o, g, and q

Lowercase o: Start at the waterline, swim up and over to the boat line. Then swim backwards and down to the waterline and curve back up to the boat line. Swim out across the boat line.

Lowercase g: Start at the waterline, swim up and over to the boat line. Then swim backward and down to the waterline and curve back up to the boat line (this is just like the letter a so far), then go back down that same line, but this letter has a hook! Keep going down to the hook space and curve down and back to make a loop as you swim back up to flow out the waterline.

Lowercase q: Start at the waterline, swim up and over to the boat line. Then swim backward and down to the waterline and curve back up to the boat line (this is just like the letter a so far), go back down that same line, but this letter also has a hook! Keep going down to the hook space, but this time curve down and forward to make a loop that touches your line at the base of the waterline. Swim out to the waterline.

Trace the letters c, a, and d. Connect the letters and don't lift your pencil until all are written. Trace them three times, and then write them once on your own. Be sure to leave a pinky space between each set.

> "This is your time to showcase your best catch again. Use the section in the back of the book labeled "Fishing Derby: Showcasing My Best Catch." Find lesson 5 and complete the page. Remember, this is your "best" work. Ask your parents if they want to keep these in the book or remove them to showcase them."

CATCH ON TO CURSIVE
FISHING Derby
SHOWCASING MY BEST CATCH
BAIT & TACKLE 5

Hooked on Cursive

Name

TACKLE BOX 6

" Are you up for another challenge? Your next challenge is to do the Don't Tip the Boat exercise each day (from Bait & Tackle 5.4). "

" Good fishermen remember to gather their gear. Your gear has been used in other weeks but be sure to gather it. "

Gather Your Gear

Day 2:
☐ Tweezers and yarn from lesson 1

Day 3:
☐ Pushpins (thumb tacks)
☐ One of the following: cutting board, cork board, or foam sheet

Rainbow Trout: a fish from the trout species in western North America. It gets its name because of its rainbow-like coloring.

Name _____

Bait & Tackle 6.1

> "Jesus was also a storyteller. His stories are better known as parables. Read in your Bible about this parable in Matthew 13:47–50. This reminded me of how Jesus told the disciples they would be fishers of men, and in this parable, men pulled in the nets. What happens next makes me realize how much more our families need to connect with others and *catch souls* for Jesus. You know, many will come and hear the Word of God, but, unfortunately, not all will follow it. I want your family to be one that the angels count as righteous."

> "I really love mazes. Be sure to not hit the shoreline or you might tip your canoe!"

Gear Up!

Keep Your Canoe in the River: Complete the maze by drawing between the lines.

Capital C: Start at the pole line, curve back, and swim back and down to the waterline. Flow with the current out to connect to another letter.

Trace then write three capital C's here. When only writing capital cursive letters, such as your initials, we do not connect them together, and some capital letters do not connect to the lowercase letters at all. The capital C does connect just like the lowercase c does; you simply swing into the next letters' strokes. In this practice, do not connect the capital C's since they are all capital letters. We will practice connecting it to lowercase letters another day.

☐ **REMINDER:** Take some time to work on your weigh-in challenge.

Name _____

Bait & Tackle 6.2

" Just as Jesus was a storyteller, fishermen also like to tell stories. Sometimes we can use a story to make connections with others, and we can use that to share the Gospel. "

Gear Up!

Worm Squeezes: Use tweezers to pick up worms (pieces of yarn). Make sure you get 5–10 worms.

" Remember we first did this activity in Bait & Tackle 1.5. "

Bait & Tackle 6.2 83

GO FISH

Capital C: Start at the **pole line**, curve back and swim back and down to the **waterline** and then flow with the current out to connect to the next letter.

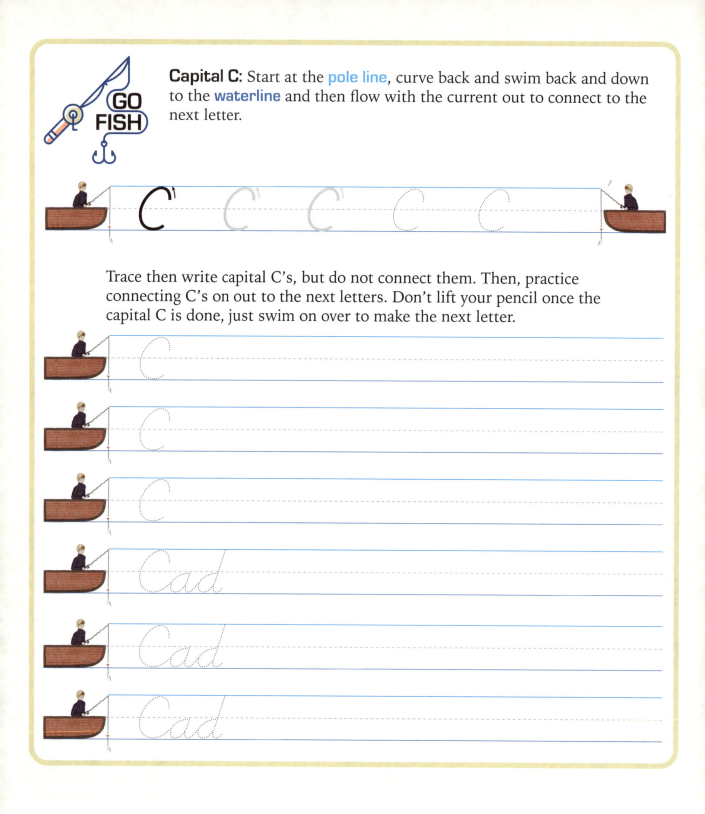

Trace then write capital C's, but do not connect them. Then, practice connecting C's on out to the next letters. Don't lift your pencil once the capital C is done, just swim on over to make the next letter.

☐ **REMINDER:** Take some time to work on your weigh-in challenge.

Name

Bait & Tackle 6.3

> There is another story about Jesus falling asleep in a boat. Here is my summary, but you can read it in Mark 4:35-41. One time, Jesus fell asleep in the boat with His disciples. A big storm came up, and the disciples were scared for their lives! Jesus kept sleeping through the storm. The disciples, fearful, woke Jesus. Jesus came out from inside the boat and commanded the wind and waves to stop by saying, "Peace, be still." WHAM! The waves and wind stopped immediately! Pretty cool, huh? You see, when Jesus is with you, there is no need to fear the storms of life. Well, I better get back to catching my dinner, and I see you have a sleeping fisherman you need to go poke to wake him up!

Gear Up!

Wake That Fisherman! Use your pushpins to poke the fisherman awake! Remember to use a cork board, cutting board, or foam behind your paper.

Capital C: Start at the pole line, curve back and swim back and down to the waterline, and flow with the current out to connect to another letter.

Trace then write two capital C's without connecting them. Then, practice connecting it on out to the next letter. Don't lift your pencil once the capital C is done, just swim on over to make the next letter. Practice the word *dog* also.

Challenge: Write the following in cursive: c, a, and d.

> Did you complete the Don't Tip the Boat challenge? If you did, you get your balance badge. Color it in, then cut it out and add it to your achievement board.
>
> Your next challenge is to use your best handwriting to make the letters given each day.

Name _____

Bait & Tackle 6.4

" You know that when the storms come, you need an anchor plan in place. Even if the storm pulls your anchor out, at least it will help drag your boat, so you aren't pulled too far. The anchor gives us hope that our boat will survive the storm. Jesus is known as our anchor. Hebrews 6:19 says, "We have this as a sure and steadfast anchor of the soul, a hope that enters into the inner place behind the curtain. . . ." Jesus is our hope, He is our soul's anchor. "

Gear Up!

Anchor Up: Stand with your feet about shoulder width apart. Bend over and pretend to pull up a heavy anchor. Give the anchor 10 good pulls all the way up. Remember, that anchor is heavy!

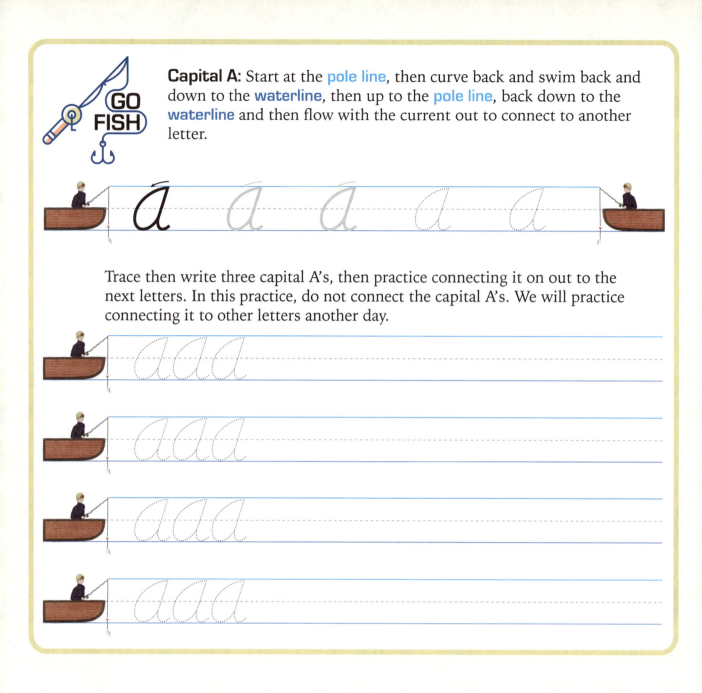

Name _____

Bait & Tackle 6.5

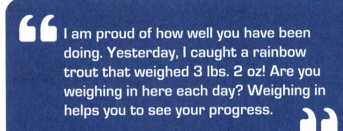
" I am proud of how well you have been doing. Yesterday, I caught a rainbow trout that weighed 3 lbs. 2 oz! Are you weighing in here each day? Weighing in helps you to see your progress. "

Gear Up!

Flow with the Current: Complete the maze of lines of the water's current.

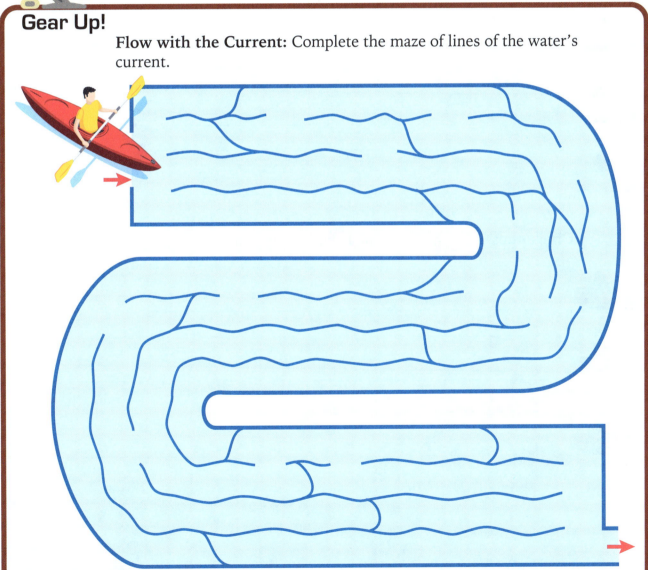

Capital A: Start at the pole line, then curve back and swim back and down to the waterline, then up to the pole line and back down to the waterline and then flow with the current out to connect to another letter.

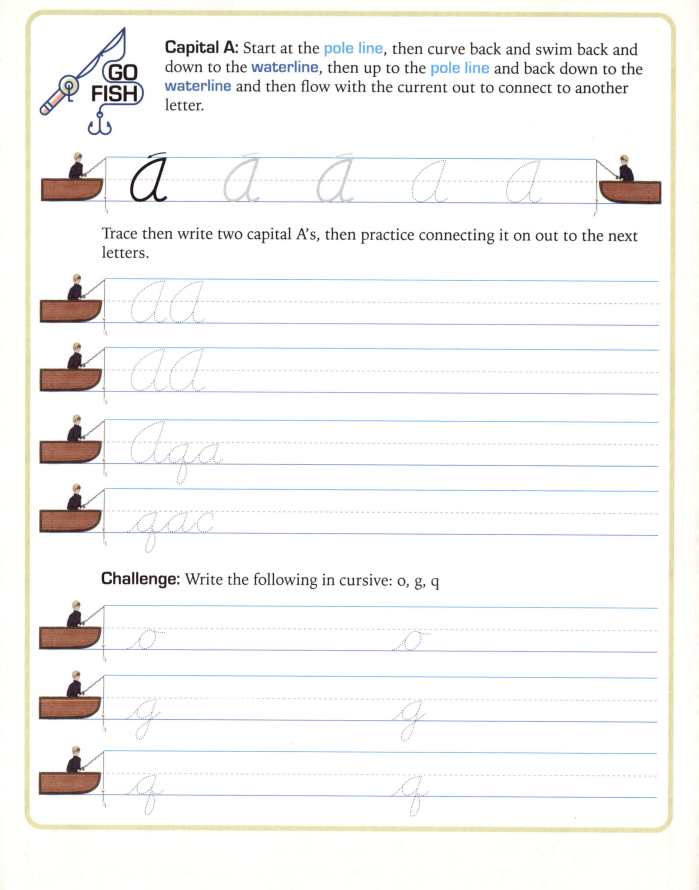

Trace then write two capital A's, then practice connecting it on out to the next letters.

Challenge: Write the following in cursive: o, g, q

Name

"Be sure to weigh in at Bait & Tackle 7.1 and 7.4. You'll also be given new challenges. I can't wait to see you win."

"You have previously done the exercises in the Gear Up section. This week you only need gear for Bait & Tackle 7.2. You'll be learning some neat fishing terms, and one is tasty!"

Gather Your Gear

Day 2
☐ Cotton swabs
☐ Sidewalk chalk

Tackle Box 7

Official GUIDE

Bream: greenish bronze freshwater fish.

Hush puppies: deep fried round balls made from cornmeal.

Buoy: anchored float with a navigation mark. It can show information or hazards for boats.

Buffalo Fish: the largest North American sucker fish. They have large lips for sucking and are grayish green with a humped back.

Name _____

Bait & Tackle 7.1

> "Bream are a type of fish. They are small and feisty. We call the place they lay their eggs a "bed," which is where the male fish guard and feed. If we get on a bed, we will catch a lot. Today I got in a bed of bream. Boy, oh boy, did I fill my live well. They sure are fun to catch! I will eat well tonight. I think I will make up some hush puppies and fresh corn on the cob to go with the bream."

Gear Up!

Live Well Reaches: Sit in a chair or side of a bathtub with your feet flat on the ground. Keep your feet spread apart. Bend over and touch the top of the ground between your feet as if you were touching the top of the live well in your boat. Do this 12 times.

Capital A: Start at the pole line and curve back, then swim back and down to the waterline, then up to the pole line, then back down to the waterline. Then flow with the current out to connect to another letter.

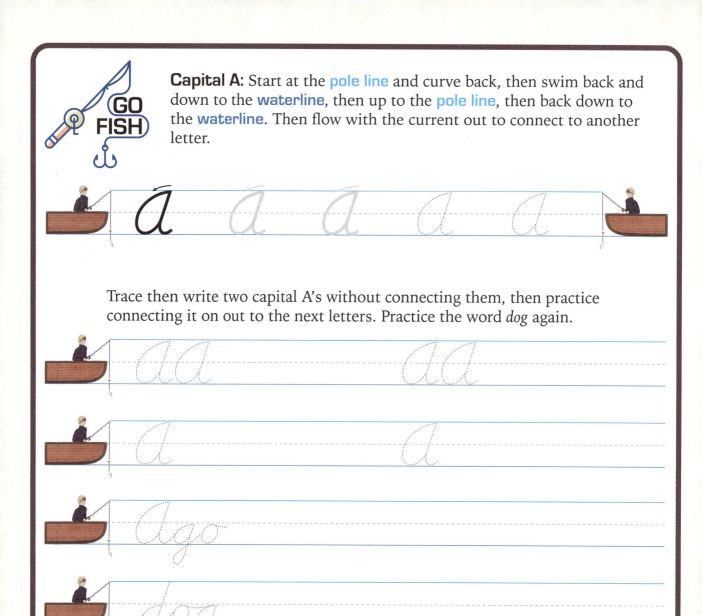

Trace then write two capital A's without connecting them, then practice connecting it on out to the next letters. Practice the word *dog* again.

> Did you complete the challenge? You were to use your best handwriting to write some of the letters you have learned.
>
> Your next challenge is to place your writing on the lines correctly. You can use the fishing guide to help you know where they should be. Try using this in your other courses as well.

Name

Bait & Tackle 7.2

> Have you ever seen a hoop net? In Arkansas, we are part of the Mississippi River Valley. Buffalo fish are often caught in hoop nets in rivers and lakes throughout the Mississippi River Valley. Buffalo fish are among our nation's most important wild food fishes. Check out this hoop net in this picture. It reminds me of the disciples casting their nets. I also think of how cursive has hoops and loops just like the net of this hoop net. Pretty cool, huh?

Gear Up!

Brighten the lures with your cotton swabs and sidewalk chalk to decorate and liven up the lures. Fish like flashy lures, so make them colorful.

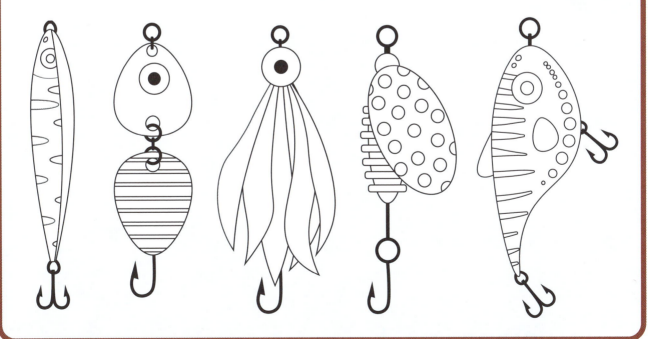

Capital O: Start at the pole line, just like with the capital C. Curve back and swim back and down to the waterline, then circle up to the pole line to connect your line and loop down and out. Capital O's do not connect to other letters.

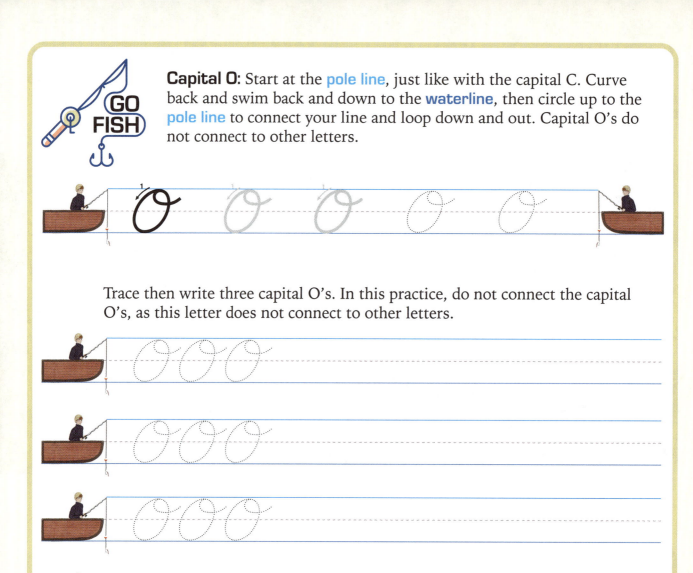

Trace then write three capital O's. In this practice, do not connect the capital O's, as this letter does not connect to other letters.

☐ **REMINDER:** Take some time to work on your weigh-in challenge.

Name _____

Bait & Tackle 7.3

> "John 12:46 says, "I have come into the world as light, so that whoever believes in me may not remain in darkness." Before lighthouses, people would build fires to guide ships home. We are like a lighthouse to the world. We have the Holy Spirit working in us which produces an outer example, or light, to others. It's often called "letting our lights shine.""

Gear Up!

Lighthouse Taps: Lighthouses flash their lights, so we are going to tap for lighthouse flashes. Bring your pinky and thumb together to tap and open, tap and open, like a lighthouse flash. Do this 12 times with both hands.

Capital O: Start at the pole line, just like with the capital C. Curve back and swim back and down to the waterline, then circle up to the pole line to connect your line, and then loop down and out.

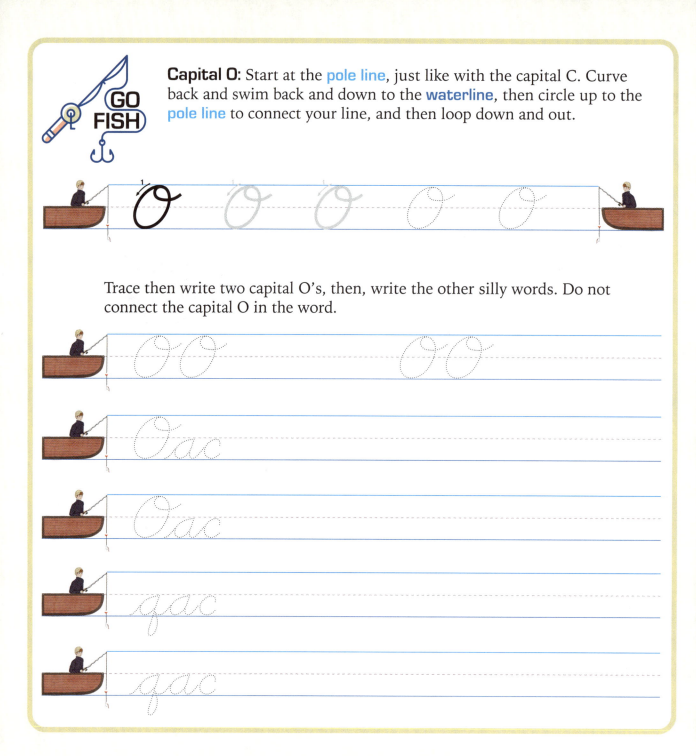

Trace then write two capital O's, then, write the other silly words. Do not connect the capital O in the word.

☐ **REMINDER:** Take some time to work on your weigh-in challenge.

Name

Bait & Tackle 7.4

" When you are in a lake or ocean, you will see buoys. Buoys are there to give us a marker or as a caution. Remember how the disciples followed the instructions Jesus gave them? Good fishermen follow the rules of the water, just like you are following the rules for *Catching on to Cursive*. "

" Be sure to keep your eyes on the buoys. This might be a challenge, but you can do it. Remember to have someone listen and watch as you read off the numbers on the buoys. "

Gear Up!

Buoy Markers: Reading from left to right, read the number on every other buoy. Call it aloud to someone as they watch you read. Try to keep a steady pace as you use your eyes to track.

Capital O: Start at the pole line, then curve back and swim back and down to the waterline, then circle up to the pole line to connect your line, and loop down and out.

Trace then write two capital O's, then practice writing the other words, but remember the capital O does not connect to the other letters.

" Did you use the guide to place your letters correctly? If so, you can color in the guide badge in the back of the book. Be sure to add this badge to your achievement board. "

Name _____

Bait & Tackle 7.5

" What are some ways you can let your light shine? Discuss this with a parent. Some suggestions are to show kindness, be honest, share with your siblings or friends, and keep a good attitude. "

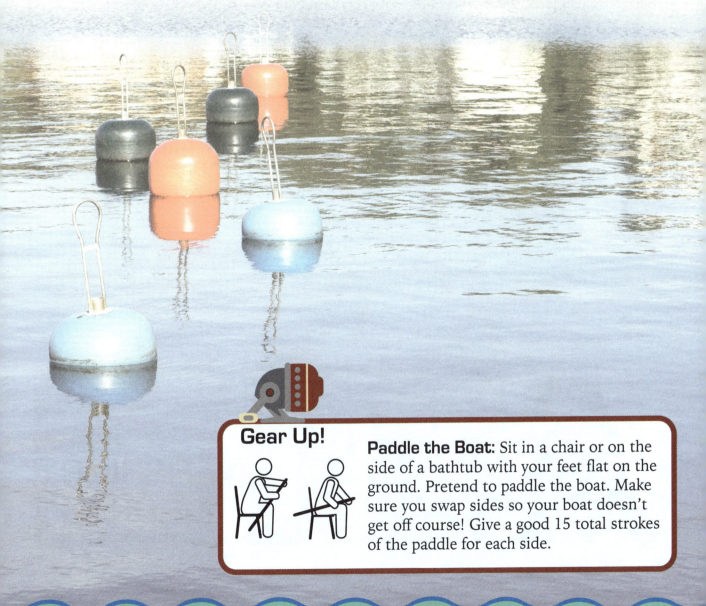

Gear Up!

Paddle the Boat: Sit in a chair or on the side of a bathtub with your feet flat on the ground. Pretend to paddle the boat. Make sure you swap sides so your boat doesn't get off course! Give a good 15 total strokes of the paddle for each side.

Review your letters: letters C, A, and O

Capital C: Start at the pole line, curve back and swim back and down to the waterline, and flow with the current out to connect to another letter.

Capital A: Start at the pole line and curve back, then swim back and down to the waterline, then up to the pole line, then back down to the waterline. Then flow with the current out to connect to another letter.

Capital O: Start at the pole line, then curve back and swim back and down to the waterline, then circle up to the pole line to connect your line, and loop down and out.

It's your turn to practice the capital letters from this week. Practice the C, A, and O. Make sure you trace them twice, but write them on your own once.

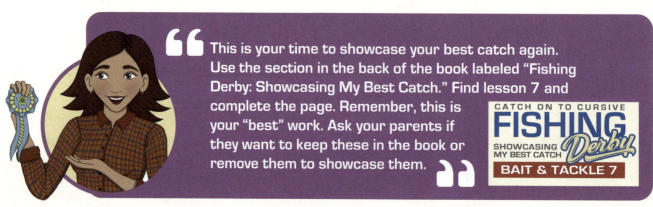

"This is your time to showcase your best catch again. Use the section in the back of the book labeled "Fishing Derby: Showcasing My Best Catch." Find lesson 7 and complete the page. Remember, this is your "best" work. Ask your parents if they want to keep these in the book or remove them to showcase them."

CATCH ON TO CURSIVE
FISHING Derby
SHOWCASING MY BEST CATCH
BAIT & TACKLE 7

Name

"Your next challenge is to use all the letters you have learned by writing the words in the lesson each day."

"Be sure to check out your gear. You have one new activity this week and others you are familiar with. We are learning about something stinky in your fishing guide."

Day 1:
☐ Pencil with eraser or pencil with pushpin in the eraser

Day 3:
☐ Paper clips

Day 4:
☐ Sticky notes or paper
☐ Ball (tennis or approx. size)

Day 5:
☐ Small objects such as beads, small buttons, or sunflower seeds
☐ Play-Doh or other dough

Tackle Box 8 103

Official GUIDE

Catfish: a freshwater fish that usually lives on the bottom of the pond or lake. They have whiskers, or barbels, like a cat, which is how they got their name.

Catfish bait: There are many kinds of bait fishermen use to lure in catfish. The one I am speaking of is round, firm, moldable balls that are like clay. Once wet, it is gummy and slimy. They make it in different scents, such as chicken liver. I wish I could describe the horrid smell that comes from this kind of bait, but it will make you sick to your stomach.

Name

Bait & Tackle 8.1

> "Genesis 1:28 tells us that God put man to rule over the fish, birds, and every living creature. Just as you rule over the fish, we are to rule ourselves also. That means to have self-control and diligence. We are told in Colossians 3:15–17,
>
> "And let the peace of Christ rule in your hearts, to which indeed you were called in one body. And be thankful. Let the word of Christ dwell in you richly, teaching and admonishing one another in all wisdom, singing psalms and hymns and spiritual songs, with thankfulness in your hearts to God. And whatever you do, in word or deed, do everything in the name of the Lord Jesus, giving thanks to God the Father through him."
>
> When we are working hard on learning cursive, we can let the peace of God rule in our hearts and be thankful. We can learn cursive in the name of the Lord! I am excited about the progress you are making. It won't be long until you will be writing lots of words in cursive."

Gear Up!

The Eye of the Hook: If you can, use a pushpin in the tip of an eraser or just a pencil with an eraser. Hold the pencil straight up and down in front of your nose. Bring it in slowly as you keep your eyes on the pin or eraser. Keep your focus. See how close you can bring it in before you see two of it. Hold this for 10 seconds, release, then do it two more times.

Capital Q: Remember how the capital O started at the top and had a loop out at the top? Well, the letter Q is a flip of that. Start at the waterline, curve back up to the pole line and then back around to the waterline to connect your lines, then loop up and out to the waterline so you will be ready to connect to other letters.

Trace then write three capital Q's. In this practice, do not connect the capital Q's. We will practice connecting it to other letters another day.

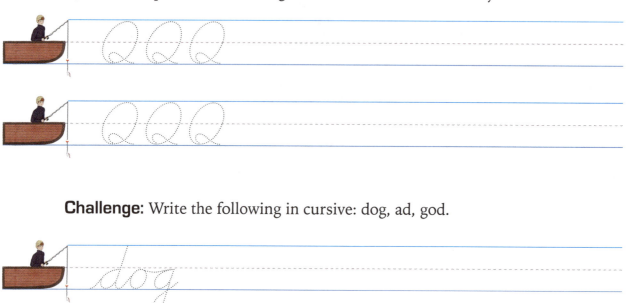

Challenge: Write the following in cursive: dog, ad, god.

☐ **REMINDER:** Take some time to work on your weigh-in challenge.

Name

Bait & Tackle 8.2

" Here's a scale for rating your attitude this week. You have been learning cursive for 8 weeks now. I told you it would take patience, persistence, and perseverance. I think you are doing a wonderful job. What rating would you give your attitude today? Be thankful we have the freedom and opportunity to learn. "

Gear Up!

Don't Hit the Bridge: The ships in the river need to get through. Place your hands flat on the ground with tips of toes on the ground and body lifted to be the bridge. Hold this for 10–15 seconds. Try to beat your time this week. (Your last time was at Bait & Tackle 4.1.) Record today's time here: _____

Capital Q: Start at the waterline, curve back up to the pole line and then back around to the waterline to connect your lines, then loop up and out to the waterline so you will be ready to connect to other letters.

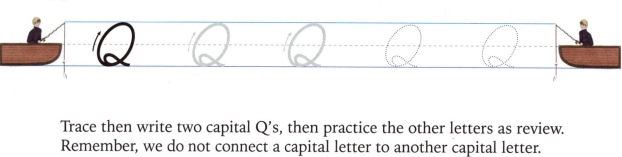

Trace then write two capital Q's, then practice the other letters as review. Remember, we do not connect a capital letter to another capital letter.

Challenge: Write the following in cursive: cog, odd, doc

☐ **REMINDER:** Take some time to work on your weigh-in challenge.

Name _____

Bait & Tackle 8.3

> "What rating would you give your attitude today? Are you ruling over your attitude? What is one thing you can thank God for today? I know when I am out fishing, I am thankful for the beautiful creation God has made and shared with me."

😀 🙂 😐 🙁 ☹️

Gear Up!

Hook the Fish: At the bottom of the page is a row of fish. Open the paper clips and secure a paper clip to each fish.

Capital Q: Start at the **waterline**, curve back up to the **pole line** and back around to the **waterline** to connect your lines, then loop up and out to the **waterline**. Be ready to connect to other letters.

Trace then write two capital Q's, then practice the other letters as review.

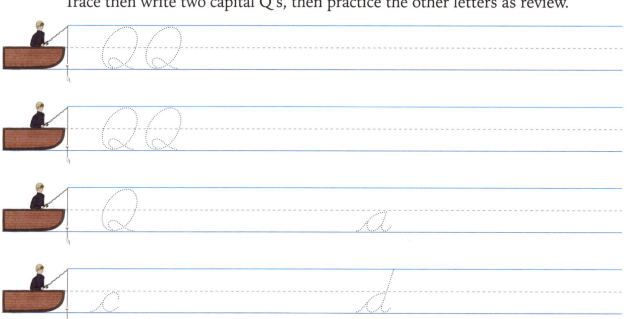

> Have you been writing your words each day? If so, trace the dot to dot.
>
> Your next challenge is to hook the fish each day (see previous page). Remember to remove the paper clips and store them until the next day.

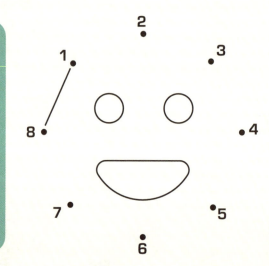

110　Hooked on Cursive

Name

Bait & Tackle 8.4

> "Attitudes really affect our effort and our thoughts. You have the power to rule over those attitudes and thoughts. Praying and asking God to help you keep a good attitude in your effort and to have a joyful heart is a great place to begin. How is your attitude today? Is it improving this week?"

Gear Up!

Aim and Cast: Place a piece of paper or sticky note on a door or wall about eye level. You can make a target on it if you'd like. Take about 10 steps back and try to AIM and CAST the ball to hit the target. If you miss three times, you can step forward one step. Try to hit the paper/target in the middle at least three times in a row.

Be sure to get your parents' permission for this exercise.

Capital E: This letter is different, as it reminds me of a backwards 3. Start at the pole line and curve back and down to the boat line, then curve back and down to the waterline. From there, float on out to connect to the next letter.

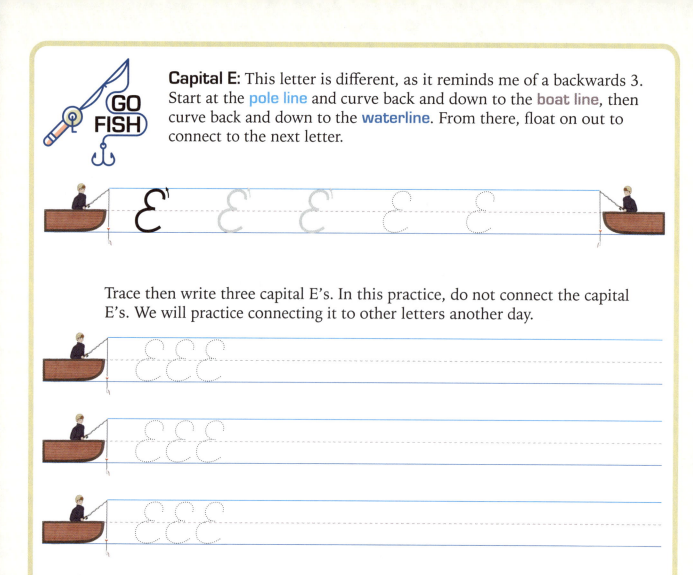

Trace then write three capital E's. In this practice, do not connect the capital E's. We will practice connecting it to other letters another day.

☐ **REMINDER:** Take some time to work on your weigh-in challenge.

Name

Bait & Tackle 8.5

> "I also like to pray the Word. One of my favorite verses to help me when I may be struggling with my attitude and thoughts is in 2 Corinthians 10:5 when it says, "take every thought captive to obey Christ." You see, I know that the Word tells me to be thankful and joyful. If my attitude is stinky like catfish bait, then I need to pray for God to help me "take every thought captive to obey Him." Have you been working to improve your attitude? Have you struggled a bit? If you have, you may want to pray this prayer. When you have a good attitude, you can keep thinking on the good things and give thanks to God."

Gear Up!

Hide the Worms: Using small objects and dough, push the small objects into the dough. Be sure to use your fingers to get them started and your thumb to get them all the way in. Remember to do at least 5 objects per hand.

Capital E: Start at the pole line and curve back and down to the boat line, then curve back and down to the waterline. From there, float on out to connect to the next letter.

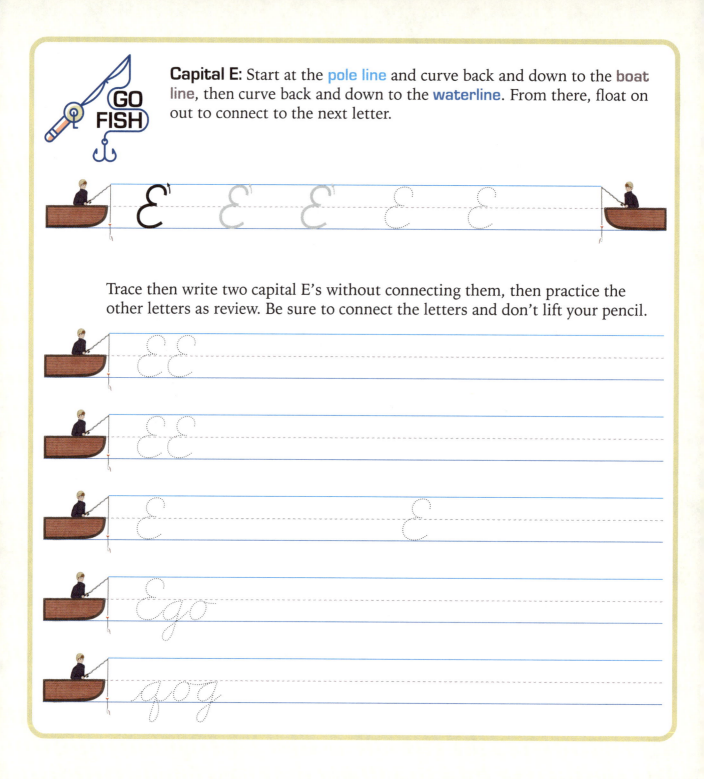

Trace then write two capital E's without connecting them, then practice the other letters as review. Be sure to connect the letters and don't lift your pencil.

☐ **REMINDER:** Take some time to work on your weigh-in challenge.

Name

TACKLE BOX 9

" Be sure to weigh in at 9.1 and get your new challenge! You're doing a great job at completing challenges. "

" This week you will have two new activities. Be sure to gather your supplies and follow directions. "

Gather Your Gear

Day 1:
☐ Painter's tape or rope or sidewalk chalk (or 2x4)

Day 3:
☐ Bicycle/scooter/skateboard items to help you balance

Day 4:
☐ Sheet of foam
☐ Sheet of plain paper

Day 5:
☐ Plastic lid with a lip or a round cake pan
☐ Marble

Official GUIDE

Whirlpool: a rapidly moving circular mass of water that has a downward pull.

DID YOU KNOW?

Summer is one of the best times to fish because you can use almost every single technique and bait because the weather is most predictable without drastic changes. (This is based on a US summer and may vary by location.)

Name _____

Bait & Tackle 9.1

"Have you ever seen a whirlpool? Whirlpools are when water is rotating due to currents or from hitting an obstacle. You might see one swirling when you let out the bath water. Whirlpools are neat and can create a soothing feeling to look at. But a real whirlpool, if large enough and in the right conditions, can be dangerous. There are things in life like whirlpools. Sin is also like this. Judas, one of the 12 disciples, had this problem. He betrayed Jesus, which means he broke his relationship with Jesus. Every time I think about Judas, I can't understand how he could have spent time with Jesus, witnessed miracles, heard Him teach, and yet he turned his back on Him. Sin is why. Sin causes division. Sin may look good, but it causes spiritual death and separates us from God. Let's pray and ask God to help us to not be lured into sin like a fish is drawn to a flashy lure. God can help us to resist sin and stand firm in our faith."

Gear Up!

Walk the Plank!
Use painter's tape, a rope, or sidewalk chalk to make a long line about 6 feet long. Walk the Plank by balancing on the line with one foot in front of the other. Do this three times. Don't fall in! There might be gators in that water!

(You can also use a 2x4 or balance beam.)

Capital E: Start at the *pole line*, and curve back and down to the *boat line*, then curve back and down to the *waterline*. From there, float on out to connect to the next letter.

Trace then write two capital E's without connecting them, then practice the other letters as review. You won't connect these letters since they are all capital letters.

"Did you strengthen your hands by hooking the fish each day? If so, color in the arrow on the strong meter.

Your next challenge is to use a capital letter in your writing when you begin a new sentence or the word I."

Name _____

Bait & Tackle 9.2

" Whirlpools are neat. They are fun to watch when you let the water out of the tub, unless you have a small toy that will fit down the drain of course! I bet the disciples saw whirlpools with as much time as they spent on the water. "

Gear Up!

Whirlpool Maze: The little fish is stuck and needs to find a way out. Help the fish swim out of the whirlpool.

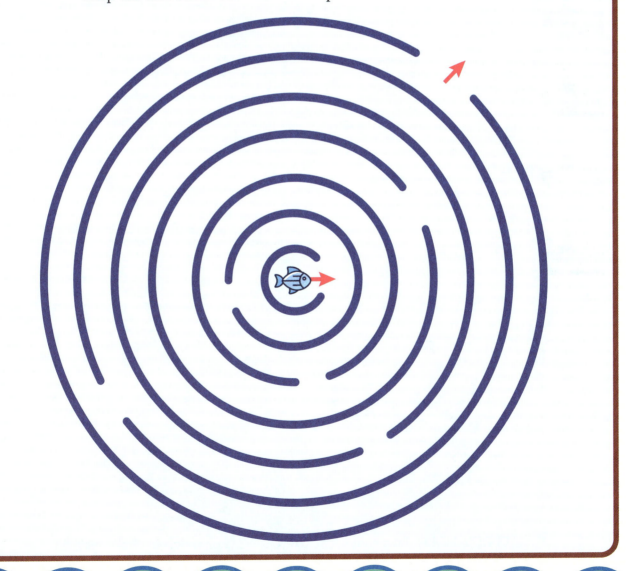

We have learned several lowercase letters. They all started like a lowercase c. Now, we will learn letters that have a different way of starting. Look at this letter t.

Lowercase t: Begin at the waterline, swim up to the pole line and straight back down and float on out to the waterline. Then, come back up and cross it at the boat line. If you are writing a word with the letter t, you will finish the whole word before coming back to cross the t.

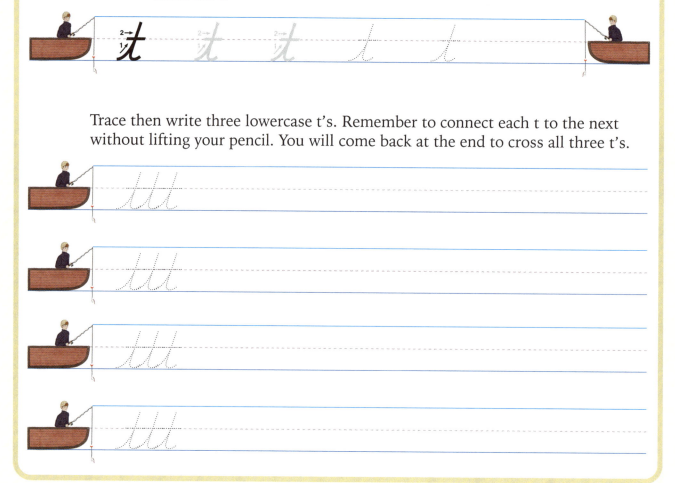

Trace then write three lowercase t's. Remember to connect each t to the next without lifting your pencil. You will come back at the end to cross all three t's.

☐ **REMINDER:** Take some time to work on your weigh-in challenge.

Name _____

Bait & Tackle 9.3

> "Another powerful force over water is a waterspout. No, not the kind of spout you turn on to get water out of, but a waterspout that is like a tornado over the water. It is like a whirlpool over the water instead of in the water. Experienced fishermen know when to get off the water or what to do if a storm does come up on them quickly. It almost becomes like an instinct that they have done so long that they no longer think about it; they just know how to respond. As you learn cursive, the more you practice and apply what you learn, the more it will become like this. You'll be an experienced writer!"

Gear Up!

Don't Tip the Boat: Balance on a bicycle, scooter, or skateboard for 15 seconds or longer. You can also use your items from the Walk the Plank activity from Bait & Tackle 9.1.

Lowercase t: Begin at the **waterline**, swim up to the **pole line** and straight back down and float on out to the **waterline**. Then, come back up and cross it at the **boat line**. If you are writing a word with the letter t, you will finish the whole word before coming back to cross the t.

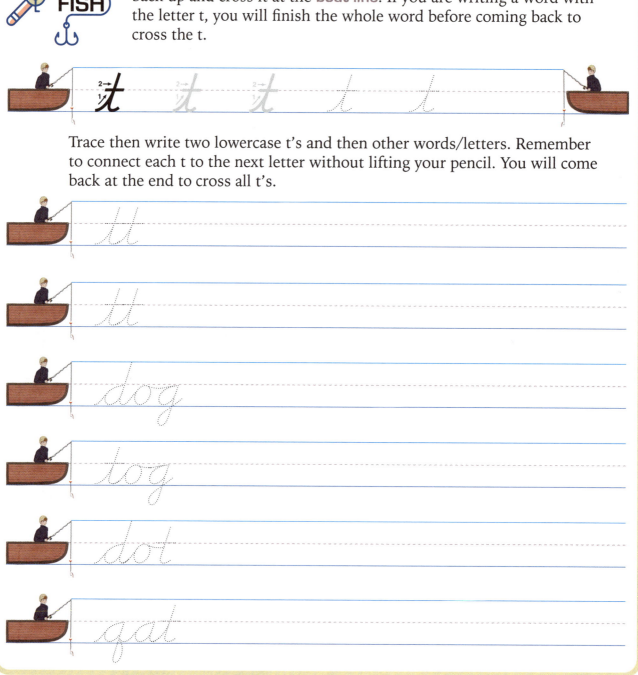

Trace then write two lowercase t's and then other words/letters. Remember to connect each t to the next letter without lifting your pencil. You will come back at the end to cross all t's.

☐ **REMINDER:** Take some time to work on your weigh-in challenge.

Name _____

Bait & Tackle 9.4

> "Most storms that are powerful must have the right conditions to gain power. Many fishermen of the Gulf of Mexico area will tell you that a few days before a strong storm hits that the bass will be aggressive eaters. My dad often says that a cool front out of the southwest is not good conditions for freshwater fishing where we live. We like fishing when our labor produces a good catch. Our hearts also must have the right conditions in order to produce spiritual fruit. The Bible tells us, "Above all else, guard your heart, for everything you do flows from it" (Proverbs 4:23, NIV). What is springing from your heart? Is the condition of your heart one that produces good fruit?"

Gear Up!

The Right Conditions: Place a plain piece of paper on a piece of foam. When you write, if you apply too little pressure, it is difficult to see your writing and it can even look shaky. If you apply too much pressure, it will cause you pain. You need the right pressure to see your words, but not too much or you'll push through the paper to the foam. Print your name to get the feel for how much pressure is the right condition for writing. Try printing your name three times.

Lowercase t: Begin at the waterline, swim up to the pole line and straight back down and float on out to the waterline. Then, come back up and cross it at the boat line. If you are writing a word with the letter t, you will finish the whole word before coming back to cross the t.

Trace then write two lowercase t's and then other words/letters. Remember to connect each t to the next letter without lifting your pencil. You will come back at the end to cross all t's.

" Have you used capital letters to start a new sentence and for the word I? If so, you earned your capital letter badge. Decorate the capital I on the badge and add it to your achievement board. "

Name

Bait & Tackle 9.5

" WOW! Look at that! Nine weeks completed today. I am enjoying our fishing and Bible talks. I am also enjoying watching you grow in fruits of the Spirit. You are persevering and showing self-control and patience too! Be proud that you have learned the letters c, a, d, o, g, q, E, t, A, O, and Q in cursive! "

Gear Up!

Marble in the Whirlpool: Using a plastic lid with a lip or a round cake pan, place a marble inside. Have someone move the lid/pan so the marble rolls in the inside edge back and forth and eventually all the way around in a circle. Follow the marble with your eyes, but do not move your head. Move only your eyes as you follow the marble back and forth. Do this for one minute.

Review your letters: letters Q, E, and t

Capital Q: Start at the waterline, then curve back up to the pole line and back around to the waterline to connect your lines, then loop up and out to the waterline. Be ready to connect to other letters.

Capital E: Start at the pole line, and curve back and down to the boat line, then curve back and down to the waterline. From there, float on out to connect to the next letter.

Lowercase t: Begin at the waterline, swim up to the pole line and straight back down and float on out to the waterline. Then, come back up and cross it at the boat line. If you are writing a word with the letter t, you will finish the whole word before coming back to cross the t.

Trace the letters Q, E, and t. Trace them three times, and then write them once on your own. Be sure to leave a pinky space between each set.

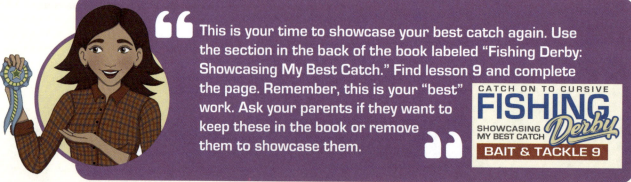

"This is your time to showcase your best catch again. Use the section in the back of the book labeled "Fishing Derby: Showcasing My Best Catch." Find lesson 9 and complete the page. Remember, this is your "best" work. Ask your parents if they want to keep these in the book or remove them to showcase them."

CATCH ON TO CURSIVE
FISHING Derby
SHOWCASING MY BEST CATCH
BAIT & TACKLE 9

Name _____

" I've got another challenge for you. In this challenge, you are to practice the Right Conditions activity each day (see Bait & Tackle 9.4.) "

" Be sure to gather your gear for each day. You're learning some neat fishing terms too. "

Gather Your Gear

Lesson 2:
☐ Wave wand from previous lessons

Day 4:
☐ Tweezers and yarn worms from previous lessons

Official GUIDE

Creation: the action and process of God bringing all things into existence.

Sunrise: the period in the morning when the sun rises over the horizon.

Sunset: the period in the evening when the sun goes below the horizon.

DID YOU KNOW?

In autumn, the lake water does a "turn over" where the cooler water from the bottom mixes with the warmer top water, and they change places. The fish also know winter is coming, and they will feed more to gain weight.

Name _____

Bait & Tackle 10.1

> In James 1:2–4 (NIV), we are told to "Consider it pure joy, my brothers and sisters, whenever you face trials of many kinds, because you know that the testing of your faith produces perseverance. Let perseverance finish its work so that you may be mature and complete, not lacking anything." Did you know the Greek word of *perseverance* gives us more understanding of this word? James wrote this in Greek. The original Greek translation of the word perseverance here means "cheerful, or hopeful endurance; constancy." In this Scripture, James is telling us how important our attitudes are. We need to keep a cheerful attitude as we are constant in our work. That is what God wants from us. Doing everything without grumbling (Philippians 2:14). I know you can do this. Some fishermen like to whistle or sing a little tune to keep their attitudes cheerful. Let's see you apply this cheerful attitude in all you do this week.

Gear Up!

Follow the numbers to complete the dot-to-dot.

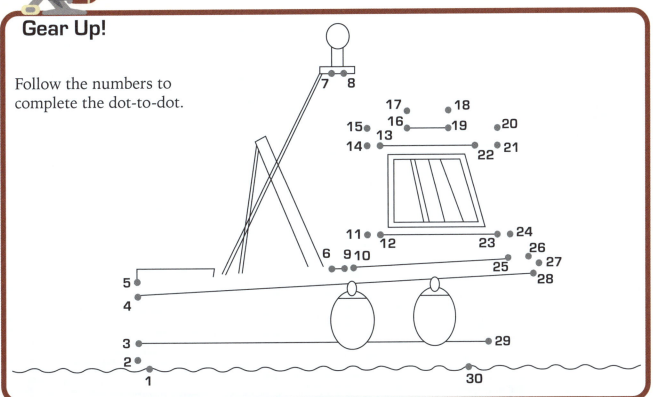

Lowercase i: Remember how we began the letter t? Today, we will start our letter the same way for the letter i. Instead of going up to the pole line, we will only go up to the boat line. Begin at the waterline, swim up to the boat line, and straight back down and float on out the waterline. Then, come back up and place your dot for your i. If you are writing a word with the letter i, you will finish the whole word before coming back to dot the i.

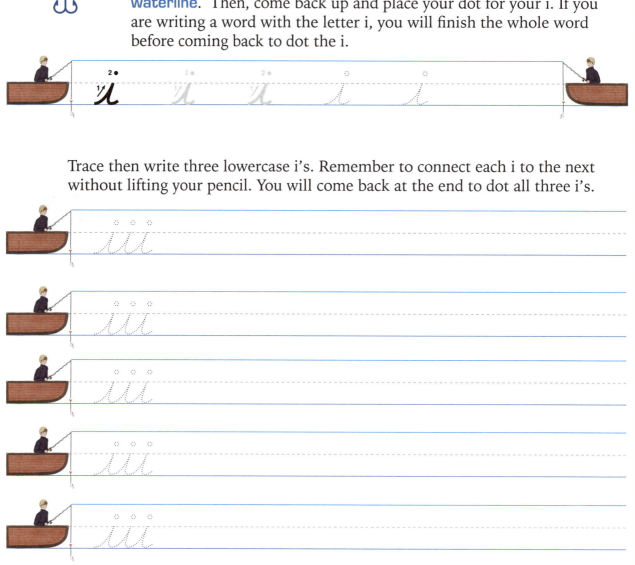

Trace then write three lowercase i's. Remember to connect each i to the next without lifting your pencil. You will come back at the end to dot all three i's.

☐ **REMINDER:** Take some time to work on your weigh-in challenge.

Name _____

Bait & Tackle 10.2

> "Read James 1:2–4 and Philippians 2:14 three times aloud in your own Bible. Try to say it without looking. Another way fishermen keep good attitudes is by giving thanks to God for the beautiful creation He made. It is difficult to be grumbling or upset when you are giving thanks. Look around you and notice something in God's creation you can be thankful for and tell your teacher. I love a sunrise or sunset. As a fisherman, I am able to see sunrises and sunsets while I fish. Remember to keep up the cheerful attitude in all you do."

Gear Up!

Making Waves: Use your wave wands from week 1 to make more waves! Be sure to make 8's sideways and upright with both hands.

Lowercase i: Begin at the waterline, swim up to the boat line, and then straight back down and float on out to the waterline. Then, come back up and place your dot for your i. If you are writing a word with the letter i, you will finish the whole word before coming back to dot the i.

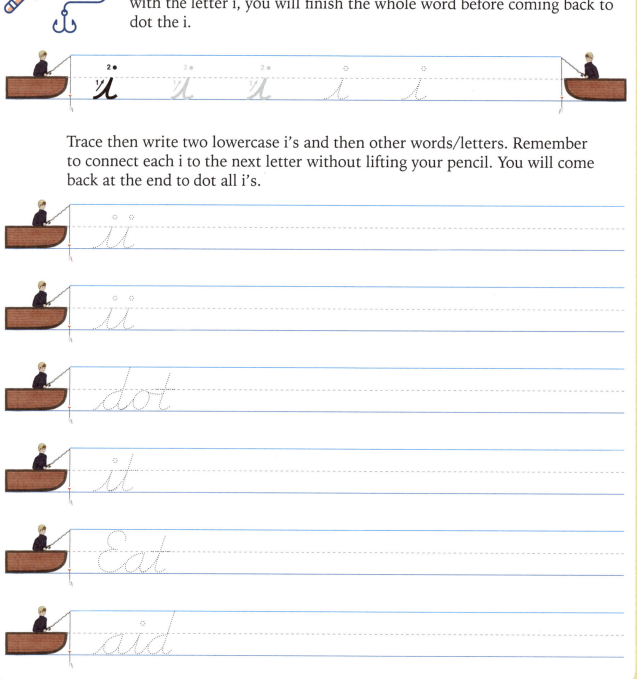

Trace then write two lowercase i's and then other words/letters. Remember to connect each i to the next letter without lifting your pencil. You will come back at the end to dot all i's.

☐ **REMINDER:** Take some time to work on your weigh-in challenge.

Name

Bait & Tackle 10.3

> Hey, "A glad heart makes a cheerful face." That is from Proverbs 15:13. If you have a happy heart, it will show on the outside. It's like that song, "If you're happy and you know it." If you are happy and have a joyful heart, then it will show in everything you do. One time I had lost a fishing contest, then my dog got sick. This made me sad. Life wasn't all happy. I needed to have joy in the sadness. I prayed and asked God to help me. That's what you can do too! If you are having a hard time with being full of joy, pray and ask God to help you. Remember, giving thanks for something in creation also helps us. Find something else you can be thankful for in God's creation.

Gear Up!

Trace the fishing lines to catch the fish and then connect that line to the fishing pole.

Lowercase i: Begin at the waterline, swim up to the boat line, and then straight back down and float on out to the waterline. Then come back up and place your dot for your i. If you are writing a word with the letter i, you will finish the whole word before coming back to dot the i.

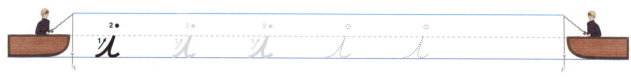

Trace then write two lowercase i's and then other words/letters. Remember to connect each i to the next letter without lifting your pencil. You will come back at the end to dot all i's.

" Did you do the Right Conditions activity? If so, you've learned to apply the right pressure as your write. Now you won't have light handwriting or broken crayons! You have earned your Right Conditions badge. Remember to add your badge to your achievement board.

Your next challenge is to practice the Marble in the Whirlpool activity from Bait & Tackle 9.5. "

134 Hooked on Cursive

Name _____

Bait & Tackle 10.4

" Hey there! Let's play a little game today. I have some words I forgot from our Scripture focus this week. Can you help by drawing a line to where they belong?
(*HINT: look back in your Bible or day 1 of this week.) "

Consider it pure _____,

my brothers and sisters,

whenever you face trials of many   joy

kinds, because you know that the

testing of your _____   perseverance

produces _____.

Let perseverance finish its work   faith

so that you may be mature and

complete, not lacking anything.

 " Don't squeeze the worms too hard or you'll have worm slime on your hands. "

Gear Up!

 Worm Squeezes: Use tweezers to pick up worms (pieces of yarn). Make sure you get 5–10 worms.

Lowercase j: Today, we will start our letter the same way as we did the letter i. Begin at the waterline, swim up to the boat line and straight back down, but keep on going to the hook space and then loop it back and up to the waterline to flow on out. If you are writing a word with the letter j, you will finish the whole word before coming back to dot the j.

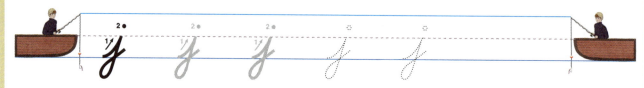

Trace then write three lowercase j's. Remember to connect each j to the next without lifting your pencil. You will come back at the end to cross all three j's.

☐ **REMINDER:** Take some time to work on your weigh-in challenge.

Name _____

Bait & Tackle 10.5

> "Hey, did you know that if you sing, it helps bring joy? Read James 1:2–4 and Philippians 2:14 aloud again today. Keep on having a cheerful attitude in all you do. Remember that ways to keep a cheerful attitude are to sing, give thanks, and pray! Sing the song "If You're Happy and You Know It" to stir up some joy!"

(Have your parent look this up if you don't know it.)

Gear Up!

> "You know one thing I recently did that was fun? I rode a fishing boat roller coaster! Try following the path I took."

Bait & Tackle 10.5 137

Lowercase j: Begin at the waterline, swim up to the boat line and straight back down, but keep on going to the hook space and then loop it back and up to the waterline to flow on out. If you are writing a word with the letter j, you will finish the whole word before coming back to dot the j.

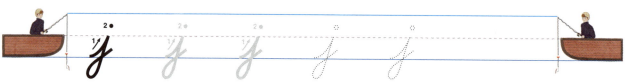

Trace then write two lowercase j's and then other words/letters. Remember to connect each j to the next letter without lifting your pencil. You will come back at the end to dot all j's.

☐ **REMINDER:** Take some time to work on your weigh-in challenge.

Name

TACKLE BOX 11

" I see you've been working on the weigh-in challenge given last week. I'll see you at the weigh-in section to see if you've won the challenge. "

" You'll only need gear for one day this week but check out the massive fish in your guide on the next page! "

Gather Your Gear

Day 4:
☐ Cotton swabs
☐ Sidewalk chalk

Official GUIDE

↑←**Goliath grouper:** large saltwater fish also known as the jewfish. This fish is usually found in shallow waters.

↓**Whale shark:** slow and filter feeding shark which is the largest living fish known.

Filter feeder: fish that feeds on living organisms it strains from the water.

Name _____

Bait & Tackle 11.1

" One of my favorite verses in the Bible is Philippians 4:13. Read that from your Bible. Now, help me fill in the missing letters by tracing the cursive letters you know. "

I can do all things through Christ who strengthens me. **(NKJV)**

" When I am feeling like I can't go on, I can pray and ask God to give me the strength to keep on going. His strength is perfect when my strength is gone. Hide that verse in your hearts so you can remember where your strength comes from. "

Gear Up!

Live Well Reaches: Sit in a chair or side of a bathtub with your feet flat on the ground. Keep your feet spread apart. Bend over and touch the top of the ground between your feet as if you were touching the top of the live well in your boat. Do this 12 times.

Lowercase j: Begin at the waterline, swim up to the boat line and straight back down, but keep on going to the hook space and then loop it back and up to the waterline to flow on out. If you are writing a word with the letter j, you will finish the whole word before coming back to dot the j.

Trace then write two lowercase j's and then other words/letters. Remember to connect each j to the next letter without lifting your pencil. You will come back at the end to dot all j's.

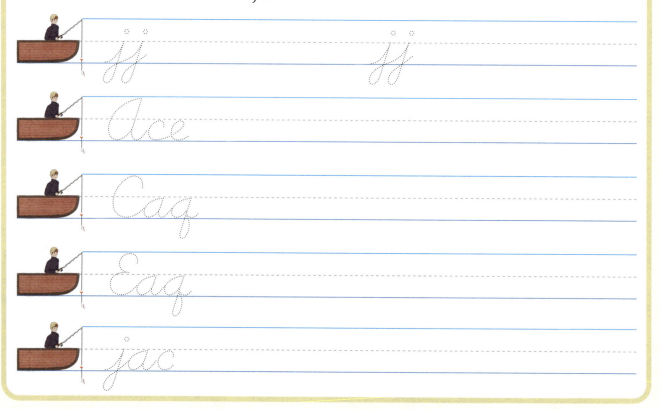

Hey there, were you able to complete the weigh-in challenge and follow the marble in the whirlpool? If you completed the weigh-in challenge, you have earned your whirlpool badge. Find it in the back, color it, then add it to your achievement board.

Your next weigh-in challenge is to use your tweezers and yarn to do 5 worm squeezes per hand each day. (See Bait & Tackle 10.4.)

Name

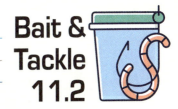 Bait & Tackle 11.2

> "Remember where our strength comes from? That's right, from God! Let's read Philippians 4:13 again. "I can do all things through Christ who strengthens me" (NKJV). Did you know that there are huge fish with great strength? The goliath grouper may be the strongest fish today, but the whale shark is the largest.
>
> In the Bible, the story of Jonah was about a great fish that swallowed Jonah. Yes, a fish swallowed a man! Jonah was running from God, but God had a plan for Jonah. The Bible says that God "prepared a great fish" and Jonah was in the belly of the fish for three days and three nights (Jonah 1:17).
>
> From the language of the Bible, "great fish" could mean any large creature of the sea, and we don't know if it was a whale, a goliath grouper, a whale shark, or some now-extinct fish. What we do know is that Jesus even referred to this great fish in Matthew 12:40 as he talked about His death, burial, and Resurrection. God has all kinds of wonderful things in His creation that are mighty and strong, but even we need to depend on the strength of God."

Gear Up!

Trace the lines to make waves.

ccccccccccccccccc

ccccccccccccccccc

Lowercase p: Once again, we begin this new letter like a letter we have learned. Begin this like the letter j. Begin at the waterline, swim up to the boat line and then straight back down to the hook line. Swim right back up your line, then up and over to bump the boat line. Circle back around to bump the waterline and your straight line. Then, flip over and swim back out toward the waterline.

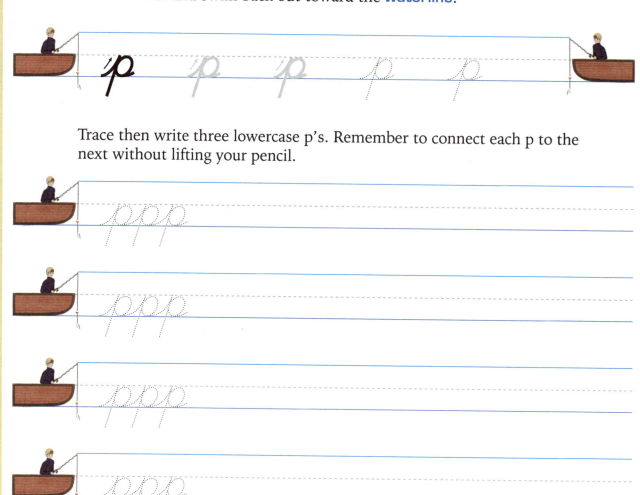

Trace then write three lowercase p's. Remember to connect each p to the next without lifting your pencil.

☐ **REMINDER:** Take some time to work on your weigh-in challenge.

Name _____

Bait & Tackle 11.3

> "Did you remember to hide that verse in your hearts this week? Let's read it, say it, and read it again. Get your Bibles out and open them to Philippians 4:13. Read it aloud, say it aloud (without looking), and read it aloud again. Ask a parent to help you research a goliath grouper and a whale shark. It is amazing to see God's wonderful creation."

Gear Up!

Lighthouse Taps: Lighthouses flash their lights, so we are going to tap for lighthouse flashes. Bring your pinky and thumb together to tap and open, tap and open, like a lighthouse flash. Do this 12 times with both hands.

Lowercase p: Begin this like the letter j. Begin at the **waterline**, swim up to the **boat line** and then straight back down to the hook line. Swim right back up your line, then up and over to bump the **boat line**. Circle back around to bump the **waterline** and your straight line. Then, flip over and swim back out toward the **waterline**.

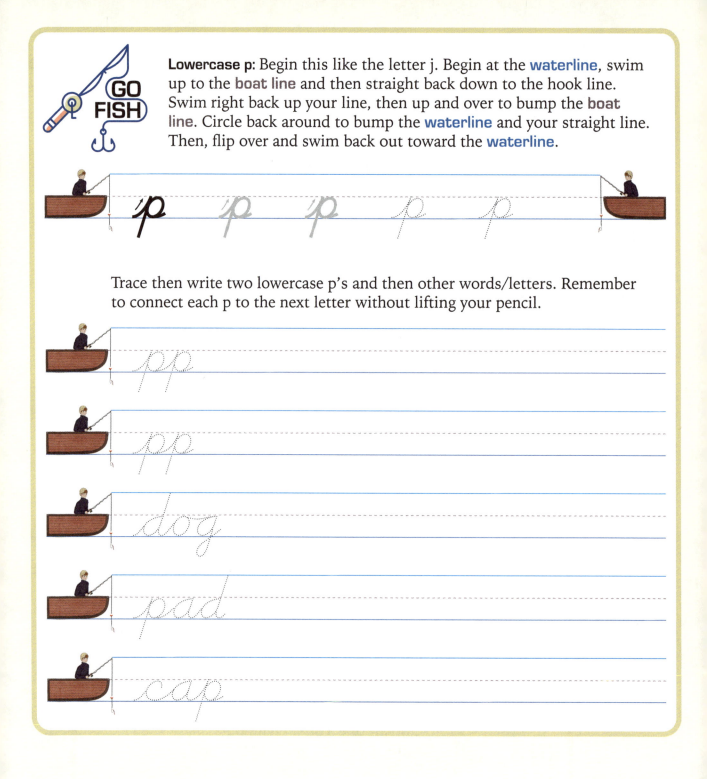

Trace then write two lowercase p's and then other words/letters. Remember to connect each p to the next letter without lifting your pencil.

☐ **REMINDER:** Take some time to work on your weigh-in challenge.

Name _____

Bait & Tackle 11.4

> " A goliath grouper is a type of bass which usually takes more than one person to reel it in. That is how strong they are. Talking about strength, my old boat needed a hole patched recently. I replaced a whole board on it so it would be stronger than just patching the hole. Now, it needs a new coat of paint. Can you help me paint it? "

Gear Up!

Paint the Boat: Use cotton swabs rubbed on sidewalk chalk to give Skeeter's boat a new coat of paint.

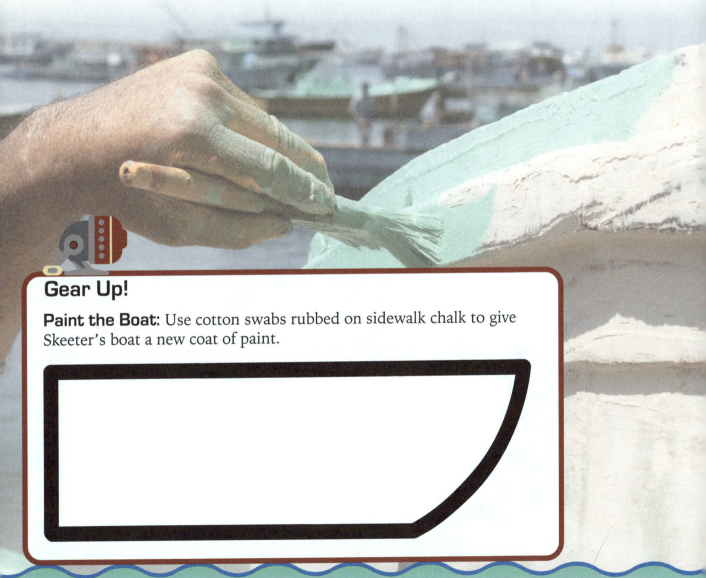

Lowercase p: Begin this like the letter j. Begin at the waterline, swim up to the boat line and then straight back down to the hook line. Swim right back up your line, then up and over to bump the boat line. Circle back around to bump the waterline and your straight line. Then, flip over and swim back out toward the waterline.

Trace then write two lowercase p's and then other words/letters. Remember to connect each p to the next letter without lifting your pencil.

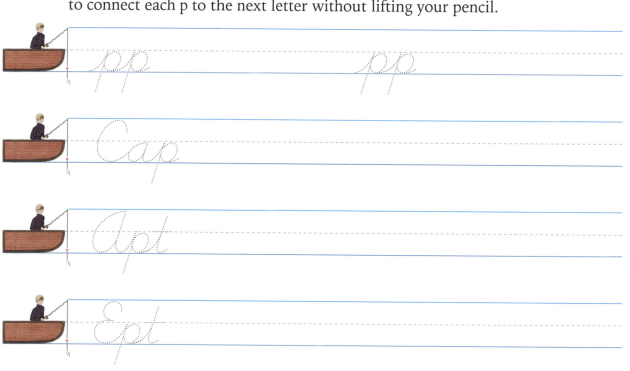

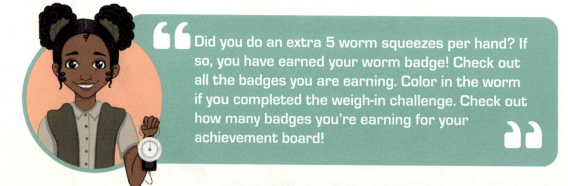

" Did you do an extra 5 worm squeezes per hand? If so, you have earned your worm badge! Check out all the badges you are earning. Color in the worm if you completed the weigh-in challenge. Check out how many badges you're earning for your achievement board! "

Name _____

Bait & Tackle 11.5

> "Remember where our strength comes from? That's right, from God! Let's read Philippians 4:13 again. "I can do all things through Christ who strengthens me." His strength is perfect! Jonah needed to learn to rely on God's strength and not his own. He also needed to learn that obedience to God brings blessings. What other lessons do you think Jonah could learn?"

Gear Up!

Paddle the Boat: Sit in a chair or on the side of a bathtub with your feet flat on the ground. Pretend to paddle the boat. Make sure you swap sides so your boat doesn't get off course! Give a good 15 total strokes of the paddle for each side.

Review your letters: letters i, j, and p

Lowercase i: Begin at the waterline, swim up to the boat line, and then straight back down and float on out to the waterline. Then come back up and place your dot for your i. If you are writing a word with the letter i, you will finish the whole word before coming back to dot the i.

Lowercase j: Begin at the waterline, swim up to the boat line and straight back down, but keep on going to the hook line and then loop it back and up to the waterline to flow on out. If you are writing a word with the letter j, you will finish the whole word before coming back to dot the j.

Lowercase p: Begin this like the letter j. Begin at the waterline, swim up to the boat line and then straight back down to the hook line. Swim right back up your line, then up and over to bump the boat line. Circle back around to bump the waterline and your straight line. Then, flip over and swim back out toward the waterline.

Trace the letters j, i, and p. Connect the letters and don't lift your pencil until all are written. Trace them three times, and then write them once on your own. Be sure to leave a pinky space between each set.

> This is your time to showcase your best catch again. Use the section in the back of the book labeled "Fishing Derby: Showcasing My Best Catch." Find lesson 11 and complete the page. Remember, this is your "best" work. Ask your parents if they want to keep these in the book or remove them to showcase them.

CATCH ON TO CURSIVE
FISHING Derby
SHOWCASING MY BEST CATCH
BAIT & TACKLE 11

Hooked on Cursive

Name

 TACKLE BOX 12

"Hey there, I've got another challenge for you to complete. Use the cotton swabs, sidewalk chalk, and a piece of paper to make your own painting of a fish. Be creative as you'll be earning your artist badge. (See Bait & Tackle 7.2 for inspiration.)"

"Remember, good fishermen gather their gear and are prepared for what is ahead. Be sure to gather your gear for your Gear Up sections."

Gather Your Gear

Day 3:
☐ Paper clips

Day 5:
☐ Pushpins
☐ One of the following: cutting board, cork board, or foam sheet

GUIDE

Fly fishing: a fishing method which uses "flies" or fly lures to catch fish. The fly is cast using a fly rod, reel, and specialized weighted line. This is different from other methods of rod and reel fishing and requires more skill and technique.

Fly lures: fishing bait that is used in fly fishing. The bait looks like natural insects or other organisms fish eat. These float or "land" on the water.

Brown trout: a freshwater trout with a slim body. Brown trout vary in color from silvery with relatively few spots and a white belly to the more common reddish-brown with a creamy white on the fish's belly. Both brown and rainbow trout have spots on their upper body.

Name _____

Bait & Tackle 12.1

" I have been making lures for fly fishing. We call them "flies." They take time, patience, and detail. I am proud of the ones I have made, but it took a while. I am also proud of how you have been persevering through your work. You have really shown you are growing in perseverance and patience.

The Bible tells us in Ecclesiastes 7:8, "Better is the end of a thing than its beginning, and the patient in spirit is better than the proud in spirit." Let's dig into this like we'd dig for worms so we can understand it better. Tying flies for fly fishing takes effort, time, and isn't always joyful. Yes, the final product of the finished work brings me joy. I can enjoy the feeling of accomplishment and hard work.

The word proud has two meanings. It can mean you feel pleasure about something, or it can mean you think you are more important than everyone else. In the verse we read, the word proud means to think you are more important or better than others. Try to learn patience so you can find joy in all you do and feel pleasure in all you accomplish. "

Gear Up!

Complete the dot-to-dot. First, try tracing it with your eyes before you get your pencil to complete it.

Lowercase s: We begin this new letter like the letters i, j, and p. Begin at the waterline, swim up to the boat line and then down, and curve back as you bump the waterline and your line. Then, flip over and swim back out toward the waterline.

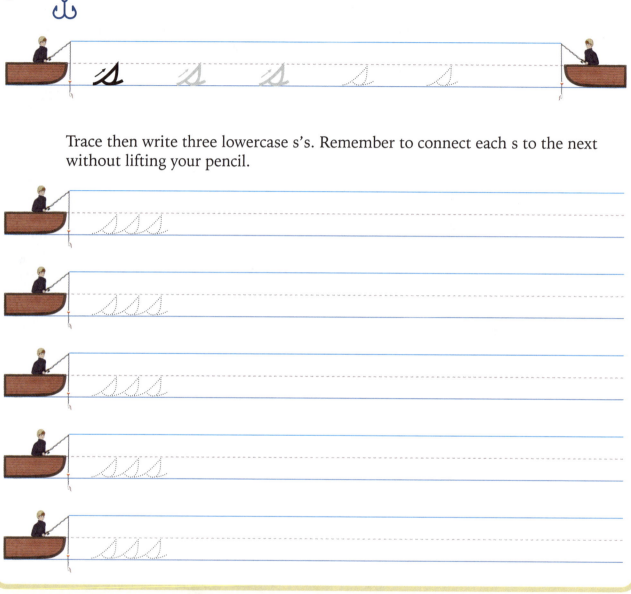

Trace then write three lowercase s's. Remember to connect each s to the next without lifting your pencil.

□ **REMINDER:** Take some time to work on your weigh-in challenge.

Name _____

Bait & Tackle 12.2

> "Fish are amazing creatures, and God created them with amazing design and instincts. The rainbow trout is a beautiful fish that has a pinkish stripe on its side with colors from green to brown to blue that will fade to a white toward its belly. They are good fish for eating, and they enjoy eating. Some people even have been known to feed them corn, but they also eat flies, which is why I have been making flies (fly lures). God's handiwork is all around us and, we have the honor of enjoying what He made."

Gear Up!

Don't Hit the Bridge: The ships in the river need to get through. Place your hands flat on the ground with tips of toes on the ground and body lifted to be the bridge. Hold this for 10–15 seconds.

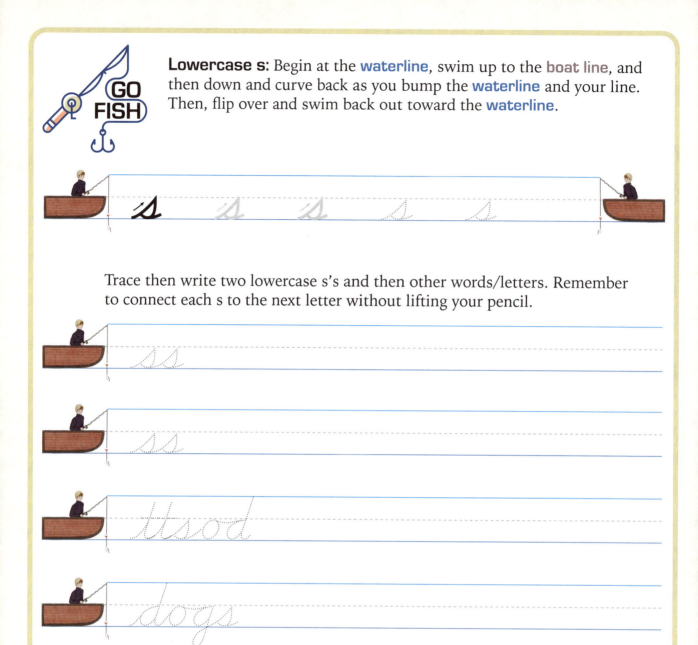

Lowercase s: Begin at the waterline, swim up to the boat line, and then down and curve back as you bump the waterline and your line. Then, flip over and swim back out toward the waterline.

Trace then write two lowercase s's and then other words/letters. Remember to connect each s to the next letter without lifting your pencil.

REMINDER: Take some time to work on your weigh-in challenge.

Name

Bait & Tackle 12.3

> "Once I have learned how to tie and make fly fishing lures, I will be able to enjoy fishing for rainbow and brown trout. I live not too far from two of the best trout fishing rivers in the United States. Fly fishing is an art and takes patience to learn how to cast just right. It's a lot like this course. You are putting in the patience and effort now so you can enjoy the benefits of writing in cursive. Keep on persevering."

> "Optional: Ask a parent to help you look up fly fishing and the White River and Little Red River in Arkansas. See if you can watch someone casting as they fly fish. Do you notice how it is an art?"

Gear Up!

Hook the Fish: At the bottom of the page is a row of fish. Open paper clips and secure a paper clip to each fish.

Lowercase s: Begin at the waterline, swim up to the boat line, and then down and curve back as you bump the waterline and your line. Then, flip over and swim back out toward the waterline.

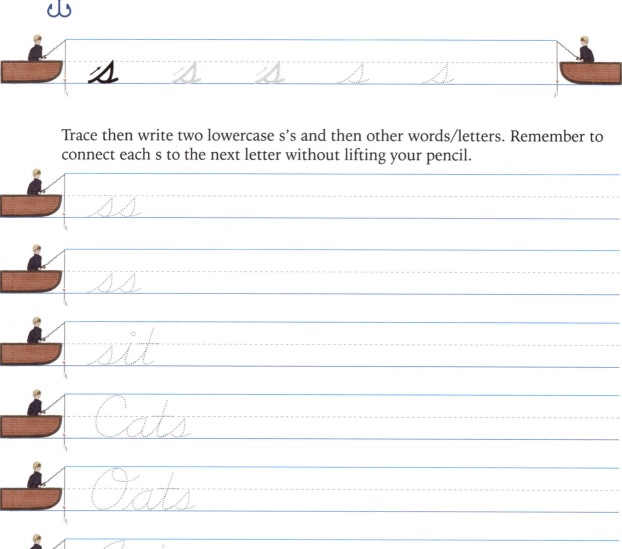

Trace then write two lowercase s's and then other words/letters. Remember to connect each s to the next letter without lifting your pencil.

"How did your artwork turn out? I'm sure it is fabulous! If you did the artist's challenge, you earn your artist's badge. Color in the artist's pallet on the badge. I just love this badge! It will look so good on your achievement board.

Your next challenge is to hold the Don't Hit the Bridge activity for 15 seconds and a 10-second break between. Do three each day. (See Bait & Tackle 12.2.)"

Name _____

Bait & Tackle 12.4

> "You know, this talk of perseverance, being patient, and proud when we have put in the good work reminds me that I was able to get all of my flies tied and I am ready to go fishing for trout. There are also brown trout. Trout are part of the salmon family and are healthy for you to eat. I love how God has given us fish we can catch to eat that are healthy for our bodies. God always provides for us."

Gear Up!

Hoist the Sails: These are called side planks and are like a side pushup where you hold your body up. Lay on your side, lift your body up with the arm closest to the ground. Your foot should be on its side on the ground. Your body makes a triangle shape like a sail.

Hold the position for 8 seconds, relax, and repeat two times. Do both sides of your body.

Lowercase u: We begin this new letter like the letter i also. It is actually like two connected letter i's without the dots. Begin at the waterline, swim up to the boat line, and then down and curve out as you bump the waterline. Then swim up to the boat line and then down and curve out.

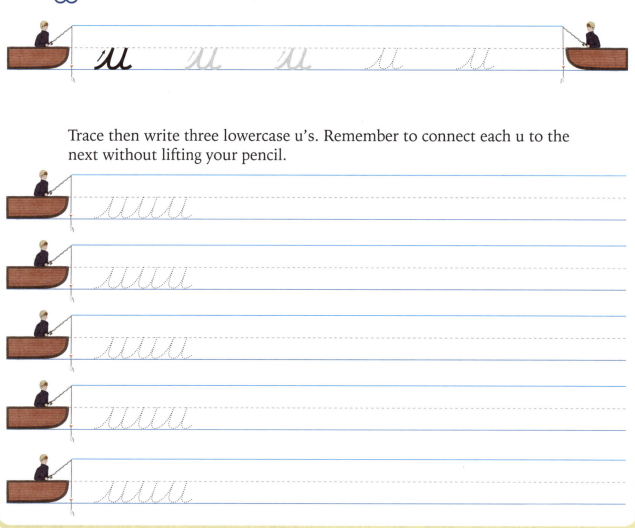

Trace then write three lowercase u's. Remember to connect each u to the next without lifting your pencil.

☐ **REMINDER:** Take some time to work on your weigh-in challenge.

160   Hooked on Cursive

Name _____

 Bait & Tackle 12.5

 "Help me finish this verse by tracing the letters you know."

Better is the end of a thing than the beginning, and the patient in spirit is better than the proud in spirit.

 "Awesome job! God's creation is simply amazing. I love learning about fish and all the things in creation that God made for us to enjoy."

Gear Up!

Trim the Fish: Use pushpins to poke the dotted edges of the fish. Be sure to use your thumb to help you poke the fish and remember to do equal amounts of pushes with each hand.

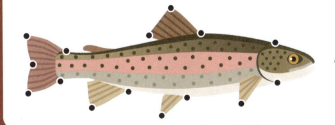 

Lowercase u: Begin at the **waterline**, swim up to the **boat line**, and then down and curve out as you bump the **waterline**. Then swim up to the **boat line** and then down and curve out.

u u u u u

Trace then write two lowercase u's and then other words/letters. Remember to connect each u to the next letter without lifting your pencil.

uu

uu

quit

Quit

it

dit

☐ **REMINDER:** Take some time to work on your weigh-in challenge.

Name _____

"Oh, we sure have some fun challenges this week! I can't wait to see how well you do. I hope you're earning your badges."

"There is gear for three days you will need to gather. You should have it all but be sure to gather it together."

Gather Your Gear

Day 1:
☐ Sticky notes or paper
☐ Ball (tennis or approx. size)

Day 2:
☐ Small objects such as beads, small buttons, or sunflower seeds
☐ Play-Doh or other dough

Day 3:
☐ Painter's tape or rope or sidewalk chalk

Official GUIDE

Guppies: small freshwater fish, mainly in aquariums, and sometimes used to eat mosquito larvae (eggs). Guppies do not lay eggs like most fish, but rather give birth to their babies.

Mollies: a large variety of freshwater fish which are social. They are sometimes called short-finned molly or common molly.

DID YOU KNOW?

Fishing during autumn is different than summer. The fish's appetites have increased, and you can use large bait such as large minnows and lures. The fish are looking for a place to feed and so their metabolisms are able to digest the larger bait.

Name

Bait & Tackle 13.1

> "I love God's creation. Have you ever sat out on a lake in a boat or by a pond? Think about how the water in a lake in the evening calms or how the pond water is still and quiet. God often speaks to us in the quiet. If you have a lake or pond near you, try to visit there and just sit and listen. Pray and talk with God. Thank Him for the beauty of creation. What sounds do you hear? What do you see all around? Here is a picture for you to imagine what it might be like or the sounds you might hear. God's creation is magnificent.
>
> Psalm 8:3–4
> "When I look at your heavens, the work of your fingers, the moon and the stars, which you have set in place, what is man that you are mindful of him, and the son of man that you care for him?"
> God cares so much for you. It is good to learn to enjoy His handiwork."

Gear Up!

Aim and Cast: Place a piece of paper or sticky note on a door or wall about eye level You can make a target on it if you'd like. Take about 10 steps back and try to AIM and CAST the ball to hit the target. If you miss three times, you can step forward one step. Try to hit the paper/target in the middle at least three times in a row.

Lowercase u: Begin at the waterline, swim up to the boat line, and then down and curve out as you bump the waterline. Then swim up to the boat line and then down and curve out.

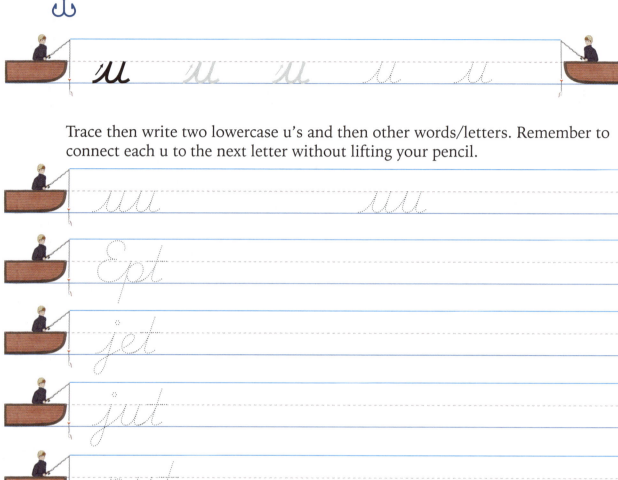

Trace then write two lowercase u's and then other words/letters. Remember to connect each u to the next letter without lifting your pencil.

Did you complete the bridges? Were you able to hold them for 15 seconds each? That shows how strong you are getting! If you completed the bridges, you have earned a bridge's badge. Color in the bridge on the badge in the back of the book. How many badges are on your achievement board after you add this one?

Your next challenge is to aim and cast each day. The catch is to do it three times with each arm and try to see how many times you hit the bullseye.

Keep track each day of how many bullseyes you hit by coloring in the bullseye on the bottom of your page.

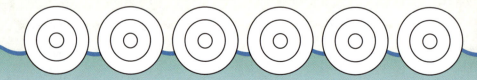

Name _____

Bait & Tackle 13.2

" Yesterday we talked about how the pond waters or lake can be still and calm. Did you know that fish, well, nature in general, can help calm you and relieve stress? Fishing is also a stress reliever. There is something peaceful about watching a fish swim. I think it is one of the reasons God created all of nature, and it is why so many people have them as pets. One peaceful and friendly fish is a type called mollies. Guppies, another type of fish, are also peaceful. Both types of fish are peaceful with other fish. Do you have a fish as a pet? "

Gear Up!

Lures in Mud: Push at least 5 small objects with each hand into dough. Be sure to use your fingers to get them started and your thumb to get them all the way in.

Lowercase w: We begin this new letter like the letter u. Begin at the waterline, swim up to the boat line and then down and curve out as you bump the waterline. Then swim up to the boat line, then down and curve out, bumping the waterline. Swim back up to the boat line and drift on over to just below the boat line to make a line for connecting to other letters. As you connect each w, you won't start at the waterline, but use the connector you made just below the boat line.

Trace then write three lowercase w's. Remember to connect each w to the next without lifting your pencil.

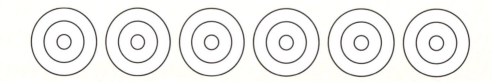

☐ **REMINDER:** Take some time to work on your weigh-in challenge.

Name _____

Bait & Tackle 13.3

> "All this talk about peaceful waters and fish makes me think about Psalms 29:11 and it says, "The LORD gives strength to his people; the LORD blesses his people with peace" (NIV). It says the Lord blesses us with peace. Peace is truly a blessing and something our world needs. We can have the peace of God and others will see that peace. We can be like the mollies and guppies as we get along well with others, and this will be a witness to others of God working in us."

Gear Up!

Walk the Plank: Use painter's tape, a rope, or sidewalk chalk to make a long line about 6 feet long. Walk the Plank by balancing on the line with one foot in front of the other. Do this three times. Don't fall in! There might be gators in that water!

(You can also use a 2x4 or balance beam.)

Lowercase w: Begin at the waterline, swim up to the boat line and then down and curve out as you bump the waterline. Swim up to the boat line, then down and curve out bumping the waterline. Swim back up to the boat line and drift on over to just below the boat line to make a line for connecting to other letters. As you connect each w, you won't start at the waterline, but use the connector you made just below the boat line.

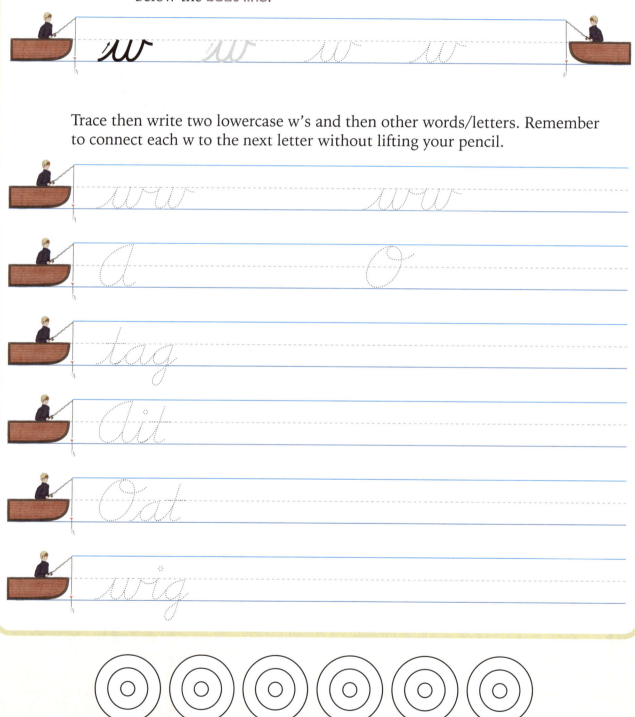

Trace then write two lowercase w's and then other words/letters. Remember to connect each w to the next letter without lifting your pencil.

☐ **REMINDER:** Take some time to work on your weigh-in challenge.

Name _____

Bait & Tackle 13.4

" Did you know that a guppy is an intelligent fish? Scientists have observed them as they interact with predators (the fish trying to eat them) and how they can dodge being caught by confusing their predator. They also have created mazes for the guppies, and they are able to go through a maze! I love learning neat things about God's creation, how He created fish with amazing design, and how fish are intelligent. Guppies also learn to adapt to their environment. God's design in fish is truly remarkable! "

Gear Up!

Help the guppies find each other.

Lowercase w: Begin at the waterline, swim up to the boat line and then down and curve out as you bump the waterline. Then swim up to the boat line, then down and curve out bumping the waterline. Swim back up to the boat line and drift on over to just below the boat line to make a line for connecting to other letters. As you connect each w, you won't start at the waterline, but use the connector you made just below the boat line.

Trace then write two lowercase w's and then other words/letters. Remember to connect each w to the next letter without lifting your pencil.

> Did you complete the aim and cast activity and hit the bullseye? How many total did you hit? _____
> Wow! That's great! You earned your bullseye badge.
>
> Color in the bullseye on the badge and be sure to add it to your achievement board.

Name _____

Bait & Tackle 13.5

> "Remember how we talked this week about the molly fish? I discovered they can live in fresh water or salt water! This fish is one more example of God's magnificent design. He created this fish to be able to adapt to its environment. That's neat that this little, peaceable fish is able to live and thrive in both types of water. Hmm . . . I wonder if there are any in the stream in my backyard."

Gear Up!

Don't Tip the Boat: Balance on a bicycle, scooter, or skateboard for 20 seconds or use your items from the Walk the Plank activity in Bait & Tackle 13.3.

Review your letters: letters s, u, and w

Begin at the waterline, swim up to the boat line, and then down and curve back as you bump the waterline and your line. Then, flip over and swim back out toward the waterline.

Begin at the waterline, swim up to the boat line, and then down and curve out as you bump the waterline. Then swim up to the boat line and then down and curve out.

Begin at the waterline, swim up to the boat line and then down and curve out as you bump the waterline. Then swim up to the boat line, then down and curve out bumping the waterline. Swim back up to the boat line and drift on over to just below the boat line to make a line for connecting to other letters. As you connect each w, you won't start at the waterline, but use the connector you made just below the boat line.

Trace the letters s, u, and w. Connect the letters and don't lift your pencil until all are written. Trace them three times, and then write them once on your own. Be sure to leave a pinky space between each set.

> "This is your time to showcase your best catch again. Use the section in the back of the book labeled "Fishing Derby: Showcasing My Best Catch." Find lesson 13 and complete the page. Remember, this is your "best" work. Ask your parents if they want to keep these in the book or remove them to showcase them."

CATCH ON TO CURSIVE
FISHING Derby
SHOWCASING MY BEST CATCH
BAIT & TACKLE 13

174 Hooked on Cursive

Name

 TACKLE BOX 14

"Your next challenge is to do the lures in mud activity (See Bait & Tackle 13.2.) Be sure to put 5 objects per hand in the dough."

"Oh look, we're talking about Skeeter's favorite fish!"

Gather Your Gear

Day 1:
☐ Wave wand from previous lessons

Day 3:
☐ Tweezers and yarn worms from previous lessons

Official GUIDE

Salmon: a pink fish good for eating and most valued for its pink flesh. Salmon are born in freshwater, grow and live adult lives in saltwater, and then return to freshwater to lay eggs.

Evolutionist: a person who believes that creation happened by chance or some catastrophic event and that living things evolve into other kinds of living things.

Creationist: a person who believes there is an Intelligent Designer, God the Creator, who created all things.

Name _____

Bait & Tackle 14.1

> "One of my favorite fish to catch and eat is salmon. Salmon are healthy for us also. When God created the world, His design included everything to sustain us. Genesis 9:3 is after the Fall when Adam and Eve sinned, and God tells them, "Every moving thing that lives shall be food for you. And as I gave you the green plants, I give you everything" (ESV). Salmon are one of the fish we now use for food. There are various species (types) of salmon. In Alaska alone there are 5 types of salmon. Check out the types here in this picture. I think salmon are a pretty fish, and they taste good!"

Chum Salmon (sometimes called dog)

King Salmon (or chinook)

Silver Salmon (coho)

Pink Salmon (humpys)

Red Salmon (sockeye)

Gear Up!

Making Waves: Use your wave wands from week 1 to make more waves! Be sure to make 8's sideways and upright with both hands.

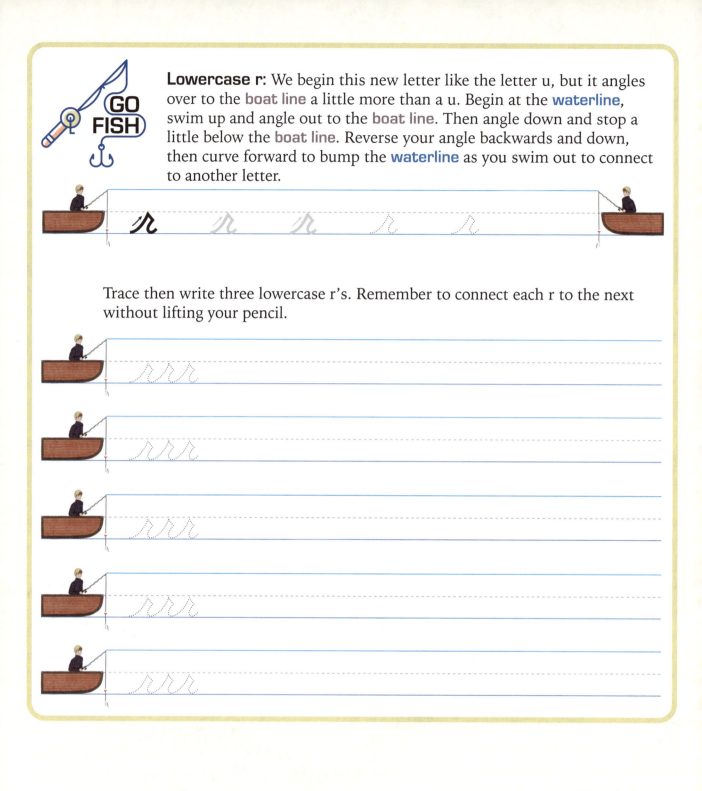

Lowercase r: We begin this new letter like the letter u, but it angles over to the **boat line** a little more than a u. Begin at the **waterline**, swim up and angle out to the **boat line**. Then angle down and stop a little below the **boat line**. Reverse your angle backwards and down, then curve forward to bump the **waterline** as you swim out to connect to another letter.

Trace then write three lowercase r's. Remember to connect each r to the next without lifting your pencil.

☐ **REMINDER:** Take some time to work on your weigh-in challenge.

Name _____

Bait & Tackle 14.2

" I read a book called *Marvels of Creation: Sensational Sea Creatures*, and it had a section on salmon. The books states, "Salmon travel thousands of miles in the ocean but have a God-given instinct to return to the river where they were hatched. Scientists are not quite sure how the salmon find their way back. Some studies indicate they find their way by taste or smell. Some scientists think that the thyroid gland is involved somehow. There is even speculation that they use the position of the sun, moon, and stars to find their special river. The accuracy of the salmon's journey can be explained by the wonderful design of the Creator. The salmon's journey back to its birthplace is a dangerous one with many obstacles such as rapids, falls, and predators along the way. When the salmon reaches the river, it reverts back to freshwater."[1] This is where the salmon will lay its eggs. How amazing is it that God created the salmon with this instinct to return to where they were born? How amazing is it that the salmon adapts from freshwater to sea water and back to fresh water? Even scientists cannot explain this, but we know this is one more design example from God, our divine, intelligent Creator. "

Gear Up!

Salmon are a-MAZE-ing. Help the salmon get from the ocean back to where it was born.

[1] Davis, Buddy, and Kay Davis. *Marvels of Creation: Sensational Sea Creatures*. Green Forest, AR: Master Books, 2005. p. 49.

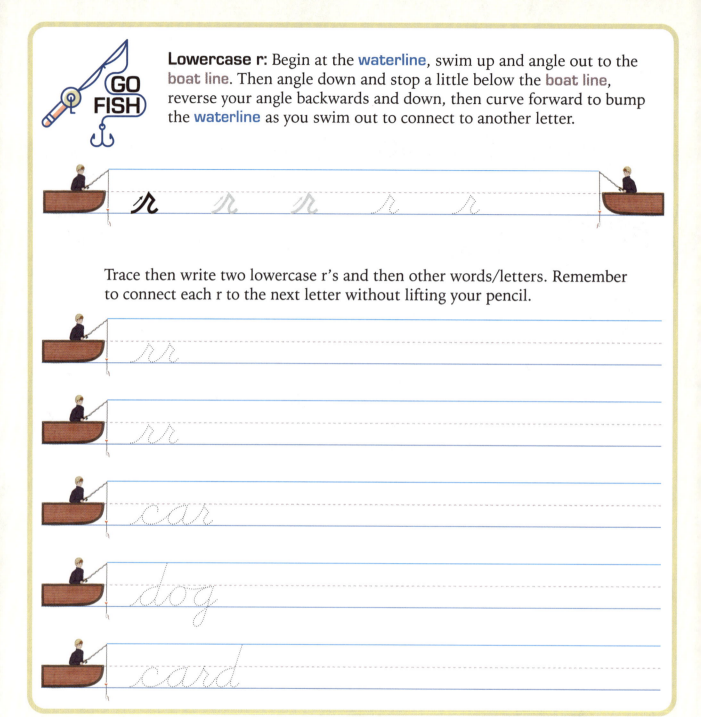

Lowercase r: Begin at the **waterline**, swim up and angle out to the **boat line**. Then angle down and stop a little below the **boat line**, reverse your angle backwards and down, then curve forward to bump the **waterline** as you swim out to connect to another letter.

Trace then write two lowercase r's and then other words/letters. Remember to connect each r to the next letter without lifting your pencil.

☐ **REMINDER:** Take some time to work on your weigh-in challenge.

Name

Bait & Tackle 14.3

"I think salmon are one of God's amazing creations. I stand in awe of his creation. Psalm 145:10–12 says it so well.

"All your works shall give thanks to you, O Lord, and all your saints shall bless you! They shall speak of the glory of your kingdom and tell of your power, to make known to the children of man your mighty deeds, and the glorious splendor of your kingdom!"

Give thanks and tell others about the wonderful creation God has designed for us to enjoy."

Gear Up!

Worm Squeezes: Use tweezers to pick up worms (pieces of yarn). Make sure you get 5–10 worms.

Lowercase r: Begin at the **waterline**, swim up and angle out to the **boat line**. Then angle down and stop a little below the **boat line**, reverse your angle backwards and down, then curve forward to bump the **waterline** as you swim out to connect to another letter.

Trace then write two lowercase r's and then other words/letters. Remember to connect each r to the next letter without lifting your pencil.

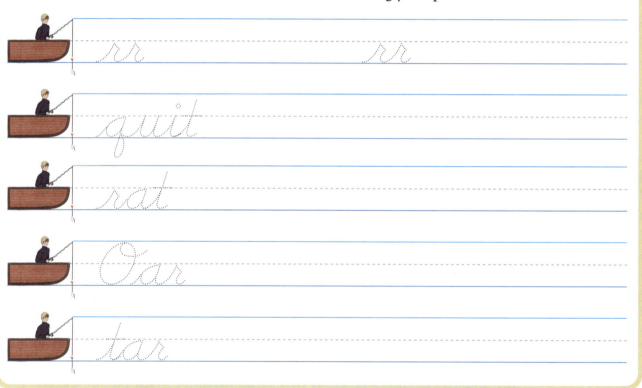

> I hope you completed the challenge and pushed objects into dough. If so, mark it off on your weigh in!
>
> Your next challenge is to write as many words as you can in cursive using these letters:
>
> c, a, d, o, g, q, A, O, C, Q, E, i, t, j, p, s, w, u, r.
>
> Do some each day on the pages coming up.

Name _____

Bait & Tackle 14.4

> "Salmon are amazing. Evolutionists think salmon help prove that animals evolve because they adapt to their environment. They think this change proves that a salmon can change into something else. This is as silly and untrue as thinking a salmon could turn into a dog. We know that God designed animals with the ability to adapt and change with their environment, but we do not have any evidence showing that a salmon can become something else. No matter how it adapts to its environment, it remains a salmon. In Genesis 1:21, we find that God said He "created the great sea creatures and every living creature that moves, with which the waters swarm, according to their kinds.""

Gear Up!

Anchor Up: Stand with your feet about shoulder width apart. Bend over and pretend to pull up a heavy anchor. Give the anchor 10 good pulls all the way up. Remember, that anchor is heavy!

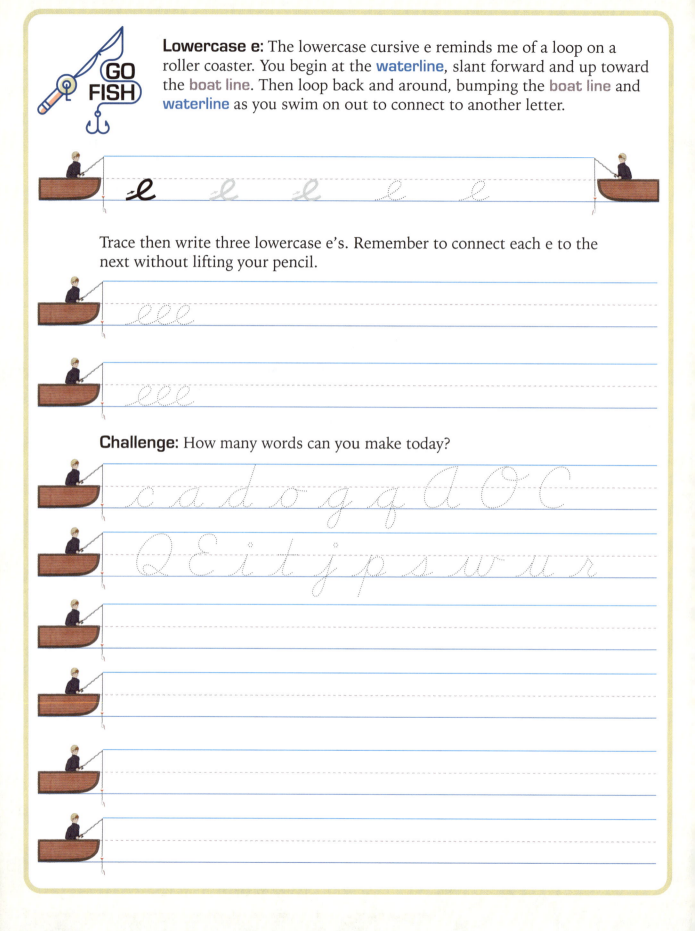

Name _____

Bait & Tackle 14.5

"Speaking about kinds, how many types of fish are there? According to World Atlas website, there are approximately 33,600; however, we also know that scientists are still exploring the ocean. At this time, they have only explored about 5% of the ocean floor, which means several creatures in the ocean have yet to be found. Yet, God created them all and knows the exact number. Wow! That's amazing!"

Gear Up!

Complete the dot-to-dot. You may color it when you're done.

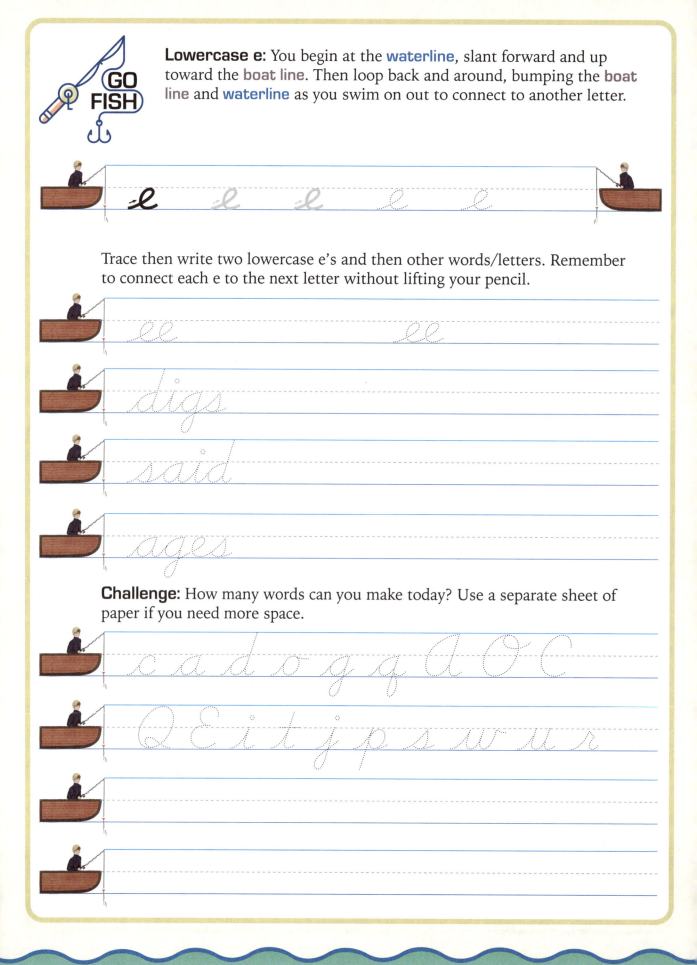

Name _____

TACKLE BOX 15

> " I hope you've been doing well on your challenge. I will see you at the weigh in. "

> " Wow, you only need gear on one day this week. Check out the neat animals you are learning about. I love turtles! "

Gather Your Gear

Day 2:
☐ Cotton swabs and sidewalk chalk

Bass: a wide variety of perch-like bony edible fish which mainly live in fresh water, but some live in salt water.

Crappie (crop-pee): North American freshwater fish which are usually silvery white with black speckles. Crappie is a type of sunfish.

Crawdad/Crayfish: freshwater crustacean which is from the same animal kind as a lobster.

Name _____

Bait & Tackle 15.1

"Sometimes when I am fishing at my pond, I see these little heads pop up out of the water. Do you know what they are? Turtles! Usually these are slider turtles. Turtles will sometimes eat my worm, and I won't even feel them do it! Turtles are amazing in their design also. God created them with a hard shell to protect them. When they sense danger, they can pull their whole body inside their shell, and the front has a hinge that pulls up to completely close the turtle inside the shell. Proverbs 18:10 says, "The name of the Lord is a strong tower; the righteous man runs into it and is safe." Just like God created turtles to pull inside their shells for protection, we can run to God, our strong tower, for protection. God is our refuge, or our safe place."

Gear Up!

Live Well Reaches: Sit in a chair or side of a bathtub with your feet flat on the ground. Keep your feet spread apart. Bend over and touch the top of the ground between your feet as if you were touching the top of the live well in your boat. Do this 12 times.

Lowercase e: You begin at the waterline, slant forward and up towards the boat line. Then loop back and around, bumping the boat line and waterline as you swim on out to connect to another letter.

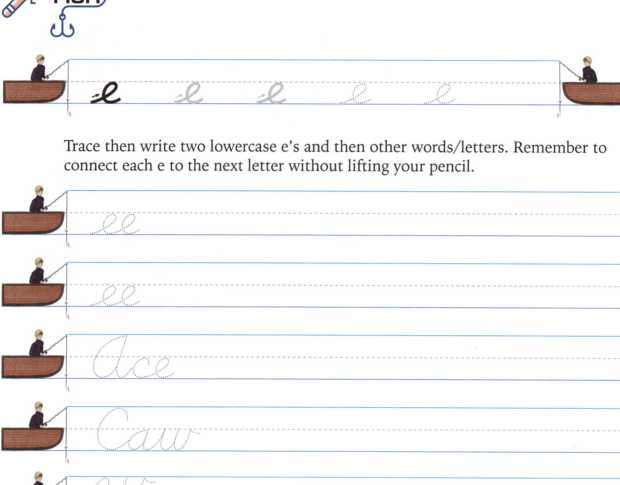

Trace then write two lowercase e's and then other words/letters. Remember to connect each e to the next letter without lifting your pencil.

> How many words were you able to make all together? _____ That's awesome! You are making progress. You should be proud. If you completed the challenge, you earned the cursive word's badge. Color it in below. Wow! Check out your achievement board. You have so many badges!
>
> Your next challenge is to complete three dot-to-dots from the Weigh-In Challenges section in the back of the book. There are three total, which is one for each day of this challenge. Please complete only one per day.

Name _____

Bait & Tackle 15.2

" Some of the best fish in our pond that the turtles love are the smaller bass and crappie. They also love to feed on the bugs like water striders or mosquitoes. Did you know a water strider can "walk" on water? Remember in Matthew 14 how Jesus walked on the water and Peter said "Lord, if it is you, command me to come to you on the water." He said, "Come." So Peter got out of the boat and walked on the water and came to Jesus (Matthew 14:28–29 ESV). I think it is amazing how God created an insect that can walk, or paddle, on top of the water. That is fascinating. "

Gear Up!

Use cotton swabs and sidewalk chalk to paint the fish.

Bait & Tackle 15.2   191

Lowercase l: The lowercase cursive l is like the lowercase cursive e, but taller. You begin at the waterline, slant forward and up toward the pole line. Then loop back and down, bumping the waterline as you swim on out to connect to another letter.

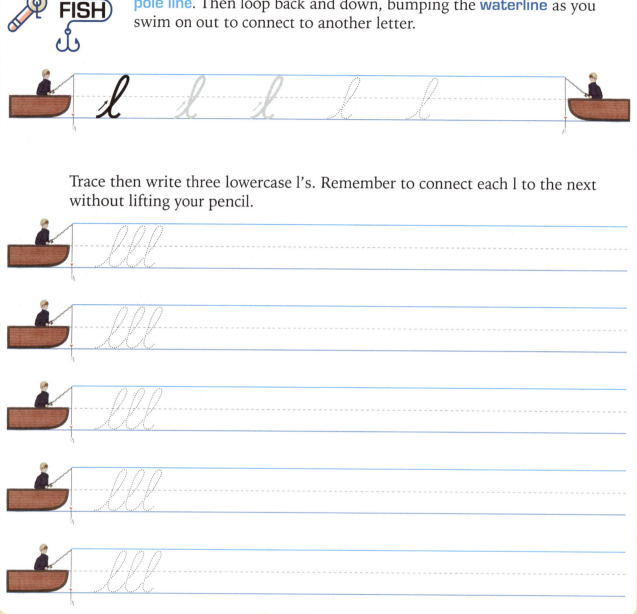

Trace then write three lowercase l's. Remember to connect each l to the next without lifting your pencil.

☐ **REMINDER:** Take some time to work on your weigh-in challenge.

Name _____

Bait & Tackle 15.3

> "Water striders cannot see clearly, which makes them easy prey for the fish and birds at our pond. That makes me think of a story of a man that couldn't see at all, and he was brought to Jesus. Read this story from Mark 8:22–25: And they came to Bethsaida. And some people brought to him a blind man and begged him to touch him. And he took the blind man by the hand and led him out of the village, and when he had spit on his eyes and laid his hands on him, he asked him, "Do you see anything?" And he looked up and said, "I see people, but they look like trees, walking." Then Jesus laid his hands on his eyes again; and he opened his eyes, his sight was restored, and he saw everything clearly.
>
> After his first touch from Jesus, the man wasn't seeing clearly like a water strider doesn't see clearly. After his second touch from Jesus his sight was clear. Sometimes it is like this with us too. When we pray for God to help us in an area we struggle with, such as lying or anger, God begins the work in us, but it isn't always immediately answered. Sometimes it takes time for God to change us to overcome things such as lying or anger."

Gear Up!

Lighthouse Taps: Lighthouses flash their lights, so we are going to tap for lighthouse flashes. Bring your pinky and thumb together to tap and open, tap and open, like a lighthouse flash. Do this 12 times with both hands.

Lowercase l: Begin at the waterline, slant forward and up toward the pole line. Then loop back and down, bumping the waterline as you swim on out to connect to another letter.

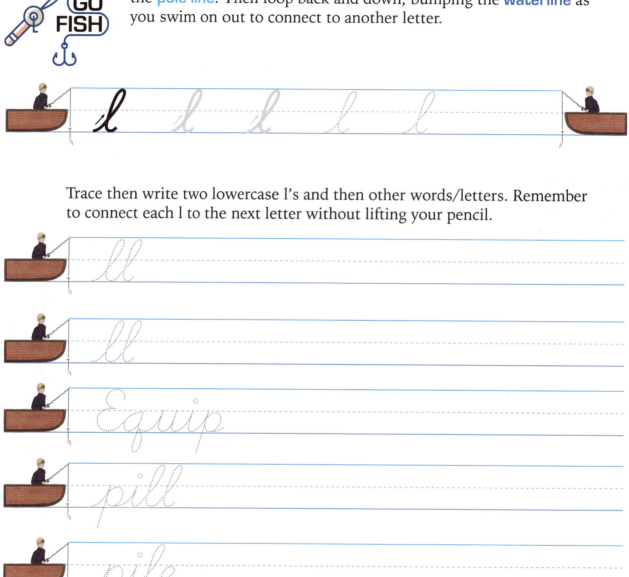

Trace then write two lowercase l's and then other words/letters. Remember to connect each l to the next letter without lifting your pencil.

☐ **REMINDER:** Take some time to work on your weigh-in challenge.

Name

Bait & Tackle 15.4

"Another pond and creek creature we enjoy catching are called crayfish. We call them crawdads around here. They look like small lobsters. When I was a little boy, I would play in a creek in the back yard and catch crawdads. Now, Anna plays in the creek and pond and catch crawdads. Crawdads also hide under rocks. Remember how the turtle hides in its shell? Well, crawdads hide under the rock. The rock is their refuge (shelter) much like God is our refuge. Psalm 18:2 says, "The Lord is my rock and my fortress and my deliverer, my God, my rock, in whom I take refuge, my shield, and the horn of my salvation, my stronghold." That one verse tells us a lot about God. Just as the crawdad finds refuge under a rock, we can find refuge in God, our Rock."

Gear Up!

Oh fun! You are going to spell the word fish. Be sure to keep your eyes on each row as you go across. Check out the example below before you begin.

Follow and loop to spell FISH.

L S K **F** G E **I** P J N **S** B W Q Z **H** B K S J

K J F H K L S I E A H J M S L P O H E W

D F S G T I K L P N S C Z N H J K W F H

E W Q Z X F N H U I Q R F C L S K H G E

P J F S B I Q Z H B K S J K F H G E P J

Bait & Tackle 15.4   195

Lowercase l: Begin at the waterline, slant forward and up toward the pole line. Then loop back and down, bumping the waterline as you swim on out to connect to another letter.

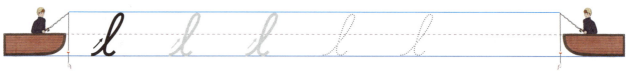

Trace then write two lowercase l's and then other words/letters. Remember to connect each l to the next letter without lifting your pencil.

" Did you complete the dot-to-dot challenge? If you did then you have earned another badge! It's the dot-to-dot badge in the back of the book. Color it in and add it to your achievement board if you completed the challenge. "

Name _____

Bait & Tackle 15.5

"Everything in our pond needs to be watchful for the kingfishers. Kingfishers are a type of bird that sits on branches near the pond and watches for anything it sees it can eat. Then it swoops down, catches it, and returns to the branch to eat. God's creation is truly remarkable. The Bible talks about the birds in Matthew 6:26 and it says, "Look at the birds of the air: they neither sow nor reap nor gather into barns, and yet your Heavenly Father feeds them. Are you not of more value than they?" God provides for the birds, and if He cares that much for the birds then we know He cares for us and will take care of us."

Gear Up!

Paddle the Boat: Sit in a chair or on the side of a bathtub with your feet flat on the ground. Pretend to paddle the boat. Make sure you swap sides, so your boat doesn't get off course! Give a good 15 total strokes of the paddle for each side.

Review your letters: letters r, e, and l

Lowercase r: Begin at the waterline, swim up and angle out to the boat line. Then angle down and stop a little below the boat line, reverse your angle backwards and down, then curve forward to bump the waterline as you swim out to connect to another letter.

Lowercase e: The lowercase cursive e reminds me of a loop on a roller coaster. You begin at the waterline, slant forward and up towards the boat line. Then loop back and around, bumping the boat line and waterline as you swim on out to connect to another letter.

Lowercase l: Begin at the waterline, slant forward and up toward the pole line. Then loop back and down, bumping the waterline as you swim on out to connect to another letter.

Trace the letters r, e, and l. Connect the letters and don't lift your pencil until all are written. Trace them three times, and then write them once on your own. Be sure to leave a pinky space between each set.

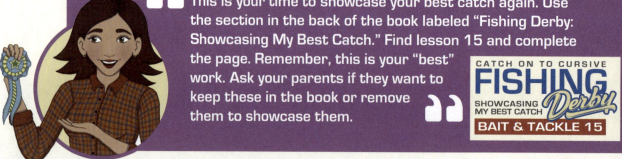

This is your time to showcase your best catch again. Use the section in the back of the book labeled "Fishing Derby: Showcasing My Best Catch." Find lesson 15 and complete the page. Remember, this is your "best" work. Ask your parents if they want to keep these in the book or remove them to showcase them.

198 Hooked on Cursive

Name

TACKLE BOX 16

" Are you up for another challenge? Here it is! In the back of the book is a section called Weigh-In Challenges. Find that section and use the Tracking Practice sheet to practice finding words/letters as you track with your eyes and loop with your hand (see Gear Up from Bait & Tackle 15.4). There are a total of three, which is one for each day of this challenge. "

" This week you'll be learning a new activity in the Gear Up section as well as learning about a very neat fish. "

Gather Your Gear

Day 1:
☐ Pencil with eraser or pencil with pushpin in the eraser

Day 3:
☐ Paper clips

Day 4:
☐ Sticky notes or paper
☐ Ball (tennis or approx. size)

Coelacanth (see-luh-canth): a large bony saltwater fish. It has a special hinge in its skull to help it open its mouth extra wide.

Name _____

Bait & Tackle 16.1

> "Did you know that sometimes scientists think a fish is extinct (none of that kind living), but then a fisherman will catch that fish? It's true! In 1938, a fisherman captured a coelacanth off the coast of South Africa. Scientists thought this fish was extinct, but it was still alive. That is neat that fishermen play a role in science."[1]

Gear Up!

The Eye of the Hook: If you can, use a pushpin in the tip of an eraser or just a pencil with an eraser. Hold the pencil straight up and down in front of your nose. Bring it in slowly as you keep your eyes on the pin or eraser. Keep your focus. See how close you can bring it in before you see two of it. Hold it for 10 seconds, then release and do these two more times.

---

1 "Sorry, But You Are Extinct: The Coelacanth's Story on August 4, 2007 by Answers in Genesis," Answers in Genesis, 8/4/2007, https://answersingenesis.org/fossils/living-fossils/sorry-but-you-are-extinct-the-coelacanths-story/.

Lowercase k: The lowercase cursive k begins the same as a lowercase cursive l. You begin at the waterline, slant forward and up towards the pole line. Then loop back and straight down to the waterline as you swim straight back up and circle around under the boat line, then swim out and down to bump the waterline.

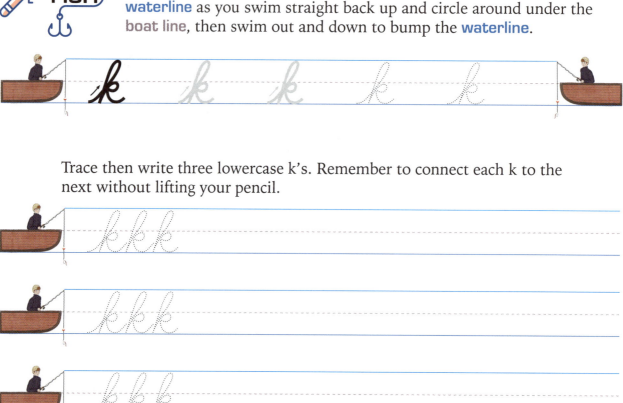

Trace then write three lowercase k's. Remember to connect each k to the next without lifting your pencil.

☐ **REMINDER:** Take some time to work on your weigh-in challenge.

Name _____

Bait & Tackle 16.2

> " Do you know what the best part about the coelacanth being discovered was? Scientists noticed it looked just like its ancestors (older fish in its family). It had not changed. We know the coelacanth was created the same day as all the other fish and cannot be 300 million years old. Evolutionists think that the coelacanth is 300 million years old, but this catch from the fisherman proved that is wrong and this fish has not changed since God created it. Counter what isn't true with what is true. This example is more evidence that the biblical account is true, and animals do not evolve. "

Gear Up!

Don't Hit the Bridge: The ships in the river need to get through. Place your hands flat on the ground with tips of toes on the ground and body lifted to be the bridge. Hold this for 10–15 seconds.

Lowercase k: Begin at the waterline, slant forward and up toward the pole line. Then loop back and straight down to the waterline as you swim straight back up and circle around under the boat line, then swim out and down to bump the waterline.

Trace then write two lowercase k's and then other words/letters. Remember to connect each k to the next letter without lifting your pencil.

kk

kk

wrote

tow

took

week

☐ **REMINDER:** Take some time to work on your weigh-in challenge.

Name _____

Bait & Tackle 16.3

> " A coelacanth is a round, plump fish. They can live for 60 years or more. The coelacanth we see today are considered a living fossil. "Living fossils" are organisms that can be found both living in the world today and found preserved in the rock record as fossils. Living fossils are reminders to us of the Creator and how marvelous His works are. "

Gear Up!

Hook the Crawdads: At the bottom of the page is a row of crawdads (crayfish). Open paper clips and secure a paper clip to each one.

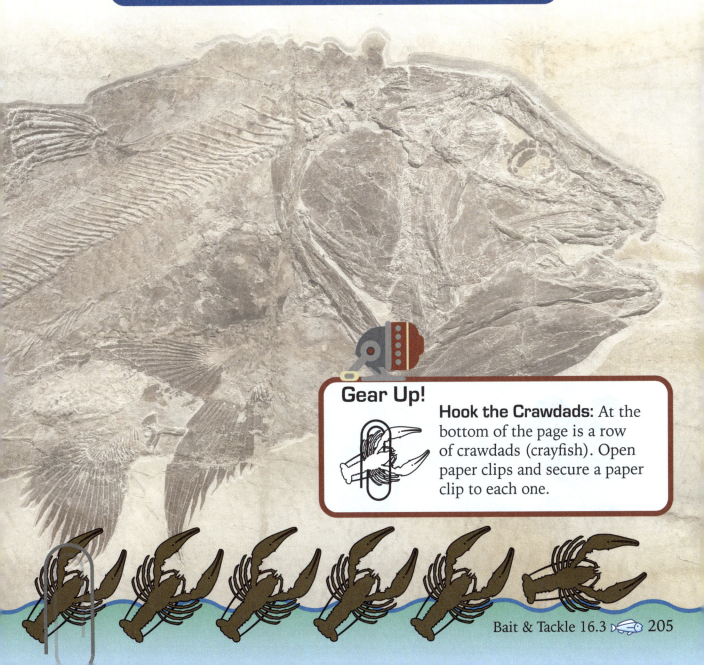

Lowercase k: Begin at the waterline, slant forward and up toward the pole line. Then loop back and straight down to the waterline as you swim straight back up and circle around under the boat line, then swim out and down to bump the waterline.

Trace then write two lowercase k's and then other words/letters. Remember to connect each k to the next letter without lifting your pencil.

> How did you do on tracking your letters? If you completed this challenge, you have earned the Eye Tracking badge, and you may color it in the back of the book then add it to your achievement board.
>
> Your next challenge is to hook the crawdads (crayfish) each day.

Name

Bait & Tackle 16.4

> "There are many fish that God designed to adapt to their environments. God's design is complete. His design doesn't leave room for errors. We also know the Bible is truth. In Genesis, we read that God created all things. We know that we do not have evidence of evolution. I know I've never seen a fish grow legs and begin walking and talking."

Gear Up!

Aim and Cast: Place a piece of paper or sticky note on a door or wall about eye level. You can make a target on it if you'd like. Take about 10 steps back and try to AIM and CAST the ball to hit the target. If you miss three times, you can step forward one step. Try to hit the paper/target in the middle at least three times in a row.

Lowercase b: The lowercase cursive b is the same as a lowercase cursive l with one last piece. Begin at the waterline, slant forward and up toward the pole line. Then loop back and straight down to the waterline, swim back up to bump the bottom of the boat line, and slant out and down.

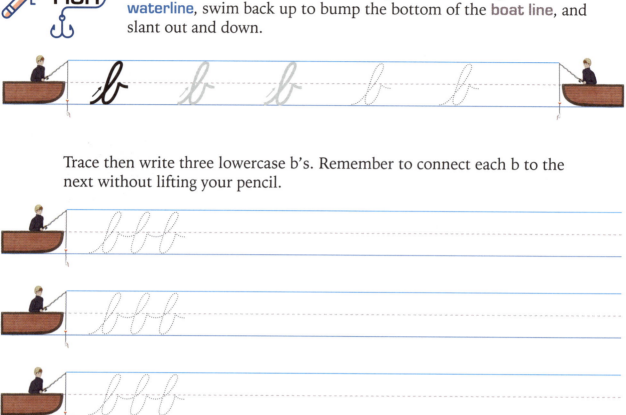

Trace then write three lowercase b's. Remember to connect each b to the next without lifting your pencil.

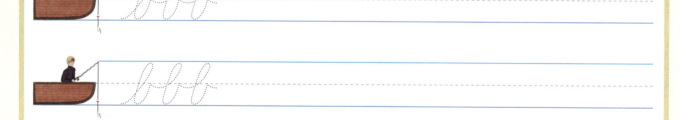

☐ **REMINDER:** Take some time to work on your weigh-in challenge.

Name

Bait & Tackle 16.5

" With all this talk about the coelacanth being a plump fish, it is making me hungry. I think I need to get my line in the water and see what I can catch. I doubt it will be a coelacanth, but I bet it will make a nice dinner. "

Gear Up!

It's time for a new activity. This activity is called Under & Over.

Under & Over: You will help the fish swim over the obstacles. On the top row, begin by going under the first obstacle and back up between the next obstacles. You want to try to stay in the middle of the two obstacles you are going under and over. See the example to help you complete this activity.

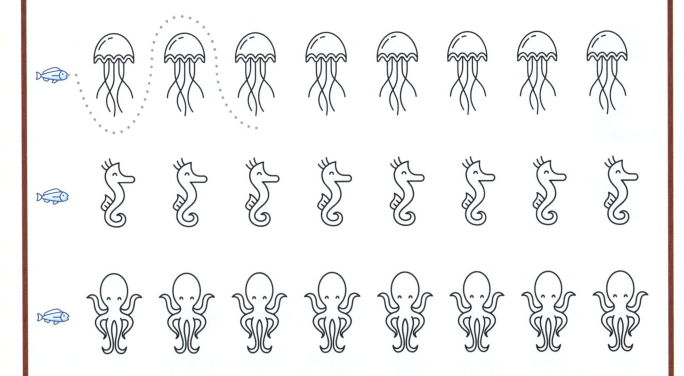

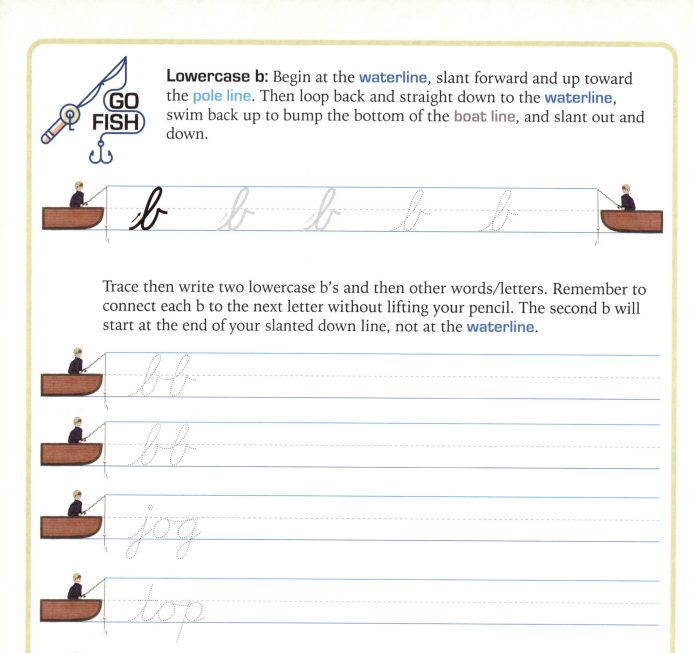

Name

"I can't wait to check in with you at the weigh-in section."

"Oh, I see Skeeter is talking about minnows and God's magnificent creation this week. Be sure to complete Skeeter's challenge."

Gather Your Gear

Day 1:
☐ Painter's tape or rope or sidewalk chalk

Day 2:
☐ Sheet of foam
☐ Sheet of plain paper

Day 5:
☐ Plastic lid with a lip or a round cake pan
☐ Marble

Name _____

Bait & Tackle 17.1

> "If you go swimming in a lake, near the shallow parts of the water, you will find small fish called minnows. There are many types of minnows, and some are baby fish while others are simply smaller fish. Minnows like to sometimes suck on your legs, and it tickles! Minnows are very fast. They dart in and out between things. I'm sure that is part of their survival in God's design. It doesn't matter how big or small, God created them all. Have you ever seen a minnow?"

Gear Up!

Walk the Plank: Use painter's tape, a rope, or sidewalk chalk to make a long line about 6 feet long. Walk the Plank by balancing on the line with one foot in front of the other. Do this three times. Don't fall in! There might be gators in that water!

(You can also use a 2x4 or balance beam.)

Lowercase b: Begin at the waterline, slant forward and up toward the pole line. Then loop back and straight down to the waterline, swim back up to bump the bottom of the boat line, and slant out and down.

Trace then write two lowercase b's and then other words/letters. Remember to connect each b to the next letter without lifting your pencil. The second b will start at the end of your slanted down line, not at the waterline.

How has your challenge of hooking crawdads been going? Crawdads are fast and not always easy to catch! If you completed this challenge, you have earned the Hook Badge. Color in the hook on your badge from the back of the book.

Your next challenge is to do the Paddle the Boat activity from Bait & Tackle 15.5 each day. If you complete this activity, you will get another badge.

Name _____

Bait & Tackle 17.2

" Did you know minnows are used as bait for larger fish? In our pond, the bass and crappie love minnows. What is amazing is that in all of creation no matter how big or small, God knows and cares for it all. The Bible says that he even knows the number of hairs on our heads (Luke 12:7). Now think of all the people in the world, and how many heads that is! God is truly amazing. His creation is just one way we get to know God. "

Gear Up!

The Right Conditions: Place a plain piece of paper on a piece of foam. When you write, if you apply too little pressure, it is difficult to see your writing and it can even look shaky. If you apply too much pressure, it will cause you pain. You need the right pressure to see your words, but not too much or you'll push through the paper to the foam. Print your name to get the feel for how much pressure is the right condition for writing.

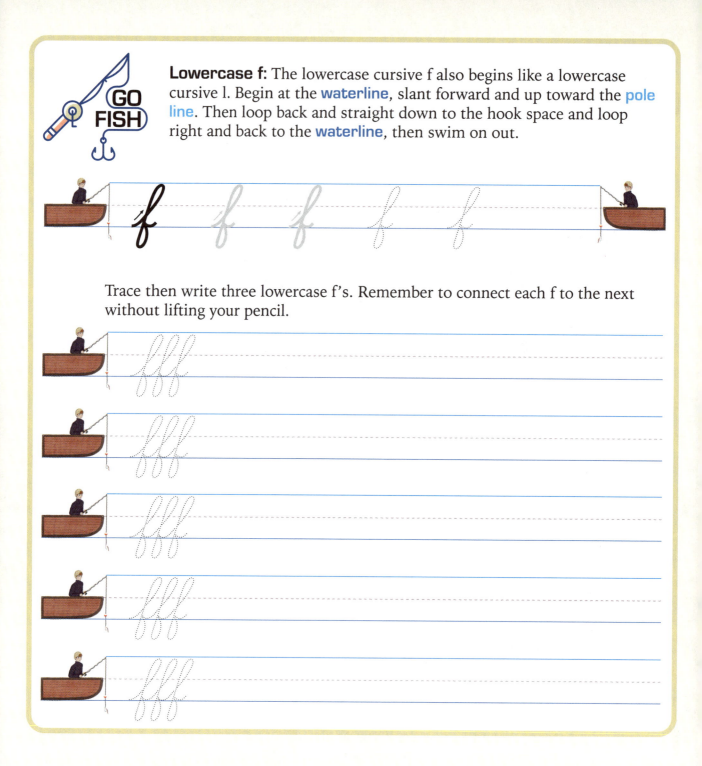

Lowercase f: The lowercase cursive f also begins like a lowercase cursive l. Begin at the waterline, slant forward and up toward the pole line. Then loop back and straight down to the hook space and loop right and back to the waterline, then swim on out.

Trace then write three lowercase f's. Remember to connect each f to the next without lifting your pencil.

☐ **REMINDER:** Take some time to work on your weigh-in challenge.

Name _____

Bait & Tackle 17.3

> "The phrase "big or small, God made it all" has made me think about this verse in Psalm 104:25 which says "Here is the sea, great and wide, which teems with creatures innumerable, living things both small and great."
>
> No matter how many are in the seas or their size, God is over all."

Gear Up!

Don't Tip the Boat: Balance on a bicycle, scooter, or skateboard for 20 seconds or use your items from the Walk the Plank activity.

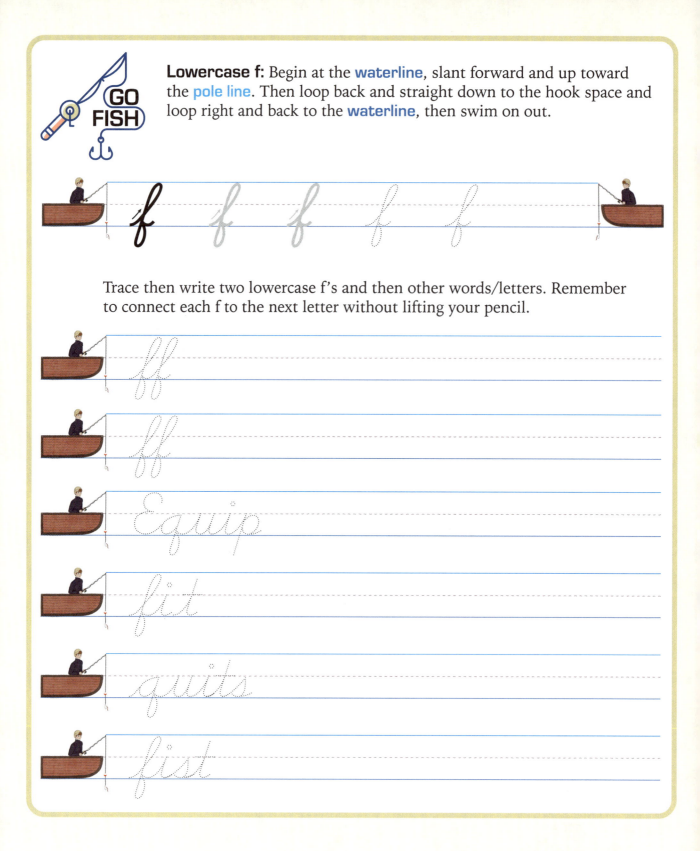

Lowercase f: Begin at the waterline, slant forward and up toward the pole line. Then loop back and straight down to the hook space and loop right and back to the waterline, then swim on out.

Trace then write two lowercase f's and then other words/letters. Remember to connect each f to the next letter without lifting your pencil.

ff

ff

Equip

fit

quits

fist

☐ **REMINDER:** Take some time to work on your weigh-in challenge.

Name _____

Bait & Tackle 17.4

" As I stand on the pond banks early in the morning, I am in awe of all creation. From the beauty of the sunset to the minnows darting, or the early bird getting a worm, it is a new masterpiece for us each day. Psalm 104:31 says, "May the glory of the Lord endure forever; may the Lord rejoice in his works." I rejoice daily at the works of God. "

 Gear Up!

Help the minnows navigate through the rocks to join their fish friends.

Bait & Tackle 17.4 219

Lowercase f: Begin at the waterline, slant forward and up toward the pole line. Then loop back and straight down to the hook space and loop right and back to the waterline, then swim on out.

Trace then write two lowercase f's and then other words/letters. Remember to connect each f to the next letter without lifting your pencil.

> Did you complete the Paddle the Boat activity? If so, you have earned another badge for your achievement board and you may color in the paddle on the badge.

Name _____

Bait & Tackle 17.5

> "I know my niece Anna has been giving you challenges, but today I have a challenge for you. I would like for you to make a masterpiece of something in creation. You can choose to make your own artwork or simply photograph some amazing things you see in creation today. Job 12:7–10 says we are to ". . . ask the beasts, and they will teach you; the birds of the heavens, and they will tell you; or the bushes of the earth, and they will teach you; and the fish of the sea will declare to you. Who among all these does not know that the hand of the LORD has done this? In his hand is the life of every living thing and the breath of all mankind." All of creation is teaching us about the goodness and magnificence of God.

Gear Up!

Marble in the Whirlpool: Using a plastic lid with a lip or a round cake pan, place a marble inside. Have someone move the lid/pan so the marble rolls in the inside edge back and forth and eventually all the way around in a circle. Follow the marble with your eyes, but do not move your head. Move only your eyes as you follow the marble back and forth. Do this for one minute.

Review your letters: letters k, b, and f

lowercase k: The lowercase cursive k begins the same as a lowercase cursive l. You begin at the waterline, slant forward and up toward the pole line. Then loop back and straight down to the waterline as you swim straight back up and circle around under the boat line, then swim out and down to bump the waterline.

lowercase b: Begin at the waterline, slant forward and up toward the pole line. Then loop back and straight down to the waterline, swim back up to bump the bottom of the boat line, and slant out and down.

lowercase f: Begin at the waterline, slant forward and up toward the pole line. Then loop back and straight down to the hook space and loop right and back to the waterline, then swim on out.

Trace the letters k, b, and f. Connect the letters and don't lift your pencil until all are written. Trace them three times, and then write them once on your own. Be sure to leave a pinky space between each set.

> "This is your time to showcase your best catch again. Use the section in the back of the book labeled "Fishing Derby: Showcasing My Best Catch." Find lesson 17 and complete the page. Remember, this is your "best" work. Ask your parents if they want to keep these in the book or remove them to showcase them."

CATCH ON TO CURSIVE
FISHING Derby
SHOWCASING MY BEST CATCH
BAIT & TACKLE 17

Name

> We have another a-MAZE-ing challenge for you. Your challenge is to complete three of the mazes in the Weigh-In section in the back of the book under A-MAZE-ing Mazes. You should complete one each day for this challenge.

> I see Skeeter is talking about catfish this week. He sure does love catfish. I can't blame him though; they are tasty!

Gather Your Gear

Day 2:
☐ Wave wands from previous lesson

Official GUIDE

Cutthroat Trout: a large spotted trout with reddish marks on its jaw, usually found in northwestern North America.

DID YOU KNOW?

In autumn, it is also important to go fishing during mid-day, so the water temperature is just right for the fish to be moving and biting. Because fish are wanting to gain weight for winter, they want to limit their movement. Reeling slower and using a larger bait is best. This time of year, the larger the bait, the larger the fish you'll catch.

Name _____

Bait & Tackle 18.1

> " I really love mountain lakes. I think one of the most beautiful mountain lakes is in Yellowstone National Park and is called Yellowstone Lake. It has good fishing, as the lake has native cutthroat trout. When I was younger, my parents took us to Yellowstone National Park. I think it is one of the most amazing places and displays God's beautiful creation everywhere you look. Psalms 104:8–11 says, "The mountains rose, the valleys sank down to the place that you appointed for them. You set a boundary that they may not pass, so that they might not again cover the earth. You make springs gush forth in the valleys; they flow between the hills; they give drink to every beast of the field; the wild donkeys quench their thrist." These verses make me think about how God's natural design is truly remarkable. Do you live near any mountains or lakes? If so, do you enjoy them? "

Gear Up!

Complete the dot-to-dot below. Try to use only your eyes to follow the dots before you begin tracing.

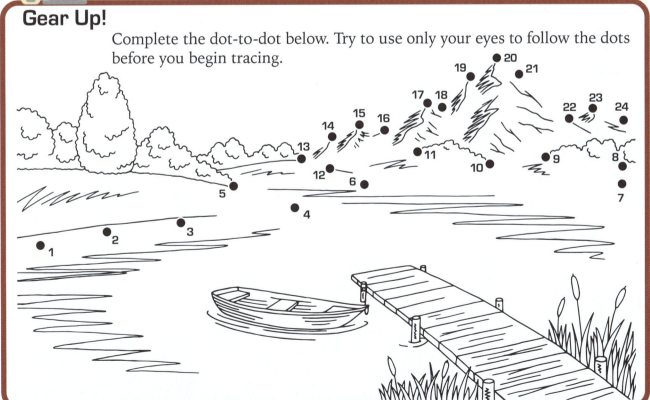

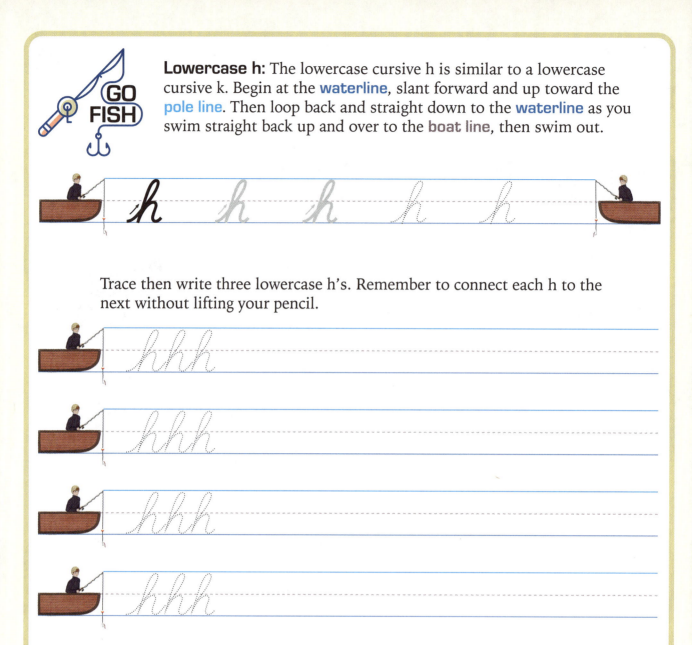

Lowercase h: The lowercase cursive h is similar to a lowercase cursive k. Begin at the waterline, slant forward and up toward the pole line. Then loop back and straight down to the waterline as you swim straight back up and over to the boat line, then swim out.

Trace then write three lowercase h's. Remember to connect each h to the next without lifting your pencil.

☐ **REMINDER:** Take some time to work on your weigh-in challenge.

Name

Bait & Tackle 18.2

> "When I was a little boy, my parents would take us to a large lake that was man-made. This means that men used a dam to block the natural flow of a river and flood a section to make a lake. They flooded a town and named the lake after the town. It is called Greers Ferry Lake, and the Little Red River is the river that feeds this lake. You might wonder why they would do this, but it serves many purposes today. The lake provides a natural water source to many homes. My grandfather loved to fish on the lake as do many others. It is a beautiful lake that is one more example of God's amazing handiwork. This is an example of us using inventions to use what God has given us to help us. I think Psalm 104:10 describes this area as it says, "You make springs gush forth in the valleys; they flow between the hills.""

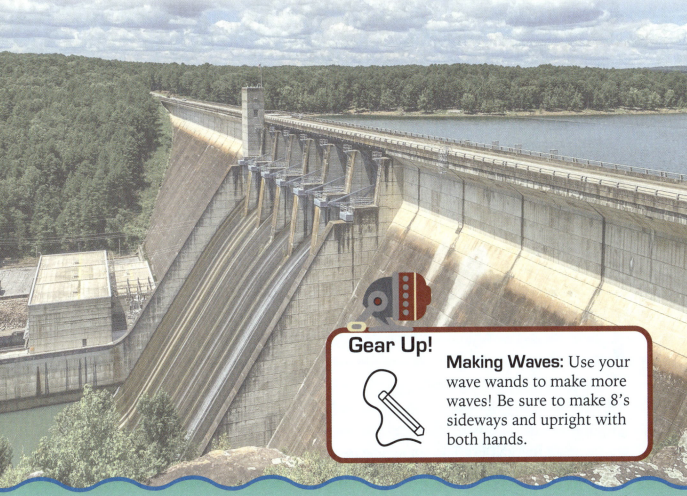

Gear Up!

Making Waves: Use your wave wands to make more waves! Be sure to make 8's sideways and upright with both hands.

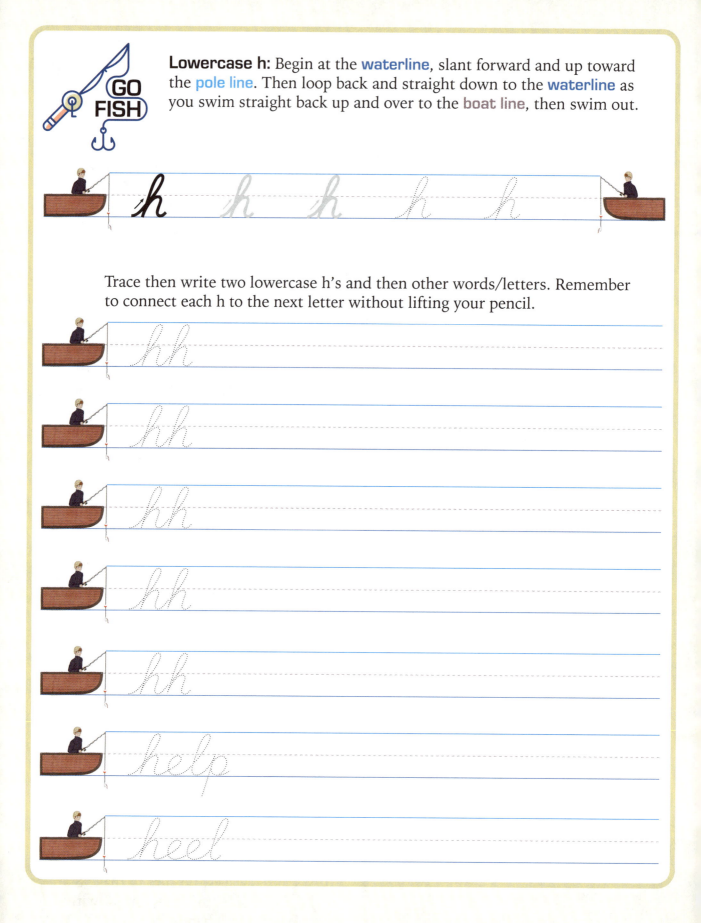

Name

Bait & Tackle 18.3

> "I remember watching my grandpa bring home his catch of catfish. Have you ever seen a catfish? Catfish make a funny croaking sound. They are called catfish because of their cat-like whiskers. Grandpa would have a fish fry (frying fish) to feed everyone. If he didn't catch enough fish or have extra put up in the freezer, we wouldn't be able to feed everyone. That reminds me of the Bible story when Jesus used 2 fish and 5 loaves to feed a large group of people (Matthew 14:17–21). Jesus not only fed all the people until they were full, but they had baskets of fish and bread left over. It was a miracle. God can take what we have and make it more."

Gear Up!

Hoist the Sails: These are called side planks and are like a side pushup where you hold your body up. Lay on your side, and lift your body up with the arm closest to the ground. Your foot should be on its side on the ground. Your body makes a triangle shape like a sail. Hold the position for 8 seconds, relax, and repeat two times. Do both sides of your body.

Lowercase h: Begin at the waterline, slant forward and up toward the pole line. Then loop back and straight down to the waterline as you swim straight back up and over to the boat line, then swim out.

Trace then write two lowercase h's and then other words/letters. Remember to connect each h to the next letter without lifting your pencil.

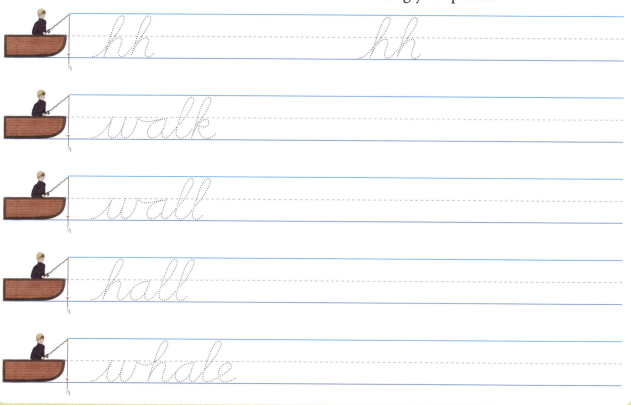

"Did you complete the a-MAZE-ing challenge? If you did, you have earned your maze badge and may color it. Remember to add your badge to your achievement board.

Your next challenge is to Hoist the Sails (see above) each day to earn a sail badge."

Name _____

Bait & Tackle 18.4

> "Anna loves to fish. One time she forgot her tackle box in my car. When I opened the car to get back in, I was blown away by the most horrid smell. It was her catfish bait. Pee-yew! Catfish are what we call bottom-feeders. This means they eat on the bottom of their homes. They do sometimes eat dead fish, but they also eat algae, other plants, and other fish. They help keep the waters clean. Once again, we see God's handiwork in fish having a job of being a cleaner of the waters."

Gear Up!

Lighthouse Taps: Lighthouses flash their lights, so we are going to tap for lighthouse flashes. Bring your pinky and thumb together to tap and open, tap and open, like a lighthouse flash. Do this 12 times with both hands.

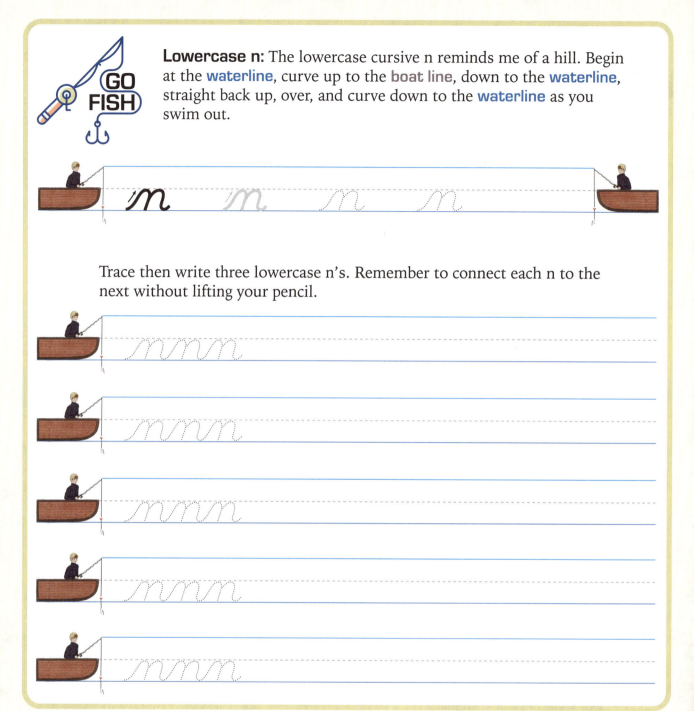

Lowercase n: The lowercase cursive n reminds me of a hill. Begin at the waterline, curve up to the boat line, down to the waterline, straight back up, over, and curve down to the waterline as you swim out.

Trace then write three lowercase n's. Remember to connect each n to the next without lifting your pencil.

☐ **REMINDER:** Take some time to work on your weigh-in challenge.

Name _____

Bait & Tackle 18.5

> " If you have never seen or heard a catfish, ask your parent to look one up so you can hear the sound a catfish makes. I'm always amazed at how each animal has such unique traits designed so neatly by our Creator. His design truly is intelligent. What has been your favorite fish we have learned about? Draw a picture of it. "

Gear Up!

Can you help me get down the river to the lake?

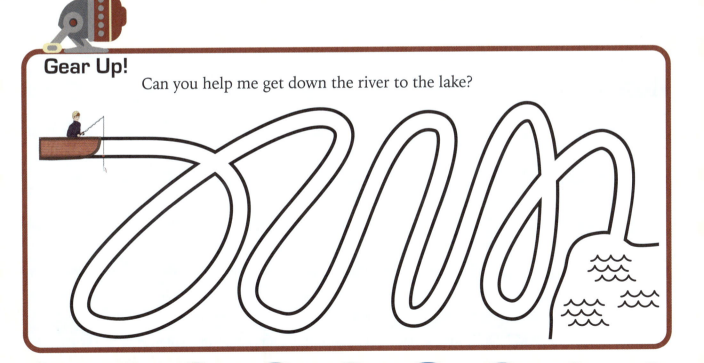

Lowercase n: Begin at the **waterline**, curve up to the **boat line**, down to the **waterline**, straight back up, over, and curve down to the **waterline** as you swim out.

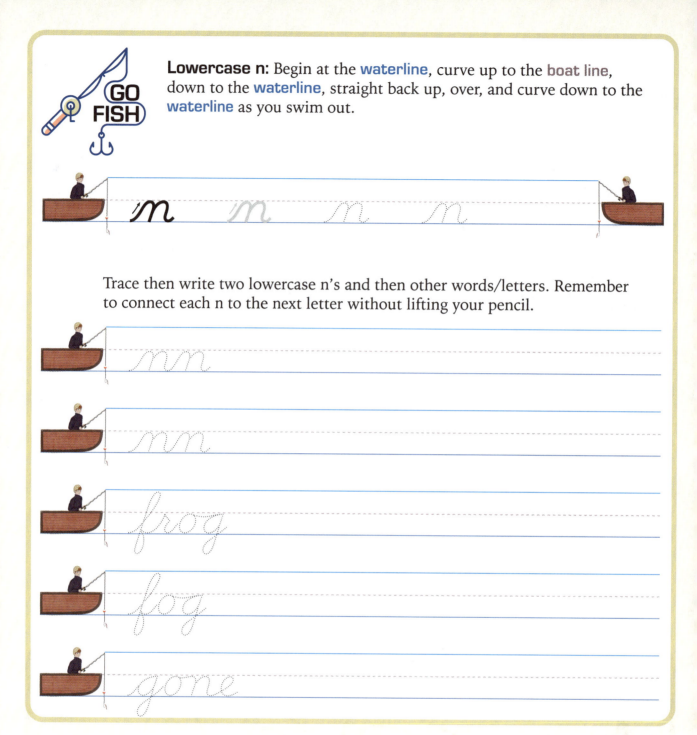

Trace then write two lowercase n's and then other words/letters. Remember to connect each n to the next letter without lifting your pencil.

☐ **REMINDER:** Take some time to work on your weigh-in challenge.

Name

TACKLE BOX 19

"It's almost time for you to weigh in! I hope you earn your badge."

"We have a fun activity for you to do this week. Don't feel like you have to do the whole word search today, but do a few words each day."

Gather Your Gear

Day 1:
☐ Cotton swabs and sidewalk chalk

Day 3:
☐ Pencil with eraser or pencil with pushpin in the eraser

Day 4:
☐ Tweezers and yarn worms from previous lessons

Since we don't have any fishing terms this week, here is a word search for some of the terms we have had! Word searches are good for tracking with your eyes and hand-eye coordination.

BAIT	CAST	HOOK
BASS	CATFISH	LURE
BUOY	CRAWDAD	SAILS
BREAM	DOCK	TROUT

B	J	B	U	O	Y	B	Q	E	B	N	T	Z	P	J	B	T	G
N	D	D	Q	J	B	H	H	F	Y	A	L	B	N	N	Q	B	G
B	Z	W	O	J	D	R	O	X	K	G	I	D	V	W	A	B	G
A	W	H	R	C	G	I	U	O	P	Q	N	T	U	F	M	L	H
S	B	Q	R	H	K	Q	L	N	K	S	L	T	L	U	L	Y	B
S	S	X	T	X	Y	H	C	R	A	W	D	A	D	U	E	N	N
A	O	H	A	R	V	G	V	D	A	S	U	S	S	F	F	H	C
I	C	T	D	Z	O	E	E	F	I	S	O	T	L	D	F	S	Y
L	S	R	X	N	I	U	M	P	X	W	J	F	U	B	E	H	Q
S	C	F	M	E	G	Y	T	U	H	I	N	O	R	N	M	Y	S
C	A	S	T	C	A	T	F	I	S	H	D	X	E	R	N	P	M
E	N	B	R	E	A	M	E	N	D	C	M	W	J	A	S	G	Q

Name _____

Bait & Tackle 19.1

> "Hey, it's Skeeter. We are beginning the third 9 weeks of this course. Can you believe it? This 9 weeks we are shifting our focus from nature and fishing to a sermon and instructions that Jesus gave to His disciples. Because Jesus used everyday people to be His disciples, we need everyday people to be disciples now. People just like you. You will be reading from your Bibles a few times this week. Today, I want you to read Matthew 5:1–12. Write the word blessed in cursive here:"

Gear Up!

Use cotton swabs and sidewalk chalk to decorate the word *blessed*.

Lowercase n: Begin at the waterline, curve up to the boat line, down to the waterline, straight back up, over, and curve down to the waterline as you swim out.

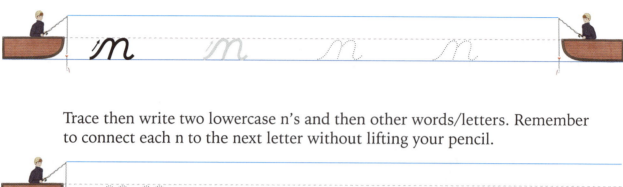

Trace then write two lowercase n's and then other words/letters. Remember to connect each n to the next letter without lifting your pencil.

> If you completed the Hoist the Sails activity each day, you have earned your sail badge and may color it. You're filling up that achievement board!
>
> Your next weigh-in challenge is to make your own maze with a fishing theme. Work on this each day adding artwork around the maze.

Name _____

Bait & Tackle 19.2

"We will continue looking at the sermon and instructions Jesus gave to His disciples. Remember, following instructions has helped you learn cursive just as it has helped many people in the Bible. Today, I want you to read Luke 6:19–23. Write the word *blessed* in cursive here:"

 blessed

Gear Up! Find your way through the word blessed.

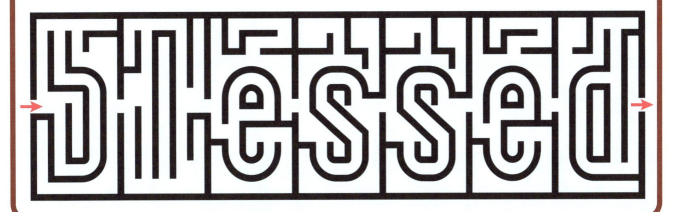

Lowercase m: The lowercase cursive m is like the letter n, but with one more hill. Begin at the **waterline**, curve up to the **boat line**, down to the **waterline**, straight back up, over, and curve down to the **waterline**. Then, straight back up, over, and curve down to the **waterline** as you swim out.

Trace then write three lowercase m's. Remember to connect each m to the next without lifting your pencil.

☐ **REMINDER:** Take some time to work on your weigh-in challenge.

Name

Bait & Tackle 19.3

> Before we cast ourselves into learning the instructions Jesus gave, also called the Beatitudes, let's talk about this sermon. It is known as the Sermon on the Mount. The reason it is called this is because Jesus had been in large crowds of people and they were craving to touch Him or be near Him so they could be healed. Jesus often left the large crowds to disciple (teach and train) His disciples. He knew His ministry on earth would be short, and the disciples would be the ones to share and carry the good news of the Gospel. He had to keep His focus on teaching the 12 disciples, so they were equipped to share the message of Jesus. Jesus left the crowd and He and His disciples went up on a mountain, which is why we call it the Sermon on the Mount.

Gear Up!

The Eye of the Hook: If you can, use a pushpin in the tip of an eraser or just a pencil with an eraser. Hold the pencil straight up and down in front of your nose. Bring it in slowly as you keep your eyes on the pin or eraser. Keep your focus. See how close you can bring it in before you see two of it. Hold it for 10 seconds, then release and do these 2 more times.

Lowercase m: Begin at the waterline, curve up to the boat line, down to the waterline, straight back up, over, and curve down to the waterline. Then, straight back up, over, and curve down to the waterline as you swim out.

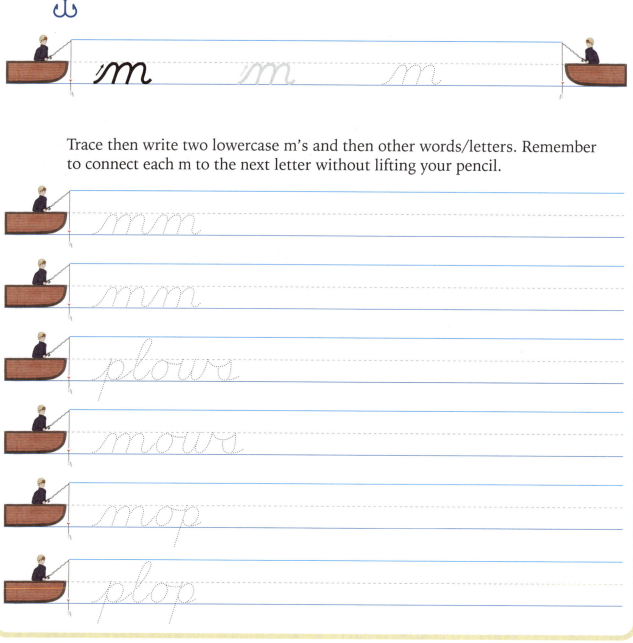

Trace then write two lowercase m's and then other words/letters. Remember to connect each m to the next letter without lifting your pencil.

☐ **REMINDER:** Take some time to work on your weigh-in challenge.

Name _____

Bait & Tackle 19.4

> "There is a word repeated in each verse. Do you know what it is? (Refer to Matthew 5:3–10 if needed.) Yes, it is *blessed*. For us to be blessed is an example of the goodness of God in our lives as believers. It doesn't mean that there will never be negative things that happen, because we know since the Fall that our world has consequences of sin. What it does mean is that by the grace of God we experience favor from God. He desires for us to be blessed and experience His goodness. I am blessed because of His goodness, not my goodness."

Gear Up!

Worm Squeezes: Use tweezers to pick up worms (pieces of yarn) one at a time. Make sure you get 5–10 worms.

Lowercase m: Begin at the waterline, curve up to the boat line, down to the waterline, straight back up, over, and curve down to the waterline. Then, straight back up, over, and curve down to the waterline as you swim out.

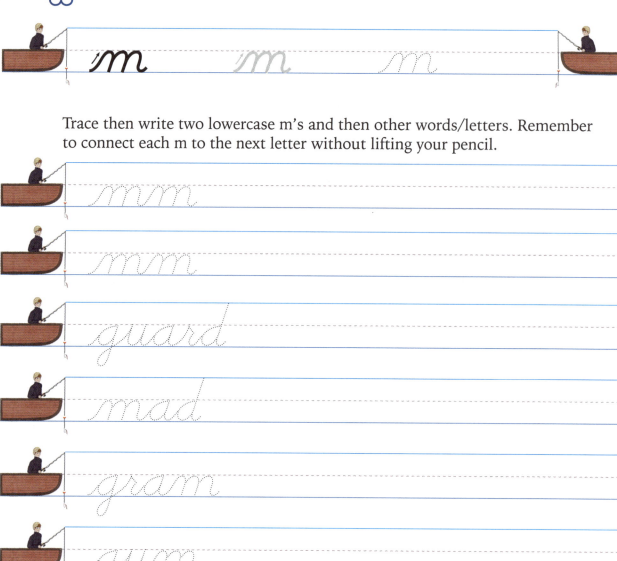

Trace then write two lowercase m's and then other words/letters. Remember to connect each m to the next letter without lifting your pencil.

" How did your maze turn out for the weigh in? I love doing mazes! Did you have someone complete yours? "

Name _____

Bait & Tackle 19.5

"A goal of the Beatitudes is in verse 12 of Matthew 5. "Rejoice and be exceedingly glad, for great is your reward in heaven, for so they persecuted the prophets who were before you" (NKJV). When our focus is on our heavenly reward, we can rejoice and be glad."

Gear Up!

Under & Over: You will help the fish swim over the obstacles. On the top row, begin by going under the first obstacle and back up between the next obstacles. You want to try to stay in the middle of the two obstacles you are going under and over. See the example to help you recall how to do this.

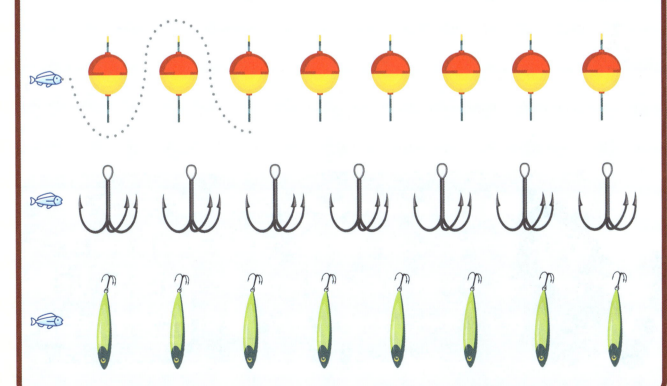

Review your letters: letters h, n, and m

Lowercase h: Begin at the waterline, slant forward and up toward the pole line. Then loop back and straight down to the waterline as you swim straight back up and over to the boat line, then swim out.

Lowercase n: Begin at the waterline, curve up to the boat line, down to the waterline, straight back up, over, and curve down to the waterline as you swim out.

Lowercase m: Begin at the waterline, curve up to the boat line, down to the waterline, straight back up, over, and curve down to the waterline. Then, straight back up, over, and curve down to the waterline as you swim out.

Trace the letters h, n, and m. Connect the letters and don't lift your pencil until all are written. Trace them three times, and then write them once on your own. Be sure to leave a pinky space between each set.

> "This is your time to showcase your best catch again. Use the section in the back of the book labeled "Fishing Derby: Showcasing My Best Catch." Find lesson 19 and complete the page. Remember, this is your "best" work. Ask your parents if they want to keep these in the book or remove them to showcase them."

CATCH ON TO CURSIVE
FISHING Derby
SHOWCASING MY BEST CATCH
BAIT & TACKLE 19

Name _____

"Are you up for another weigh-in challenge? I've got one for you! Let's have you do the Anchor Up activity in the Gear Up section of Bait & Tackle 20.1. Do these each day to build up muscles and earn your anchor badge."

"We have a new activity this week, so keep an eye out for directions from Anna."

Gather Your Gear

Day 3:
☐ Tennis ball or a ball of that size

Official GUIDE

Angelfish: freshwater fish that have a round body with long triangular fins. They are from South American basins such as the Amazon Basin.

DID YOU KNOW?

Wintertime is a great time to go ice fishing. Ice fishing is when you catch fish through a hole in the ice on a frozen body of water such as a lake. If ice fishing, or going on any frozen water, you must be safe. There is an old saying about frozen bodies of water, and I'm not sure who said it first, but it says, "Thick and blue, tried and true. Thin and crispy, way too risky." This means if the ice is thick and blue in color, it's usually safe. The ice needs to be at least 4 inches thick for you to walk on it and be safe, but you have to watch for those thin and crispy spots and stay away. *Remember, walking or driving on ice is dangerous, and you should never go on ice without an adult's permission.

Name _____

Bait & Tackle 20.1

"Last week I asked you to read two different passages of Scripture, one by Matthew and one by Luke. They were the same sermon, or instructions, known as the Sermon on the Mount. They are also called the Beatitudes. We will focus on one Beatitude each week this 9 weeks. The first one is found in Luke 6:21/Matthew 5:3. Look it up again in your Bibles. In Matthew 5:3 it says, "blessed are the poor in spirit, for theirs is the kingdom of heaven.""

Blessed are the poor in spirit,
Poor in Spirit = humble
for theirs is the kingdom of heaven.

Gear Up!

Anchor Up: Stand with your feet about shoulder width apart. Bend over and pretend to pull up a heavy anchor. Give the anchor 10 good pulls all the way up. Remember, that anchor is heavy!

Lowercase v: The lowercase cursive v begins like the lowercase n. Begin at the waterline, curve up to the boat line, down toward the waterline, but bump it as you curve back up to the boat line and slant down and out.

Trace then write three lowercase v's. Remember to connect each v to the next without lifting your pencil.

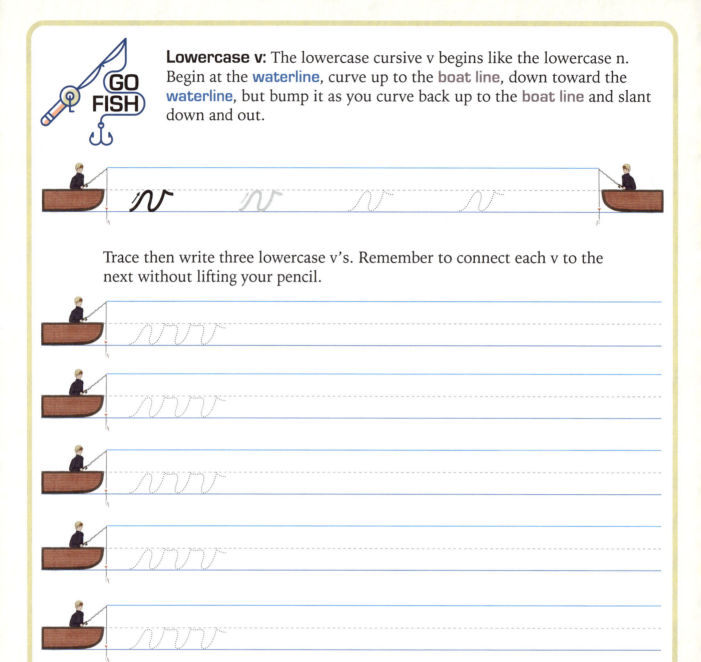

☐ **REMINDER:** Take some time to work on your weigh-in challenge.

Name _____

Bait & Tackle 20.2

> " In Matthew 5:3, the word *poor* doesn't mean poor like I would be if I wore my fishing pants that have holes in the pockets. In Greek, this word *poor* means beggar, and the word *blessed* here means fortunate or wealthy. Let's read that again by using these meanings. Fortunate are the beggars [*of*] spirit, for theirs is the kingdom of heaven. This helps us to understand the importance of our spiritual need for a Savior and seek Him with all our hearts. "

Gear Up!

Complete the maze through the angelfish.

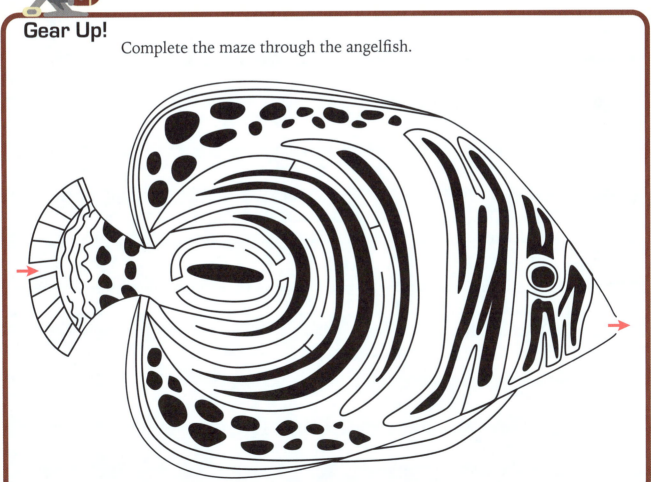

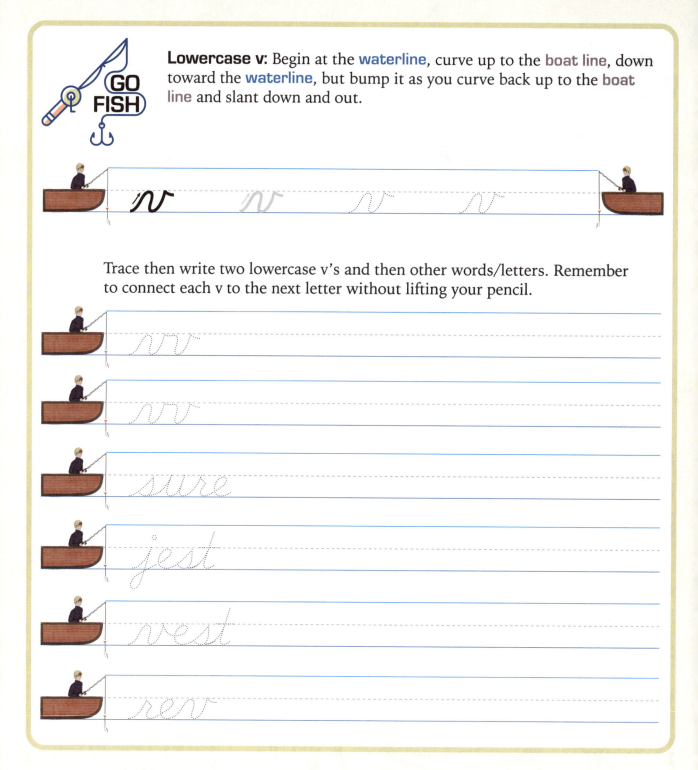

Name

Bait & Tackle 20.3

"We've talked about our need for Jesus. What are some ways we need Him? I need Him for salvation, helping me be a witness, healing in my body, and to protect me and my family. Talk with a parent about the ways we need Jesus and how He helps you."

Gear Up!

Hi there! You have a new activity this week. It is called **Crawdad Crawl.** You will use a tennis ball or a ball that size. You have two "pinchers" like the crawdad, which are your thumb and pointing finger. Start with the ball beside your foot. Using only your two pinchers (thumb and pointer finger), roll the ball up the side of your leg to your hip, across your tummy, and back down the side of the other leg. This may be difficult at first, but it will get easier with practice. Do this three times.

If you cannot do this with only two pinchers, you may add in one more to use your middle finger as well.

Lowercase v: Begin at the waterline, curve up to the boat line, down toward the waterline, but bump it as you curve back up to the boat line and slant down and out.

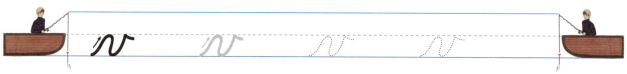

Trace then write two lowercase v's and then other words/letters. Remember to connect each v to the next letter without lifting your pencil.

" Did you complete the Anchor Up activity to earn your anchor badge? If so, you may add it to your achievement board after you color in the anchor on your badge.

Your next weigh-in challenge is to do the Crawdad Crawl once a day (see page 253). "

Name

Bait & Tackle 20.4

"Trace the following from our Beatitude found in Matthew 5:3."

Blessed are the poor in spirit, for theirs is the kingdom of heaven.

Gear Up!

Track down the angelfish. Starting at the top left row, "read" the rows and circle only the angelfish.

Lowercase y: For a lowercase y, you will make a v until the last part. Begin at the waterline, curve up to the boat line, down and drop to the hook space, then curl and loop back as you swim up and over the waterline.

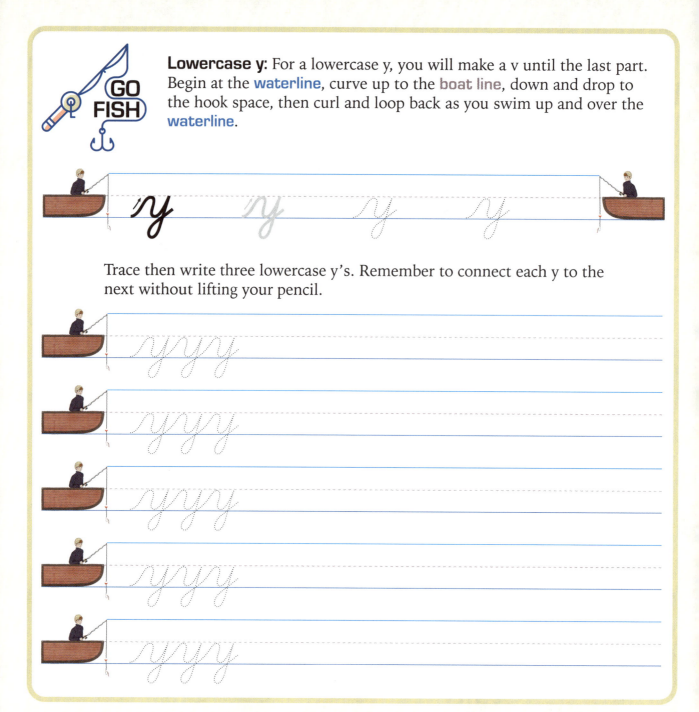

Trace then write three lowercase y's. Remember to connect each y to the next without lifting your pencil.

☐ **REMINDER:** Take some time to work on your weigh-in challenge.

Name _____

Bait & Tackle 20.5

> "The Bible says in Romans 10:9 "... if you confess with your mouth that Jesus is Lord and believe in your heart that God raised him from the dead, you will be saved." Wow! Confess (speak it) and believe is as easy as catching a hungry bream on its bed. Discuss this verse and its meaning with your teacher."

Gear Up!

Paddle the Boat: Sit in a chair or on the side of a bathtub with your feet flat on the ground. Pretend to paddle the boat. Make sure you swap sides so your boat doesn't get off course! Give a good 15 total strokes of the paddle for each side.

Lowercase y: For a lowercase y, you will make a v until the last part. Begin at the waterline, curve up to the boat line, down and drop to the hook space, then curl and loop back as you swim up and over the waterline.

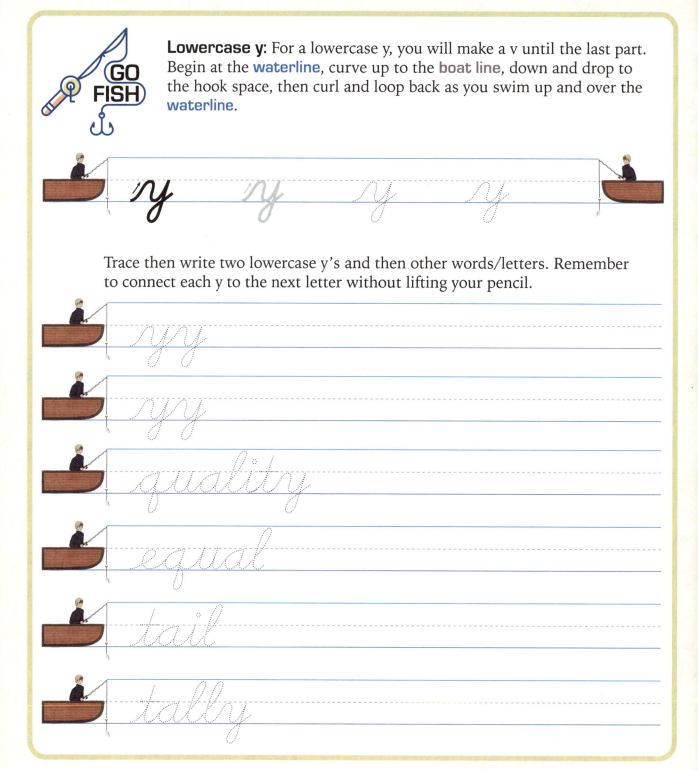

Trace then write two lowercase y's and then other words/letters. Remember to connect each y to the next letter without lifting your pencil.

yy

yy

quality

equal

tail

tally

☐ **REMINDER:** Take some time to work on your weigh-in challenge.

Name

"I'll be waiting for you at the weigh-in section. I hope you've been doing those Crawdad Crawls. See you there!"

"Oh! Check out that fun bundle of mazes you get to do this week."

Gather Your Gear

Day 1:
☐ Paper clips

Day 2:
☐ Sticky notes or paper
☐ Ball (tennis or approx. size)

Day 3:
☐ Pushpins (thumb tacks)
☐ One of the following: cutting board, cork board, or foam sheet

Name _____

Bait & Tackle 21.1

"Last week we talked about the first Beatitude, now let's talk about the second. Read it in your Bibles in Matthew 5:4. It says, "Blessed are those who mourn, for they shall be comforted.""

Blessed are those who mourn,
Mourn = grieve or sorrow
for they shall be comforted.

Gear Up!

Hook the Fish: At the bottom of the page is a row of fish. Open paper clips and secure a paper clip to each fish.

Lowercase y: Begin at the waterline, curve up to the boat line, down and drop to the hook space, then curl and loop back as you swim up and over the waterline.

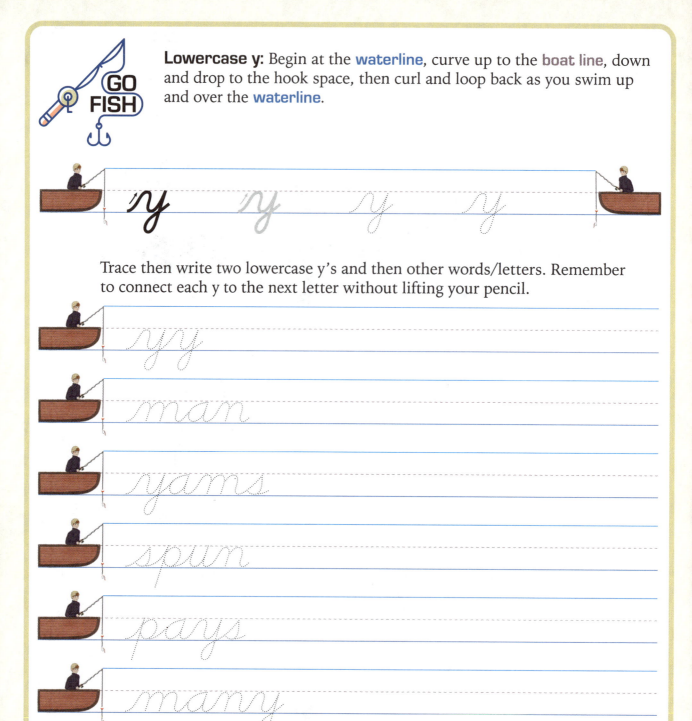

Trace then write two lowercase y's and then other words/letters. Remember to connect each y to the next letter without lifting your pencil.

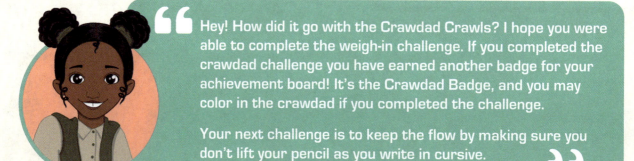

262 🐟 Hooked on Cursive

Name _____

Bait & Tackle 21.2

> Matthew 5:4 says, "Blessed are those who mourn, for they shall be comforted." In this Scripture, mourn can mean to be sad over someone's passing or someone taking a toy. It can also mean a sadness about sin and its effects. Sin separates us from God. The end of this verse says we will be comforted. The Bible says that the Holy Spirit is our comforter (John 14:26). We may be sad because of sin and its effects, but the Holy Spirit will comfort and help us. We also have the good news of knowing that Jesus will forgive us of our sins if we ask.

Gear Up!

Aim and Cast: Place a piece of paper or sticky note on a door or wall about eye level. You can make a target on it if you'd like. Take about 10 steps back and try to AIM and CAST the ball to hit the target. If you miss 3 times, you can step forward 1 step. Try to hit the paper/target in the middle at least 3 times in a row.

Capital D: Start at the pole line, go down and bump the waterline as you swim back and loop to swim back to the waterline. Bump the waterline and curve back up to the pole line, then loop down and out.

Trace then write three capital D's. The cursive capital D's do not connect to the next.

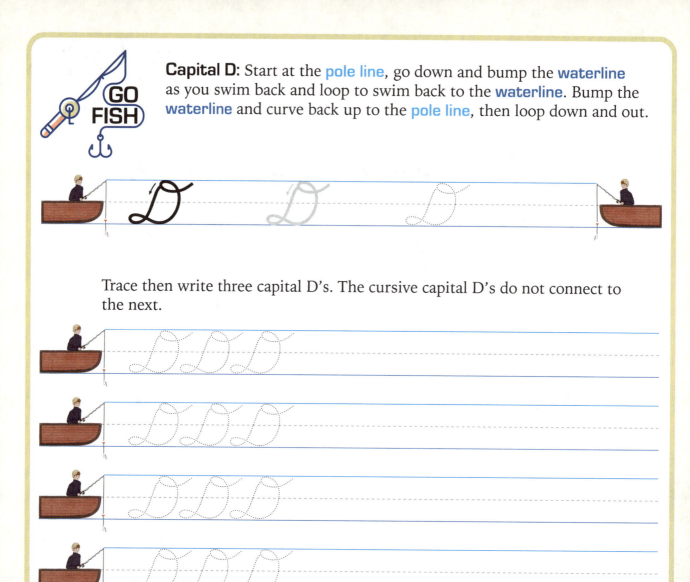

☐ **REMINDER:** Take some time to work on your weigh-in challenge.

Name _____

Bait & Tackle 21.3

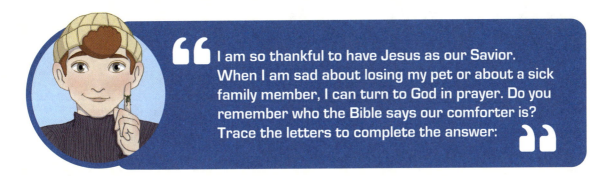

"I am so thankful to have Jesus as our Savior. When I am sad about losing my pet or about a sick family member, I can turn to God in prayer. Do you remember who the Bible says our comforter is? Trace the letters to complete the answer:"

Holy Spirit

 **Gear Up!**

Poke the Angelfish: Using pushpins (thumb tacks), make a hole in each dot. Make sure you swap hands after 10 pokes. Use your thumbs to help give you strength and stability. Be careful not to poke yourself!

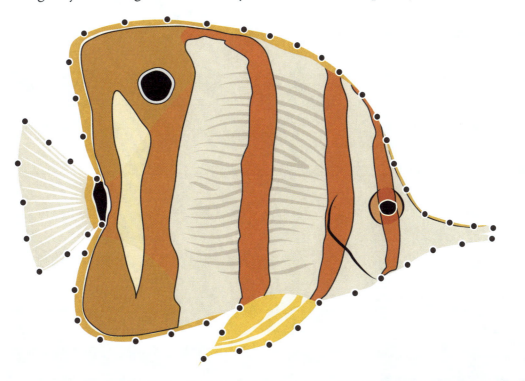

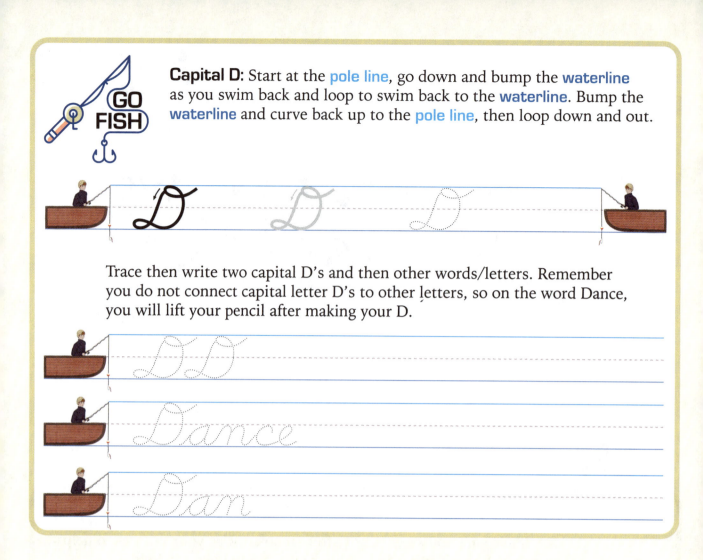

Capital D: Start at the pole line, go down and bump the waterline as you swim back and loop to swim back to the waterline. Bump the waterline and curve back up to the pole line, then loop down and out.

Trace then write two capital D's and then other words/letters. Remember you do not connect capital letter D's to other letters, so on the word Dance, you will lift your pencil after making your D.

Name

Bait & Tackle 21.4

" Trace the Beatitude in cursive. "

Blessed are those who mourn, for they shall be comforted.

Gear Up!

Don't Hit the Bridge: The ships in the river need to get through. Place your hands flat on the ground with tips of toes on the ground and body lifted to be the bridge. Hold this for 10–15 seconds. Try to beat your time this week. (Your last time was at Bait & Tackle 16.2.) Record today's time here: _____

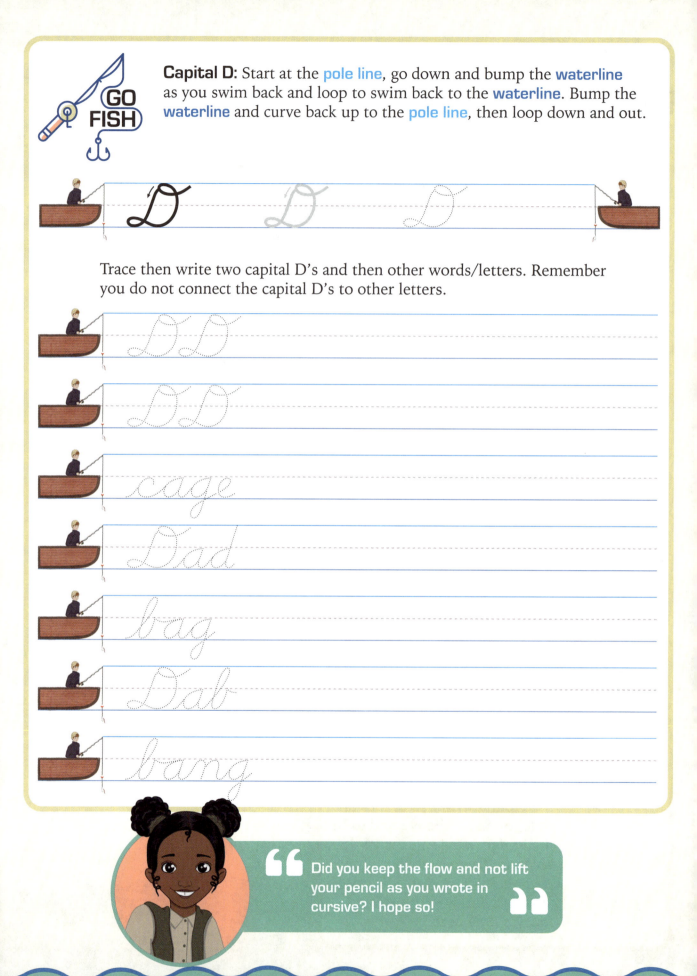

Name _____

Bait & Tackle 21.5

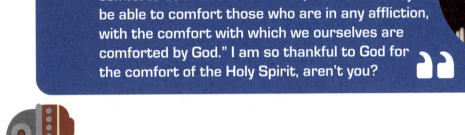

" Second Corinthians 1:3–4 says, "Blessed be the God and Father of our Lord Jesus Christ, the Father of mercies and God of all comfort, who comforts us in all our affliction, so that we may be able to comfort those who are in any affliction, with the comfort with which we ourselves are comforted by God." I am so thankful to God for the comfort of the Holy Spirit, aren't you? "

Gear Up!

Complete the dot-to-dot. Remember to first use only your eyes to find the path, then complete it.

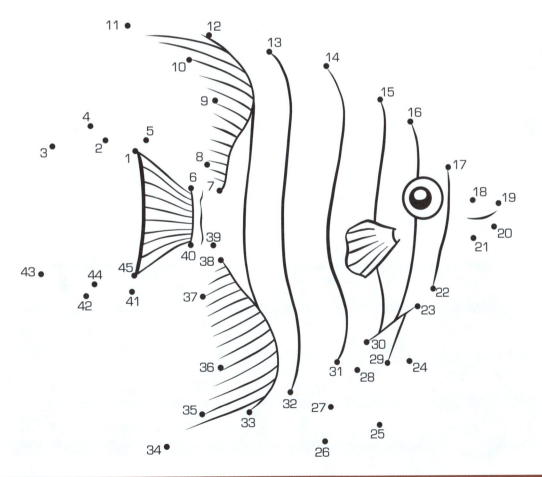

Review your letters: letters v, y, and D

Lowercase v: Begin at the waterline, curve up to the boat line, down toward the waterline, but bump it as you curve back up to the boat line and slant down and out.

Lowercase y: Begin at the waterline, curve up to the boat line, down and drop to the hook space, then curl and loop back as you swim up and over the waterline.

Capital D: Start at the pole line, go down and bump the waterline as you swim back and loop to swim back to the waterline. Bump the waterline and curve back up to the pole line, then loop down and out.

Trace the letters D, v, and y. Connect the letters v and y and do not lift your pencil until all are written. Trace them three times, and then write them once on your own. Be sure to leave a pinky space between each set.

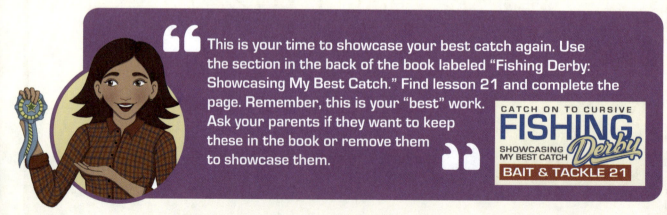

This is your time to showcase your best catch again. Use the section in the back of the book labeled "Fishing Derby: Showcasing My Best Catch." Find lesson 21 and complete the page. Remember, this is your "best" work. Ask your parents if they want to keep these in the book or remove them to showcase them.

CATCH ON TO CURSIVE
FISHING Derby
SHOWCASING MY BEST CATCH
BAIT & TACKLE 21

Hooked on Cursive

Name

"I've got another challenge for you. Your challenge is to complete two of the Under & Over activities in the weigh-in section in the back of the book (see Gear Up from Bait & Tackle 19.5). You should complete two lines each day for this challenge."

"Be sure to gather your gear and look below for a fun activity with the Beatitudes."

Gather Your Gear

Day 1:
☐ Sheet of foam
☐ Sheet of plain paper

Day 2:
☐ Painter's tape or rope or sidewalk chalk

Day 3:
☐ Plastic lid with a lip or a round cake pan
☐ Marble

Day 4:
☐ Tennis ball or ball that size

Tackle Box 22 271

Official GUIDE

We'll match the Beatitudes you've learned so far.

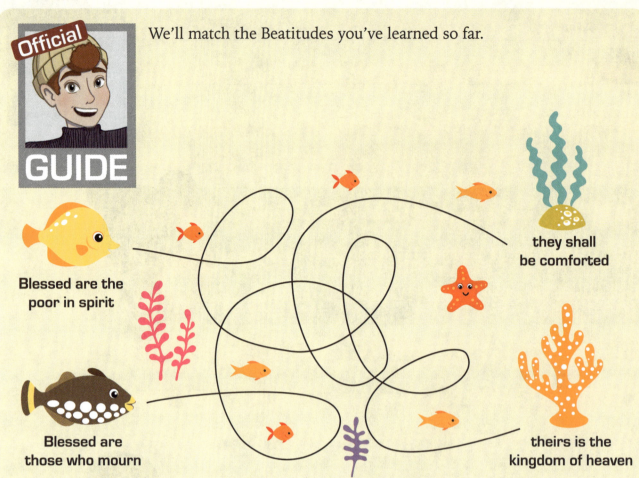

Blessed are the poor in spirit — they shall be comforted

Blessed are those who mourn — theirs is the kingdom of heaven

DID YOU KNOW?

You need an auger for ice fishing.

An auger is used to drill the hole in the ice. You want a hole about 8–10 inches wide. The most common way to ice fish is by jigging. Jigging is done with a short, light stick a little over 2 feet long with a line tied on the end — a spring bobber.

The spring bobber helps you to notice the slightest movement from a fish, and it helps to decrease your movements — it's a win-win.

Name _____

Bait & Tackle 22.1

> "We have discussed the first two Beatitudes, now let's talk about the third. Read it in your Bibles in Matthew 5:5. It says, "Blessed are the meek, for they shall inherit the earth.""

Blessed are the meek,
Meek = kind & gentle
for they shall inherit the earth.

Gear Up!

The Right Conditions: Place a plain piece of paper on a piece of foam. When you write, if you apply too little pressure, it is difficult to see your writing and it can even look shaky. If you apply too much pressure, it will cause you pain. You need the right pressure to see your words, but not too much or you'll push through the paper to the foam. Print your name 3 times and print the word *blessed* 3 times.

Capital B: Start below the pole line, curve up, bump the pole line, and go straight down to the waterline. Then go back up that line and curve up and over as you bump the pole line. Then circle out and down to the boat line. Circle down and loop out to bump the waterline as you swim back to bump the waterline, then loop down and out.

Trace then write three capital B's. The letter B does not connect to other letters.

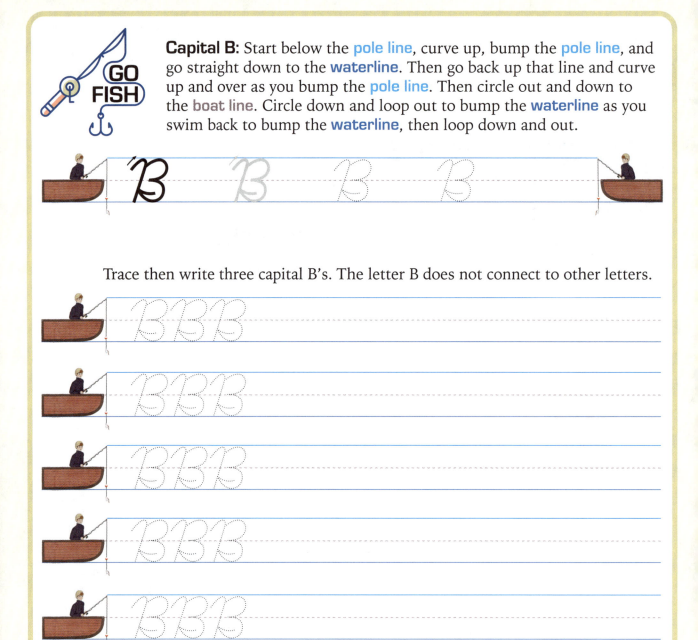

REMINDER: Take some time to work on your weigh-in challenge.

Name

Bait & Tackle 22.2

> Matthew 5:5 says, "Blessed are the meek, for they shall inherit the earth." Meek means gentle or kind. This word doesn't mean weak. It actually means that you have self-control and that you control your actions. Jesus didn't want us to be weak, but He did want us to have self-control. It's like a sailor on the sea who harnesses the power of the wind in his sail. We have to harness our emotions and be gentle and kind so we can be like Christ.

Gear Up!

Walk the Plank: Use painter's tape, a rope, or sidewalk chalk to make a long line. Walk the Plank by balancing on the line with one foot in front of the other. Don't fall in! There might be gators in that water! Do this 3 times.

(You can also use a 2x4 or balance beam.)

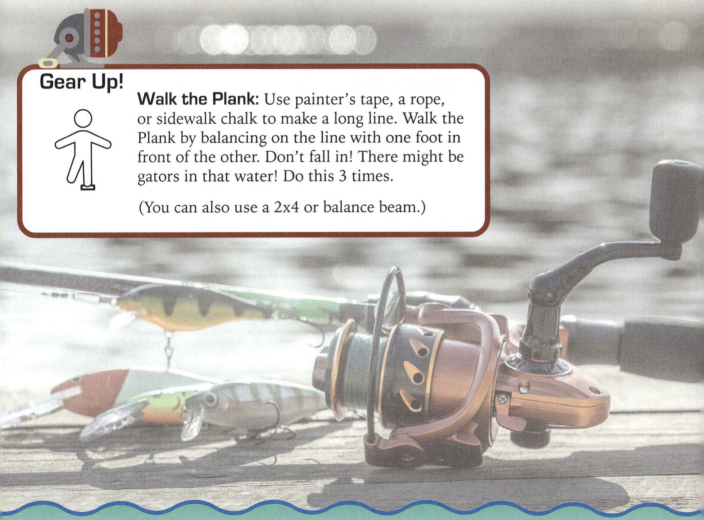

Capital B: Start below the pole line, curve up, bump the pole line, and go straight down to the waterline. Then, go back up that line and curve up and over as you bump the pole line. Then, circle out and down to the boat line. Circle down and loop out to bump the waterline as you swim back to bump the waterline, then loop down and out.

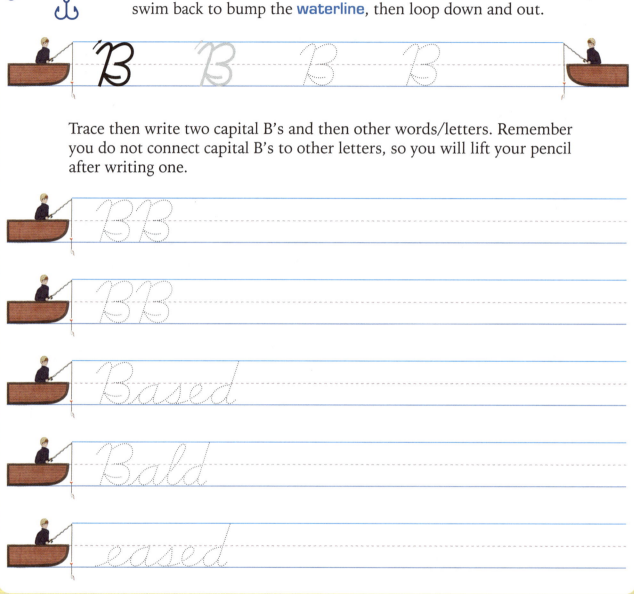

Trace then write two capital B's and then other words/letters. Remember you do not connect capital B's to other letters, so you will lift your pencil after writing one.

☐ **REMINDER:** Take some time to work on your weigh-in challenge.

Name _____

Bait & Tackle 22.3

" It isn't always easy to harness or control our emotions, especially when our friends take our toy or get the best swing first. Here's a verse to help you remember what the Bible says. Copy Proverbs 16:32 below. "

whoever is slow to anger is better than the mighty, and he who rules his spirit than he who takes a city.

Gear Up!

Marble in the Whirlpool: Using a plastic lid with a lip or a round cake pan, place a marble inside. Have someone move the lid/pan so the marble rolls in the inside edge back and forth and eventually all the way around in a circle. Follow the marble with your eyes, but do not move your head. Move only your eyes as you follow the marble back and forth. Do this for one minute.

Capital B: Start below the pole line, curve up, bump the pole line, and go straight down to the waterline. Then, go back up that line and curve up and over as you bump the pole line. Then, circle out and down to the boat line. Circle down and loop out to bump the waterline as you swim back to bump the waterline, then loop down and out.

Trace then write two capital B's and the first part of the verse in Ephesians 4:32 (NKJV). Remember that B's do not connect to the next letter, and you will lift your pencil. As we continue through your cursive writing lessons, it's time to take away our boat for the letters you already know. The boat will come back for any new letters you learn!

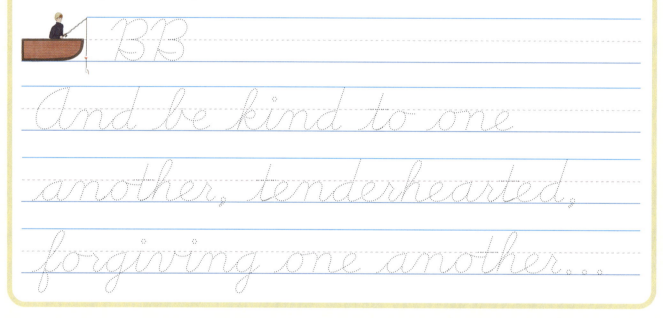

> **Did you do the Under and Over activity?** If you did, you have earned a new badge! You may color it in the back then add it to your achievement board if you completed the activity.
>
> Your next challenge is a pressure test. Use modeling clay or Play-Doh to make a ball around the end of your pencil. You may first shape it into a triangle or give grooves for your fingers. As you write, use this pencil and see if you're using the right pressure as you write. If you have more dents in the dough from too much pressure, then you need to try to reform the dough/clay and try to loosen your grip on the pencil. The goal is for the dough to not change shape as you write.

Name

Bait & Tackle 22.4

"Trace this week's Beatitude from Matthew 5:5 below."

Blessed are the meek,
for they shall inherit
the earth.

Gear Up!

Crawdad Crawl: You will use a tennis ball or a ball that size. You have two "pinchers" like the crawdad, which are your thumb and pointing finger. Start with the ball beside your foot, using only your two pinchers (thumb and pointer finger), roll the ball up the side of your leg to your hip, across your tummy, and back down the side of the other leg. This may be difficult at first, but it will get easier with practice. Do this three times.

*If you cannot do this with only two pinchers, you may add in one more to use your middle finger as well.

Capital P: The capital P begins like the capital B and also does not connect to other letters. Start below the pole line, curve up and bump the pole line and go straight down to the waterline. Circle around and bump the boat line as you connect your circle to your line.

Trace then write three capital P's. Remember you do not connect the letter P's.

☐ **REMINDER:** Take some time to work on your weigh-in challenge.

Name _____

Bait & Tackle 22.5

> "When I feel myself losing control, I can stop and ask God to help me. It's difficult to control our emotions at times, but with God's help we can win over them."

Gear Up!

Complete the maze to get from the fishing cabin to the lake.

Capital P: Start below the pole line, curve up and bump the pole line and go straight down to the waterline. Then, go back up that line and curve up and over as you bump the pole line. Circle around and bump the boat line as you connect your circle to your line.

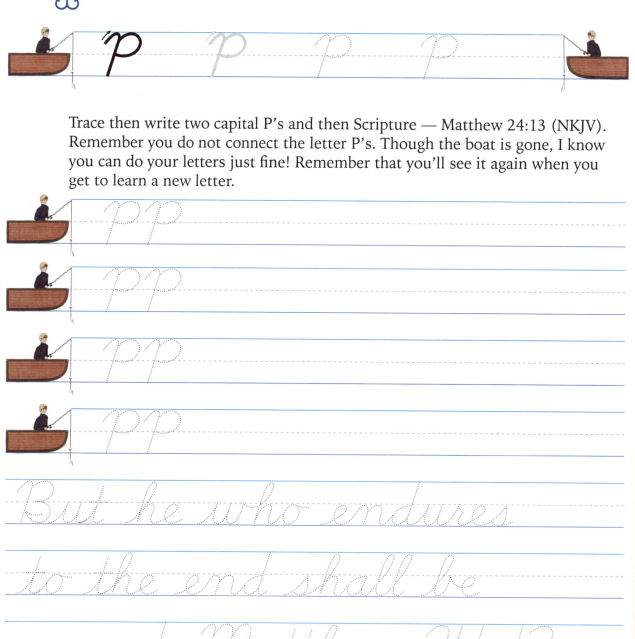

Trace then write two capital P's and then Scripture — Matthew 24:13 (NKJV). Remember you do not connect the letter P's. Though the boat is gone, I know you can do your letters just fine! Remember that you'll see it again when you get to learn a new letter.

☐ **REMINDER:** Take some time to work on your weigh-in challenge.

Name _____

"I can't wait to see you at the weigh-in section! I just know you're going to earn your badge."

"We've got another activity to help you remember your Beatitudes. Check it out below. Remember we'll be doing our Fishing Derby this week. Keep an eye out for it."

Gather Your Gear

Day 1:
☐ Hole punch (preferably single)

Day 2:
☐ Wave wands from previous lesson

Day 4:
☐ Small objects such as beads, small buttons, or sunflower seeds
☐ Play-Doh or other dough

Tackle Box 23 283

GUIDE — We'll match the Beatitudes you've learned so far.

Blessed are the poor in spirit

they shall be comforted.

Blessed are the meek

they shall inherit the earth.

Blessed are those who mourn

theirs is the kingdom of heaven.

Name

 Bait & Tackle 23.1

" We have discussed the first three Beatitudes, now let's talk about the fourth. Read it in your Bibles in Matthew 5:6. The verse says, "Blessed are those who hunger and thirst for righteousness, for they shall be satisfied." "

Blessed are those who hunger and thirst for righteousness,
hunger & thirst after righteousness = seek God & His Word
for they shall be satisfied.

Gear Up!

Under & Over: You will help the fish swim over the obstacles. On the top row, begin by going under the first obstacle and back up between the next obstacles. You want to try to stay in the middle of the two obstacles you are going under and over. See the example to help you recall how to do this.

Capital P: Start below the pole line, curve up and bump the pole line and go straight down to the waterline. Then, go back up that line and curve up and over as you bump the pole line. Circle around and bump the boat line as you connect your circle to your line.

Trace then write two capital P's and then other words. Remember, we do not connect the capital letter P's to other letters, so you do lift your pencil after writing it.

> How did the pressure test go? I bet that wasn't as easy as you thought it would be. If you completed the weigh-in challenge, you have earned the pressure test badge, and you may color it in and add it to your achievement board.
>
> Your next challenge is to warm up your hands before you write each day. You will use a hole punch and simply punch holes in a paper. Do at least 10 holes per hand before you write each day. If you complete this challenge, you will earn another badge.

Name _____

Bait & Tackle 23.2

> Matthew 5:6 says, "Blessed are those who hunger and thirst for righteousness, for they shall be satisfied." When we seek God, or hunger and thirst after His ways, He is faithful and will fill us. We can fill ourselves by reading His Word, praying, and going to church. We should desire, or want, more of God than anything else, even more than playing with our friends.

Gear Up!

Making Waves: Use your wave wands from week 1 to make more waves! Be sure to make 8's sideways and upright with both hands. Do this for 1 minute.

Capital R: The capital R begins like the capital P, but it does connect to other letters. Start below the pole line, curve up and bump the pole line and go straight down to the waterline. Circle around and bump the boat line as you connect your circle to your line, then slant out and down to bump the waterline and curve up a little.

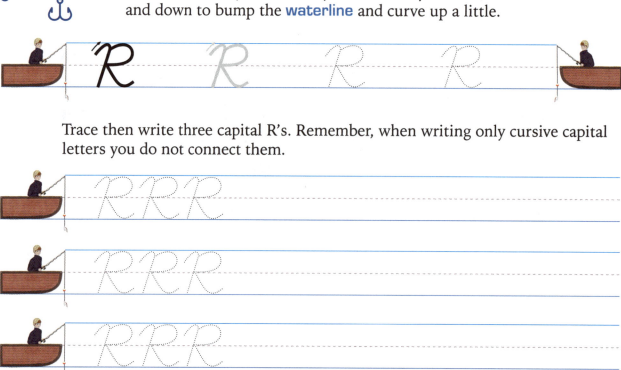

Trace then write three capital R's. Remember, when writing only cursive capital letters you do not connect them.

☐ **REMINDER:** Take some time to work on your weigh-in challenge.

Name _____

Bait & Tackle 23.3

" Here is another verse for you to remember how God is faithful to us when we seek Him. Complete the words of Proverbs 8:17 below in cursive. "

I love those who love me, and those who seek me diligently will find me.

Gear Up!

Hoist the Sails: These are called side planks and are like a side pushup where you hold your body up. Lay on your side and lift your body up with the arm closest to the ground. Your foot should be on its side on the ground. Hold the position for 8 seconds, relax, and repeat 2 times. Do both sides of your body. Your body makes a triangle shape like a sail.

Capital R: Start below the pole line, curve up and bump the pole line and go straight down to the waterline. Circle around and bump the boat line as you connect your circle to your line, then slant out and down to bump the waterline and curve up a little.

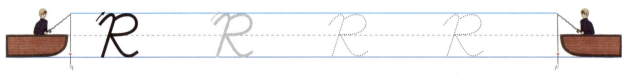

Trace then write two capital R's and Psalm 16:8 (ERV). Remember to connect each R to the next letter without lifting your pencil.

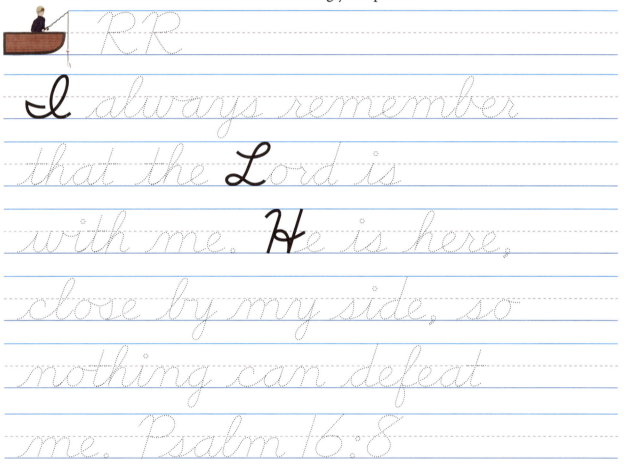

I always remember that the Lord is with me. He is here, close by my side, so nothing can defeat me. Psalm 16:8

☐ **REMINDER:** Take some time to work on your weigh-in challenge.

Name: _____

Bait & Tackle 23.4

"Copy your Beatitude from Matthew 5:6 in cursive."

Blessed are those who hunger and thirst for righteousness, for they shall be satisfied.

Gear Up!

Lures in Mud: Push the small objects into dough. Be sure to use your fingers to get them started, and your thumb to get them all the way in. Do 10 objects in dough.

Capital R: Start below the pole line, curve up and bump the pole line and go straight down to the waterline. Circle around and bump the boat line as you connect your circle to your line, then slant out and down to bump the waterline and curve up a little.

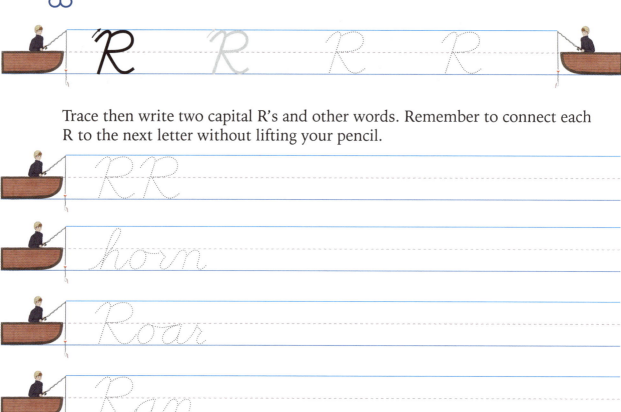

Trace then write two capital R's and other words. Remember to connect each R to the next letter without lifting your pencil.

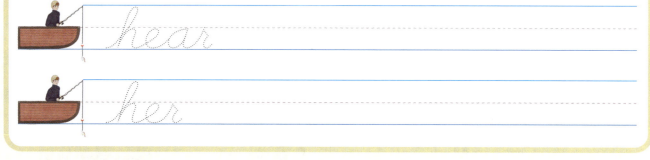

Did you complete the hand warmup activity with the hole punch each day? If so, you may color the badge in the back. Look at how many badges you have on your achievement board! Wow! You're doing a great job with the weigh-in challenges.

Hooked on Cursive

Name _____

Bait & Tackle 23.5

> "When I was younger, I listened to a song that was Scripture. It was from Matthew 6:33 (NKJV) and it says, "But seek first the kingdom of God and His righteousness, and all these things shall be added to you." That is a great verse to remind us of the promise from God as we seek to know Him more. Seek God and His ways."

Gear Up!

Paddle the Boat: Sit in a chair or on the side of a bathtub with your feet flat on the ground. Pretend to paddle the boat. Make sure you swap sides so your boat doesn't get off course! Give a good 15 total strokes of the paddle for each side.

Review your letters: letters B, P, and R

Capital B: Start below the pole line, curve up, bump the pole line, and go straight down to the waterline. Then, go back up that line and curve up and over as you bump the pole line. Then, circle out and down to the boat line. Circle down and loop out to bump the waterline as you swim back to bump the waterline, then loop down and out.

Capital P: Start below the pole line, curve up and bump the pole line and go straight down to the waterline. Then, go back up that line and curve up and over as you bump the pole line. Circle around and bump the boat line as you connect your circle to your line.

Capital R: Start below the pole line, curve up and bump the pole line and go straight down to the waterline. Circle around and bump the boat line as you connect your circle to your line, then slant out and down to bump the waterline and curve up a little.

Trace the letters B, P, and R. Trace them three times without connecting them, and then write them once on your own. Be sure to leave a pinky space between each set.

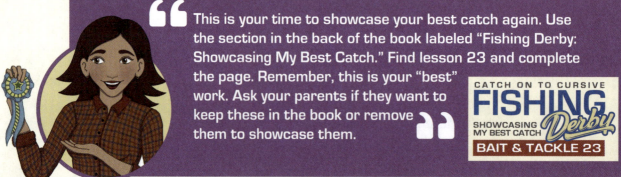

> This is your time to showcase your best catch again. Use the section in the back of the book labeled "Fishing Derby: Showcasing My Best Catch." Find lesson 23 and complete the page. Remember, this is your "best" work. Ask your parents if they want to keep these in the book or remove them to showcase them.

CATCH ON TO CURSIVE
FISHING Derby
SHOWCASING MY BEST CATCH
BAIT & TACKLE 23

Name _____

TACKLE BOX 24

> " I bet you're ready for this next weigh-in challenge. Your next challenge is to use correct size when writing. If your letter is lowercase, it should be from the boat line and to the waterline or hook space. If your letter is capital, it should be between the pole line and the waterline. "

> " On the next page is a new activity to help you remember the Beatitudes. "

Gather Your Gear

Day 1:
☐ Pencil with eraser or pencil with pushpin in the eraser

Day 4:
☐ Sheet of foam
☐ Sheet of plain paper

Day 5:
☐ Sticky notes or paper
☐ Ball (tennis or approx. size)

Tackle Box 24 295

Fill in the missing words from the Beatitudes you've learned so far.

Blessed   hunger   meek
comforted   filled   spirit
Heaven   inherit   thirst

Blessed are the poor in _____ – theirs is the kingdom of _____ Matthew 5:3

_____ are those who mourn – they shall be _____ Matthew 5:4

Blessed are the _____ – they shall _____ the earth. Matthew 5:5

Blessed are those who _____ and _____ for righteousness – they shall be _____. Matthew 5:6

Name _____

Bait & Tackle 24.1

" This week we are discussing the fifth Beatitude. Read it in your Bible. It is in Matthew 5:7. The Scripture says, "Blessed are the merciful, for they shall receive mercy." "

Blessed are the merciful,
Merciful = forgiving & compassionate
for they shall receive mercy.

Gear Up!

The Eye of the Hook: If you can, use a pushpin in the tip of an eraser or just a pencil with an eraser. Hold the pencil straight up and down in front of your nose. Bring it in slowly as you keep your eyes on the pin or eraser. Keep your focus. See how close you can bring it in before you see two of it. Hold it for 10 seconds, then release and do these 2 more times.

Capital L: The capital L is like a looping roller coaster. Begin a little below the pole line, dip down and out as you loop back up, bumping the pole line, go down to the waterline as you loop back and up to swim out the waterline.

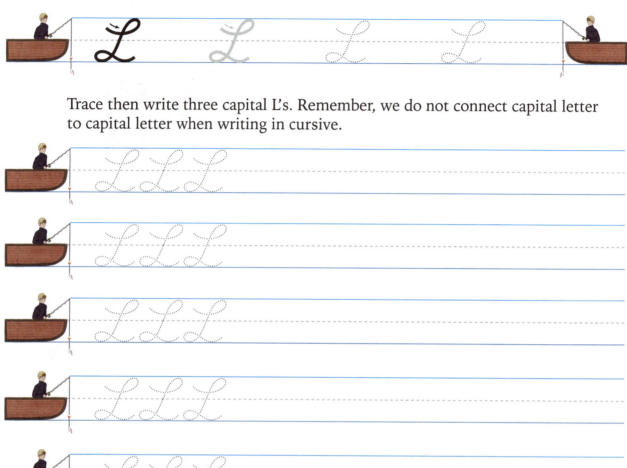

Trace then write three capital L's. Remember, we do not connect capital letter to capital letter when writing in cursive.

☐ **REMINDER:** Take some time to work on your weigh-in challenge.

Name _____

Bait & Tackle 24.2

> "Matthew 5:7 says, "Blessed are the merciful, for they shall receive mercy." Merciful is another way to say compassionate or forgiving. When we show mercy to others, we will be given mercy. Jesus was compassionate and merciful, and we are to be like Him. I want my friends and family to show mercy to me when I make a mistake."

Gear Up!

Anchor Up: Stand with your feet about shoulder width apart. Bend over and pretend to pull up a heavy anchor. Give the anchor 10 good pulls all the way up. Remember, that anchor is heavy!

Capital L: Begin a little below the pole line, dip down and out as you loop back up, bumping the pole line, go down to the waterline as you loop back and up to swim out to the waterline.

Trace then write three capital L's without connecting them, and part of Isaiah 40:31 (NKJV). Remember to connect each L to the next letters in the words without lifting your pencil.

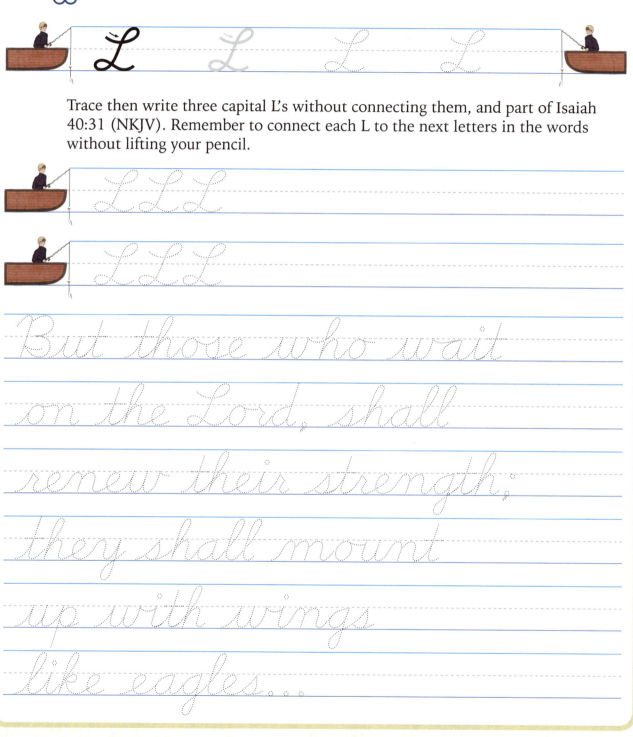

☐ **REMINDER:** Take some time to work on your weigh-in challenge.

Name

Bait & Tackle 24.3

" This verse about mercy from Luke 6:36 that says, "Be merciful, even as your Father is merciful," is another example that we are to show others mercy and compassion as God shows us mercy. "

Gear Up!

Skeeter dropped his anchor in the lake, but the rope is tangled up with another rope. Help him find which rope is attached to the anchor, then circle the correct letter.

Capital L: The capital L is like a looping roller coaster. Begin a little below the pole line, dip down and out as you loop back, bumping the pole line, go down to the waterline as you loop back and swim out to the waterline.

Trace then write three capital L's without connecting them, and part of Isaiah 40:31 (NKJV). Remember to connect each L to the next letters in the words without lifting your pencil.

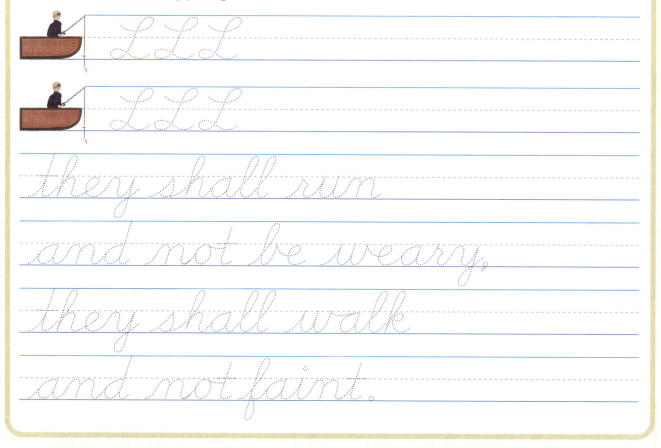

" Did you use the correct size when writing? If so, decorate the bubble letters.

Your next challenge is to color in the fish each day. This activity will help with your control of your pencil. You can choose to use colored pencils or pens to make them different colors. Please color the 5 fish provided and stay inside the lines. "

Bb

Name _____

Bait & Tackle 24.4

" Copy your Beatitude from Matthew 5:7 in cursive. "

Blessed are the merciful, for they shall receive mercy.

Gear Up!

The Right Conditions: Place a plain piece of paper on a piece of foam. When you write, if you apply too little pressure, it is difficult to see your writing and it can even look shaky. If you apply too much pressure, it will cause you pain. You need the right pressure to see your words, but not too much or you'll push through the paper to the foam. Write the verse from above.

Capital M: The capital M begins like a capital P or a lowercase m stretched tall. It reminds me of a 2-humped camel. Start below the pole line, curve up and bump the pole line as you swim down to the waterline. Then, go back up that line and curve over and down to the waterline. Go back up that line and curve over and down to the waterline again. Finally, curve up slightly after you bump the waterline.

Trace then write three capital M's. Remember, we do not connect cursive capital letters together.

Weigh-in challenge: Fill in the fish for your challenge. Remember to stay inside the lines.

Name _____

 Bait & Tackle 24.5

>  "The Bible also tells us to treat others the way we want to be treated, not how we are treated. I want to be given mercy, so I need to show mercy to others. If my friends are not being kind, I am still to show kindness."

Gear Up!

Aim and Cast: Place a piece of paper or sticky note on a door or wall about eye level. You can make a target on it if you'd like. Take about 10 steps back and try to AIM and CAST the ball to hit the target. If you miss 3 times, you can step forward 1 step. Try to hit the paper/target in the middle at least 3 times in a row.

Capital M: Start below the pole line, curve up and bump the pole line as you swim down to the waterline. Then, go back up that line and curve over and down to the waterline. Go back up that line and curve over and down to the waterline again. Finally, curve up slightly after you bump the waterline.

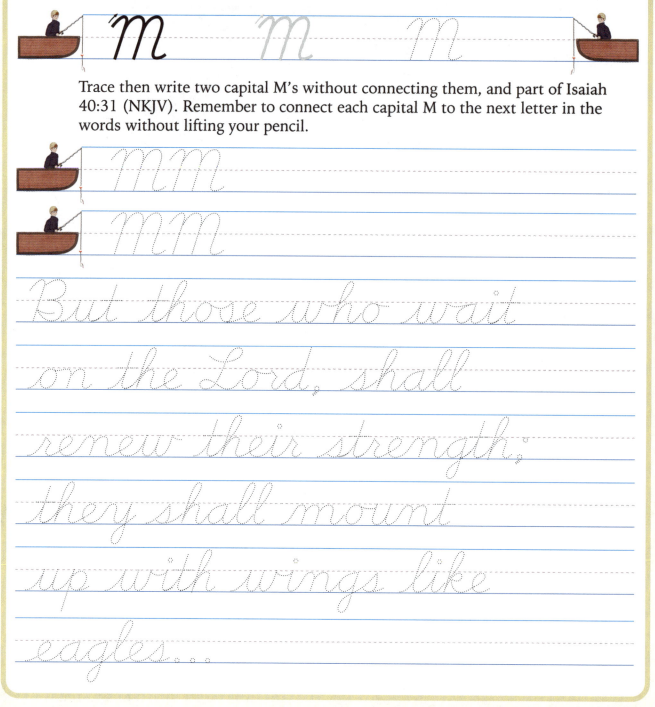

Trace then write two capital M's without connecting them, and part of Isaiah 40:31 (NKJV). Remember to connect each capital M to the next letter in the words without lifting your pencil.

Weigh-in challenge: Fill in the fish for your challenge. Be sure to stay inside the lines.

Name

"How was your weigh-in challenge? Did you stay inside the lines? I will see you at the weigh-in section."

"We have a new term this week as well as a different activity for the Beatitudes. This is a Fishing Derby week also, so be on the lookout for it."

Gather Your Gear

Day 1:
☐ Marble
☐ 2 plastic cups

Day 4:
☐ 6 2-inch x 2-inch foil squares

Official GUIDE

Weight: a metal weight used on a fishing line with a lure to increase the depth, cast distance, or movement of the bait.

Match the words from the Beatitudes you've learned so far. Use your Bible (Matthew 5).

Blessed are the poor in spirit	they shall be satisfied. Matthew 5:6
Blessed are those who mourn	theirs is the kingdom of heaven. Matthew 5:3
Blessed are the meek	they shall receive mercy. Matthew 5:7
Blessed are those who hunger and thirst for righteousness	they shall be comforted. Matthew 5:4
Blessed are the merciful	they shall inherit the earth. Matthew 5:5

DID YOU KNOW?

For jigging, you can use minnows, maggots, or wax worms. You can also use artificial bait. Another type of ice fishing is spearfishing. This takes a lot more skill and concentration. You'll also need a bait called "chum," which is fish parts, to lure the fish closer to the top.

Name _____

Bait & Tackle 25.1

" Our sixth Beatitude we will discuss is found in Matthew 5:8. Read it in your Bibles. The verse says, "Blessed are the pure in heart, for they shall see God." "

Blessed are the pure in heart,
pure in heart = resists sin & evil
for they shall see God.

" This activity is new, but it helps with your visual tracking and hand-eye coordination. Have you ever seen how a hermit crab likes to change its shell? This game is called Changing Shells. "

Gear Up!

Changing Shells: You will need 2 plastic cups for "shells," a marble, and your parent/sibling. Each of you sits across from one another at a table. Place the cup upside down over the marble. Gently push your cup toward the other person and lift it so it rolls the marble toward the other person. Both of you should remain seated during the game. They should capture the marble under their shell (cup) before it rolls off the table. Try not to roll it too hard. Then they gently push their cup forward and lift it to roll the marble toward you. You remain seated and place your shell (cup) over the marble before it rolls off the table. Each of you should do this at least 10 times.

Capital M: Start below the pole line, curve up and bump the pole line as you swim down to the waterline. Then, go back up that line and curve over and down to the waterline. Go back up that line and curve over and down to the waterline again. Finally, curve up slightly after you bump the waterline.

Trace then write two capital M's without connecting them, and part of Galatians 6:9 (NKJV). Remember to connect each M to the next letters in the words without lifting your pencil.

" I bet you did a great job coloring in the fish. If you completed the weigh-in challenge each day, you have earned your fish badge and may color it in. Remember that fishermen like to display their trophies, or badges, so be sure to add your badges to your achievement board.

Your next challenge is to play Changing Shells each day (see page 309). Keep track of your score to know who wins each day. You might make challenges like who can capture the most marbles in their shells in 5 rolls each. Have fun playing this game.
My score: _____ "

Name _____

Bait & Tackle 25.2

> Matthew 5:8 says, "Blessed are the pure in heart, for they shall see God." When we have a heart that is free from sin, we will get to go to and be with God. The actions we have come from our hearts. If our hearts are not pure, or not free of sin, then we will have negative actions like lying or unkindness. When our hearts are pure, good things come out of us and show up in our words, actions, and thoughts.

Gear Up!

Live Well Reaches: Sit in a chair or side of a bathtub with your feet flat on the ground. Keep your feet spread apart. Bend over and touch the top of the ground between your feet as if you were touching the top of the live well in your boat. Do this 12 times.

Capital N: Start below the pole line, curve up and bump the pole line as you swim down to the waterline. Then, go back up that line and curve over and down to the waterline. Finally, curve up slightly after you bump the waterline.

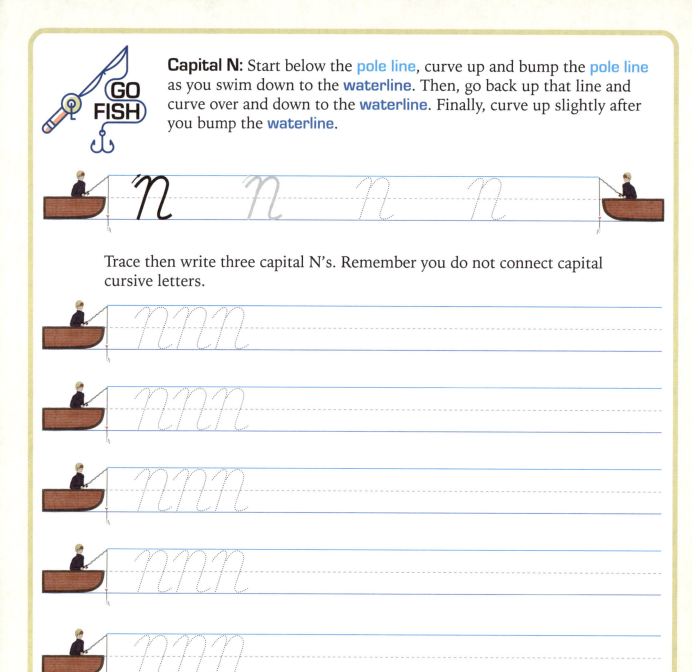

Trace then write three capital N's. Remember you do not connect capital cursive letters.

My score: _____

☐ **REMINDER:** Take some time to work on your weigh-in challenge.

Name

Bait & Tackle 25.3

> There is a verse in Luke 6:45 that says, "The good person out of the good treasure of his heart produces good, and the evil person out of his evil treasure produces evil, for out of the abundance of the heart his mouth speaks." I once heard the phrase "trash in equals trash out." This means if we keep our minds on sinful things, then we produce sinful actions, words, and thoughts. If we keep our minds focused on godly things, then we will have godly actions, thoughts, and words.

Gear Up!

Use your eyes to follow the line to find the matches, then trace the line to make the matches.

Capital N: Start below the pole line, curve up and bump the pole line as you swim down to the waterline. Then, go back up that line and curve over and down to the waterline. Finally, curve up slightly after you bump the waterline.

𝒩 𝒩 𝒩 𝒩

Trace then write two capital N's without connecting them, and Galatians 6:9. Remember to connect each N to the next letters in the words without lifting your pencil.

𝒩

𝒩

And let us not grow
weary while doing
good, for in due
season we shall reap
if we do not lose
heart. Galatians 6:9

My score: _____

☐ **REMINDER:** Take some time to work on your weigh-in challenge.

Name

Bait & Tackle 25.4

"Copy the Beatitude in cursive from Matthew 5:8."

Blessed are the pure in heart, for they shall see God.

"Hey there! Today we have a new activity for you. Fishing poles usually need a metal weight. See this picture of the round weight on the line?"

Gear Up!

We need you to **Make Weights**. Using approximately 2-inch by 2-inch squares of foil, place one hand behind your back as you use the other hand to make the foil into balls like these round weights. After you have made 3, swap hands and make 3 with your other hand.

Bait & Tackle 25.4   315

Capital N: Start below the pole line, curve up and bump the pole line as you swim down to the waterline. Then, go back up that line and curve over and down to the waterline. Finally, curve up slightly after you bump the waterline.

Trace then write two capital N's and Galatians 6:9. Remember to connect each capital N to the next without lifting your pencil.

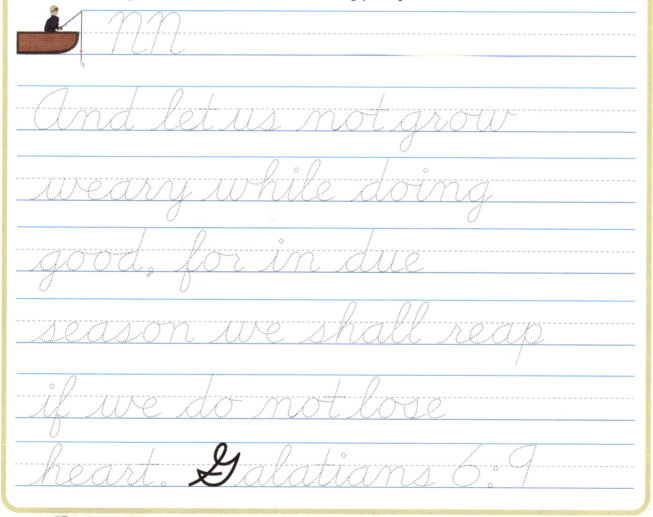

" I bet it was fun playing Changing Shells this week. If you completed the challenge, you have earned your shell badge, and you may color the shell on the badge. That's another badge for your achievement board. You sure are filling it up! "

Name _____

Bait & Tackle 25.5

> "We are to guard our hearts. This means to pay attention to what we read, watch, listen to, and even who we are friends with. If we are not making good choices, then it will show up in our actions, words, and what we say. Proverbs 4:23 (NIV) says, "Above all else, guard your heart, for everything you do flows from it.""

Gear Up!

Complete the dot-to-dot. Remember to use your eyes first before you draw.

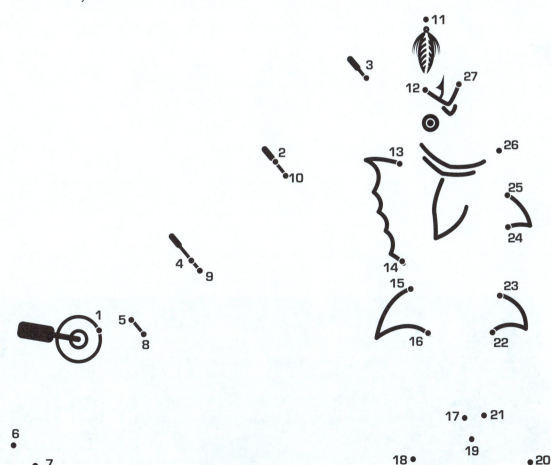

Bait & Tackle 25.5 317

Review your letters: letters L, M, and N

Capital L: The capital L is like a looping roller coaster. Begin a little below the pole line, dip down and out as you loop back, bumping the pole line, go down to the waterline as you loop back and swim out to the waterline.

Capital M: Start below the pole line, curve up and bump the pole line as you swim down to the waterline. Then, go back up that line and curve over and down to the waterline. Go back up that line and curve over and down to the waterline again. Finally, curve up slightly after you bump the waterline.

Capital N: Start below the pole line, curve up and bump the pole line as you swim down to the waterline. Then, go back up that line and curve over and down to the waterline. Finally, curve up slightly after you bump the waterline.

Trace the letters L, M, and N. Trace them three times without connecting them, and then write them once on your own. Be sure to leave a pinky space between each set.

> "This is your time to showcase your best catch again. Use the section in the back of the book labeled "Fishing Derby: Showcasing My Best Catch." Find lesson 25 and complete the page. Remember, this is your "best" work. Ask your parents if they want to keep these in the book or remove them to showcase them."

CATCH ON TO CURSIVE
FISHING Derby
SHOWCASING MY BEST CATCH
BAIT & TACKLE 25

318 Hooked on Cursive

Name

TACKLE BOX 26

"I've got a new weigh-in challenge for you. In this challenge, you will make 5 "weights" out of foil each day (see Bait & Tackle 25.4)."

"I love how well you are learning the Beatitudes. Be sure to follow the right paths on the next page."

Gather Your Gear

Day 1:
☐ Plastic lid with a lip or a round cake pan
☐ Marble

Day 3:
☐ Needle and thread

Tackle Box 26 319

Name

Bait & Tackle 26.1

> The next Beatitude is the seventh one, and it is found in Matthew 5:9. Read it in your Bibles. It says, "Blessed are the peacemakers, for they shall be called sons of God."

Blessed are the peacemakers,
peacemakers = seek peace
for they shall be called sons of God.

Gear Up!

Marble in the Whirlpool: Using a plastic lid with a lip or a round cake pan, place a marble inside. Have someone move the lid/pan so the marble rolls in the inside edge back and forth and eventually all the way around in a circle. Follow the marble with your eyes, but do not move your head. Move only your eyes as you follow the marble back and forth for one minute.

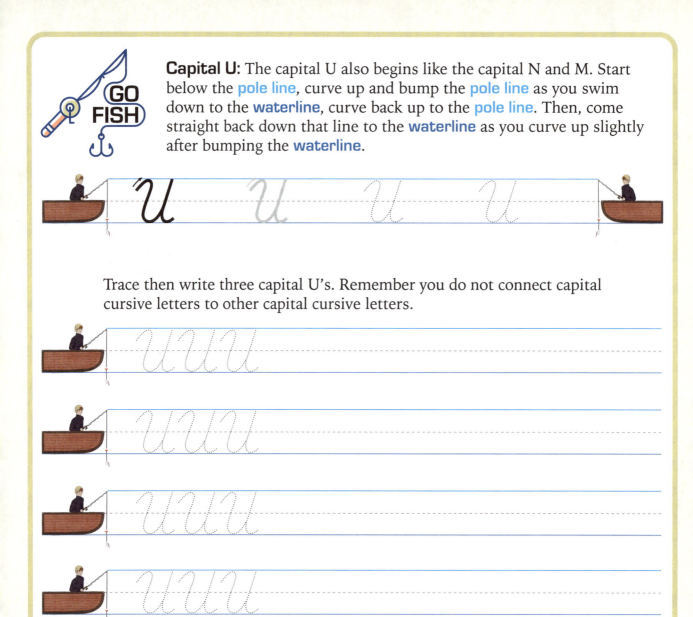

Capital U: The capital U also begins like the capital N and M. Start below the pole line, curve up and bump the pole line as you swim down to the waterline, curve back up to the pole line. Then, come straight back down that line to the waterline as you curve up slightly after bumping the waterline.

Trace then write three capital U's. Remember you do not connect capital cursive letters to other capital cursive letters.

☐ **REMINDER:** Take some time to work on your weigh-in challenge.

Name _____

Bait & Tackle 26.2

"Matthew 5:9 says, "Blessed are the peacemakers, for they shall be called sons of God." Remember how a calm comes over the lake in the evening time? Being a peacemaker is like having a calm about you all the time. A peacemaker seeks to bring peace and calm. This doesn't mean they don't stand up for what's right, but they aren't trying to pick a fight. They know that causing chaos is not a quality God desires from us. We can be peaceful in our disagreements with others."

Gear Up!

In Northern Ireland there is a maze made out of yew trees. This is called a hedge maze because the border is made from plants and trees. It was made as a symbol of peace and cooperation, just as a peacemaker has those traits.

Complete this hedge maze.

Capital U: Start below the pole line, curve up and bump the pole line as you swim down to the waterline, curve back up to the pole line. Then, come straight back down that line to the waterline as you curve up slightly after bumping the waterline.

Trace then write two capital U's without connecting them, and Psalm 118:29 (NKJV). Remember to connect each U to the next letter in the words without lifting your pencil.

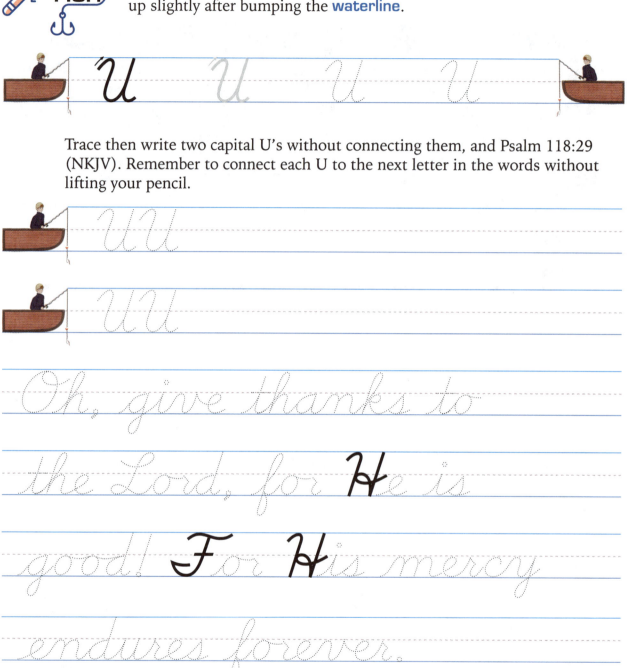

☐ **REMINDER:** Take some time to work on your weigh-in challenge.

Name _____

Bait & Tackle 26.3

> "Remember our other Beatitudes that said blessed are the meek and blessed are those who hunger and thirst after righteousness? Well, this verse in Galatians 6:8 (ESV) is almost a combination of these two Beatitudes and our one about peacemakers for this week. It says, "The one who sows to his own flesh will from the flesh reap corruption, but the one who sows to the Spirit will from the Spirit reap eternal life." Sowing to please our flesh is not being meek or seeking God. Here we see that when we have control of our emotions (meek), we seek God, and seek to bring peace, then we will reap eternal life in heaven."

Gear Up!

Anchor Up: Stand with your feet about shoulder width apart. Bend over and pretend to pull up a heavy anchor. Give the anchor 10 good pulls all the way up. Remember, that anchor is heavy!

Capital U: Start below the pole line, curve up and bump the pole line as you swim down to the waterline, curve back up to the pole line. Then, come straight back down that line to the waterline as you curve up slightly after bumping the waterline.

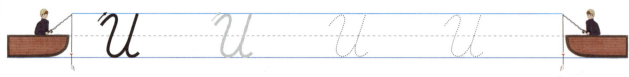

Trace then write two capital U's without connecting them, and Psalm 118:29 (NKJV). Remember to connect each U to the next letter in the words without lifting your pencil.

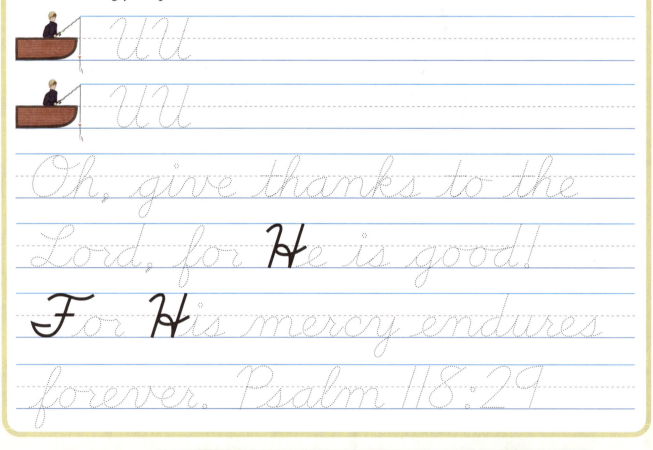

> Did you make a lot of weights? I sure hope you did. If you completed this weigh-in challenge, you have earned your Weight badge and may color it in the back of the book. Remember to add it to your achievement board.
>
> Your next challenge is to make fly lures, or at least part. You'll need a needle and thread. You will be threading a needle 5 times with each hand each day. Keep the needle and thread to do this daily.

Name _____

Bait & Tackle 26.4

" Copy the verse from Matthew 5:9 in cursive. "

Blessed are the peacemakers, for they shall be called sons of God.

 Gear Up!

Trace to complete the full image. You may color the traced portion once done.

Capital V: The capital letter V begins like a letter U. Start below the pole line, curve up and bump the pole line as you swim down to the waterline, slant back up to the pole line. Then, make a dip out and bump the pole line.

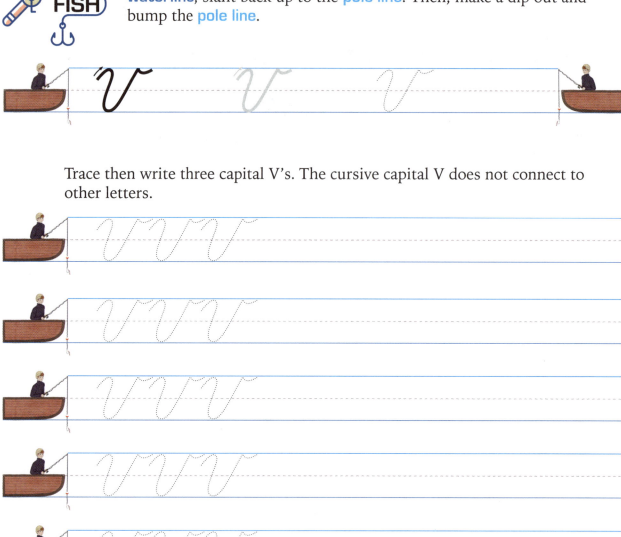

Trace then write three capital V's. The cursive capital V does not connect to other letters.

☐ **REMINDER:** Take some time to work on your weigh-in challenge.

Name _____

Bait & Tackle 26.5

"I don't like to be on the lake when it's rough and choppy. I also don't like living in a home that is full of fighting, complaining, and unkindness. I am guessing you don't either. Let's pray and ask God to help us to be peacemakers, pure in heart, and meek.

Lord, we ask that you help us to rid any sin in our hearts and make us clean. Let all things we speak, think, and do come from you. Let us control our actions, words, and thoughts and be kind to one another. Help us when someone disagrees or tempts us to become angry that we choose a peaceful way to speak and react. In Jesus' name, amen."

Gear Up!

Lighthouse Taps: Lighthouses flash their lights, so we are going to tap for lighthouse flashes. Bring your pinky and thumb together to tap and open, tap and open, like a lighthouse flash. Do this 12 times with both hands.

Capital V: Start below the pole line, curve up and bump the pole line as you swim down to the waterline, slant back up to the pole line. Then, make a dip out and bump the pole line.

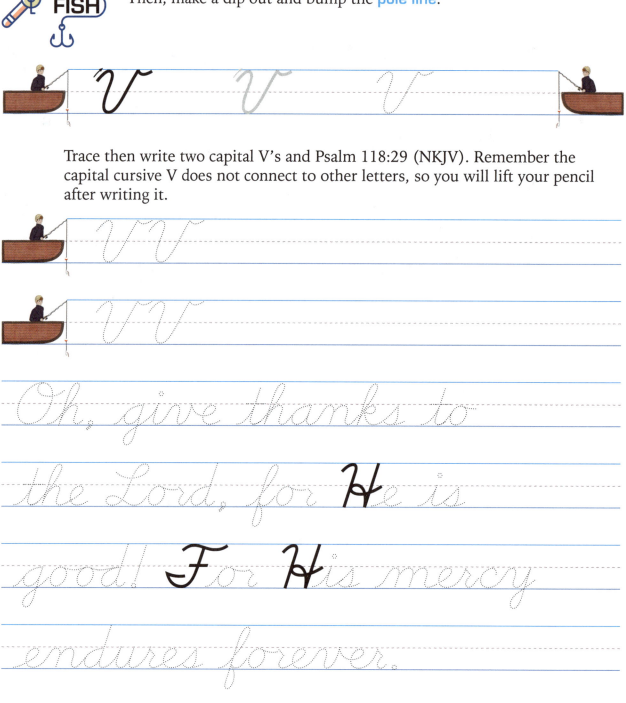

Trace then write two capital V's and Psalm 118:29 (NKJV). Remember the capital cursive V does not connect to other letters, so you will lift your pencil after writing it.

☐ **REMINDER:** Take some time to work on your weigh-in challenge.

Name

TACKLE BOX 27

" I will see you at the weigh-in challenge and issue another badge. "

" I like fishing in winter. Ice fishing can be an exciting adventure. Check out the gear you'll need this week. We have a Fishing Derby this week. Are you ready for it? "

Gather Your Gear

Day 1:
☐ Tennis ball or ball that size

Day 5:
☐ Paper clips

Official GUIDE

Complete the word search throughout this week for the words in the Beatitudes.

- BLESSED
- COMFORTED
- HEART
- HUNGER
- INHERIT
- MEEK
- MERCIFUL
- MOURN
- PEACEMAKER
- POOR
- RIGHTEOUSNESS
- SATISFIED
- SONS
- THIRST

V	V	H	U	N	G	E	R	A	P	P	Y	Z	F	H	N	Y	Z
Q	N	L	M	K	I	O	N	M	E	P	O	O	R	R	E	S	P
L	M	Y	M	F	L	U	R	H	A	W	H	E	A	R	T	A	Z
K	R	I	N	H	E	R	I	T	C	T	H	I	R	S	T	T	J
W	L	X	Y	G	L	L	G	J	E	B	L	R	T	T	R	I	K
C	O	M	F	O	R	T	E	D	M	M	L	O	Q	S	V	S	R
D	R	M	T	N	N	V	D	P	A	S	O	E	K	O	L	F	I
T	V	E	H	R	S	M	I	I	K	Q	M	U	S	N	J	I	I
Q	U	E	G	C	Q	G	J	K	E	A	T	Y	R	S	N	E	H
V	C	K	D	A	T	S	K	L	R	G	S	F	W	N	E	D	W
S	Y	V	M	E	R	C	I	F	U	L	T	O	D	H	E	D	G
X	W	R	I	G	H	T	E	O	U	S	N	E	S	S	B	W	W

DID YOU KNOW?

Bass fishing in a small lake is better than in a larger lake. The water has a chance to warm or cool quicker in a smaller body of water. Some of the best bass are caught in winter in small lakes.

Name _____

Bait & Tackle 27.1

> The next Beatitude is the eighth and final one, and it is found in Matthew 5:10. Read it in your Bibles. The verse says, "Blessed are those who are persecuted for righteousness' sake, for theirs is the kingdom of heaven."

Blessed are those who are persecuted for righteousness' sake,

persecuted for righteousness sake = rejected because they follow Christ

for theirs is the kingdom of heaven.

Gear Up!

Crawdad Crawl: You will use a tennis ball or a ball that size. You have two "pinchers" like the crawdad, which are your thumb and pointing finger. Start with the ball beside your foot, using only your two pinchers (thumb and pointer finger), roll the ball up the side of your leg to your hip, across your tummy, and back down the side of the other leg. Do this 3 times.

*If you cannot do this with only two pinchers, you may add in one more to use your middle finger as well.

Bait & Tackle 27.1 333

Capital V: Start below the pole line, curve up and bump the pole line as you swim down to the waterline, slant back up to the pole line. Then, make a dip out and bump the pole line.

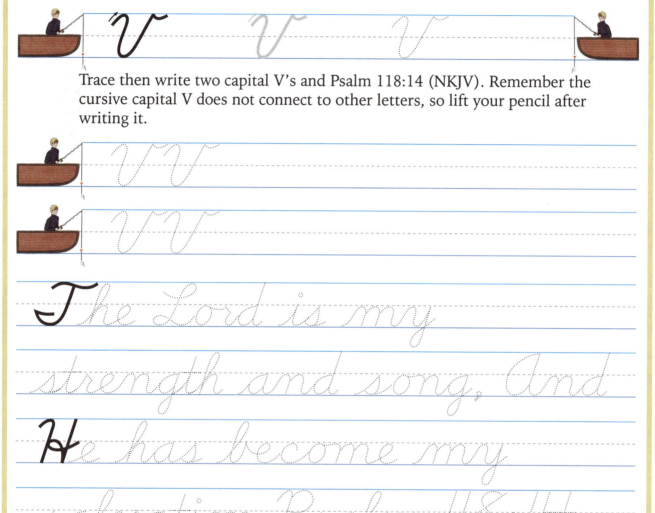

Trace then write two capital V's and Psalm 118:14 (NKJV). Remember the cursive capital V does not connect to other letters, so lift your pencil after writing it.

" Did you make "fly lures" each day by threading a needle? If you completed this weigh-in challenge you have earned another badge! I'm so proud of all the badges you're earning. You may color the badge with the fly lure then add it to your achievement board if you completed the challenge.

Your next challenge is to complete a handwriting warm-up each day before you begin to write. You can find the warm-ups in the weigh-in section in the back of the book. You should complete two lines each day for this challenge. "

Name _____

Bait & Tackle 27.2

"Matthew 5:10 says, "Blessed are those who are persecuted for righteousness' sake, for theirs is the kingdom of heaven." Persecuted means to be mistreated for your beliefs. There are people, even in America, who are persecuted for standing up for Jesus and Christianity. Jesus was persecuted. When we are mistreated for our beliefs in God, we can have hope that God is with us through it all."

Gear Up!

Under & Over: You will help the fish swim over the obstacles. On the top row, begin by going under the first obstacle and back up between the next obstacles. You want to try to stay in the middle of the two obstacles you are going under and over. See the example to help you recall how to do this.

Capital W: The capital W is like two V's. Start below the pole line, curve up and bump the pole line as you swim down to the waterline, slant back up to the pole line. Swim down to the waterline and slant back up to the pole line again. Then, make a dip out and bump the pole line.

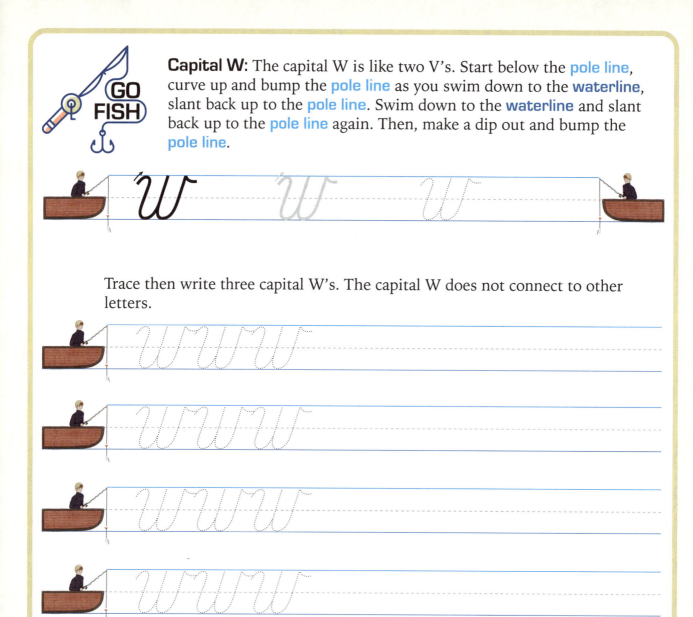

Trace then write three capital W's. The capital W does not connect to other letters.

☐ **REMINDER:** Take some time to work on your weigh-in challenge.

Name

 Bait & Tackle 27.3

> The Apostle Paul wrote to Timothy and was encouraging him about many things — 2 Timothy 3:10–11 says, "You, however, have followed my teaching, my conduct, my aim in life, my faith, my patience, my love, my steadfastness, my persecutions and sufferings that happened to me at Antioch, at Iconium, and at Lystra — which persecutions I endured; yet from them all the Lord rescued me." Notice that Paul tells Timothy of all of the persecutions he endured; the Lord rescued him from them all. Our rescuing may not be immediate, but we can have hope that God will rescue us. Paul continues that chapter by encouraging us to continue in what we know is truth and in our salvation through Christ Jesus.

Gear Up!

Follow the numbers to complete the dot-to-dot. Remember to try to use your eyes first before you begin.

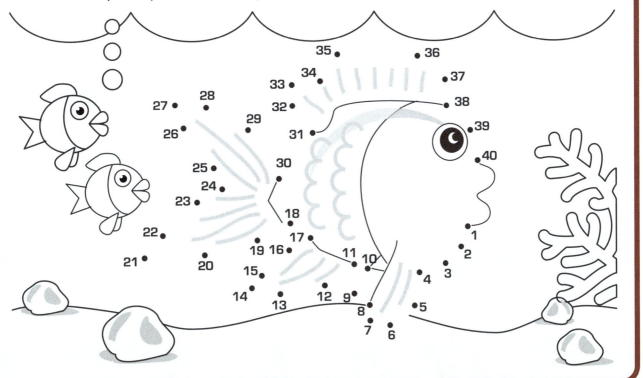

Capital W: Start below the pole line, curve up and bump the pole line as you swim down to the waterline, slant back up to the pole line. Swim down to the waterline, slant back up to the pole line again. Then, make a dip out and bump the pole line.

Trace then write two capital W's and Psalm 118:14 (NKJV). Remember the capital cursive W does not connect to other letters so you do lift your pencil after writing it.

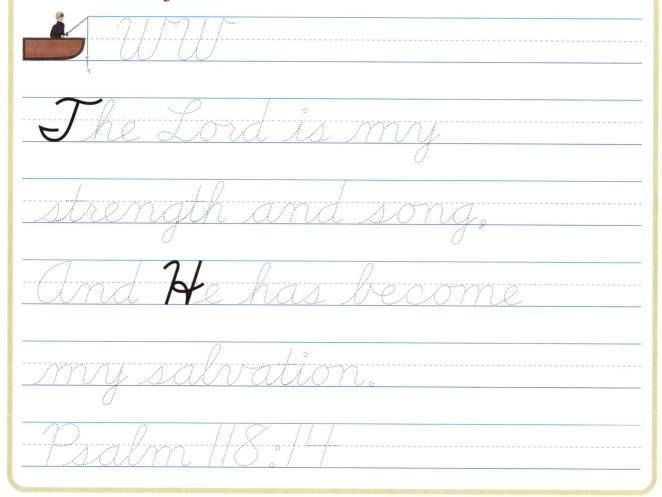

☐ **REMINDER:** Take some time to work on your weigh-in challenge.

Name _____

Bait & Tackle 27.4

" Copy the verse from Matthew 5:10 in cursive. "

Blessed are those who are persecuted for righteousness' sake, for theirs is the kingdom of heaven.

Gear Up!

Don't Hit the Bridge: The ships in the river need to get through. Place your hands flat on the ground with tips of toes on the ground and body lifted to be the bridge. Hold this for 10–15 seconds. Try to beat your time this week (your last time was at Bait & Tackle 21.4). Record today's time here: _____

Capital W: Start below the pole line, curve up and bump the pole line as you swim down to the waterline, slant back up to the pole line. Swim down to the waterline, slant back up to the pole line again. Then, make a dip out and bump the pole line.

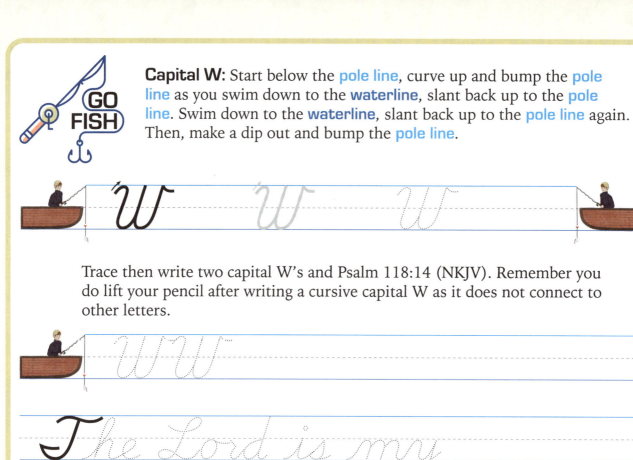

Trace then write two capital W's and Psalm 118:14 (NKJV). Remember you do lift your pencil after writing a cursive capital W as it does not connect to other letters.

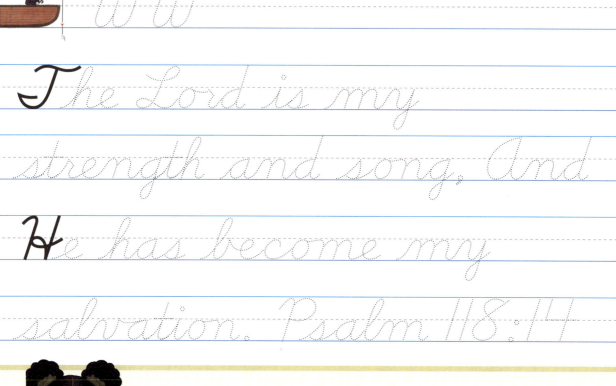

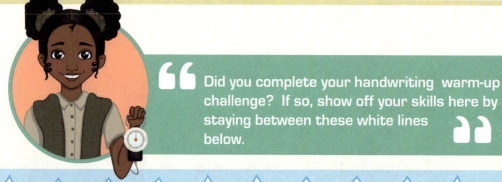

Did you complete your handwriting warm-up challenge? If so, show off your skills here by staying between these white lines below.

Name _____

Bait & Tackle 27.5

"Standing up for Christ and our beliefs may bring persecution sometimes, but we have the hope of eternal life with Christ Jesus. Praise the Lord! What a fabulous hope!"

Gear Up!

Hook the Fisherman's Boot: At the bottom of the page is a row of old boots. Open the paper clips and secure a paper clip to each boot.

Review your letters: letters U, V, and W

Capital U: Start below the pole line, curve up and bump the pole line as you swim down to the waterline curve back up to the pole line. Then, come straight back down that line to the waterline as you curve up slightly after bumping the waterline.

Capital V: Start below the pole line, curve up and bump the pole line as you swim down to the waterline, slant back up to the pole line. Then, make a dip out and bump the pole line.

Capital W: Start below the pole line, curve up and bump the pole line as you swim down to the waterline, slant back up to the pole line. Swim down to the waterline, slant back up to the pole line again. Then, make a dip out and bump the pole line.

Trace the letters U, V, and W. Trace them three times without connecting them, and then write them once on your own. Be sure to leave a pinky space between each set.

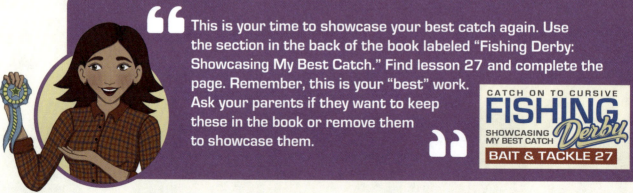

This is your time to showcase your best catch again. Use the section in the back of the book labeled "Fishing Derby: Showcasing My Best Catch." Find lesson 27 and complete the page. Remember, this is your "best" work. Ask your parents if they want to keep these in the book or remove them to showcase them.

CATCH ON TO CURSIVE
FISHING Derby
SHOWCASING MY BEST CATCH
BAIT & TACKLE 27

Name

"Hey there, I'm sending another weigh-in challenge your way. Your challenge is to do more writing warm-ups before you write each day. You'll be doing shoulder workouts each day before you write. Push your shoulders up toward your ears, then back down. Do this 5–10 times. Then, push your shoulders forward as far as you can, then push them back as far as you can. Do these 5 times."

"Remember your gear. We're going to be having fun activities and facts for you this 9 weeks, so be sure to check that out."

Gather Your Gear

Day 2:
☐ Tennis ball or ball that size

Day 3:
☐ Marble
☐ 2 plastic cups

Day 4:
☐ 6 2-inch x 2-inch foil squares

Day 5:
☐ Painter's tape or rope or sidewalk chalk

Tackle Box 28   343

Official GUIDE

Parable: simple story used to represent a moral or spiritual lesson.

Facts about Fish:

Fish are vertebrates — they have backbones/spines.

Fish have gills for breathing in water and not lungs.

Fish are cold blooded — they don't keep themselves warm, but their body temperature changes with their environment.

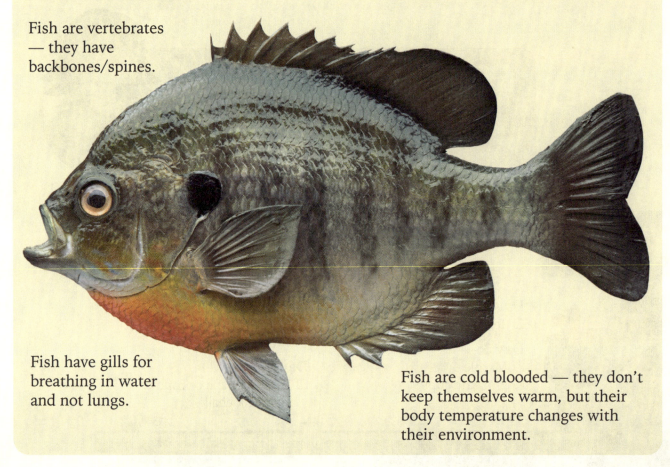

Name _____

Bait & Tackle 28.1

> "Hey, can you believe it is spring? In spring, all things become new and fresh just as our Bible topic is new. My dad is a great storyteller. He told me stories as a child and now tells every grandchild stories as they all gather around him soaking in every word. Jesus was also a great storyteller, but His stories have a lesson or moral to teach us. This 9 weeks we will look closely at different stories Jesus used to teach His disciples a lesson. We call these stories parables. Jesus had such wisdom that He knew He needed to use real-life stories to help His disciples, and us, understand kingdom concepts."

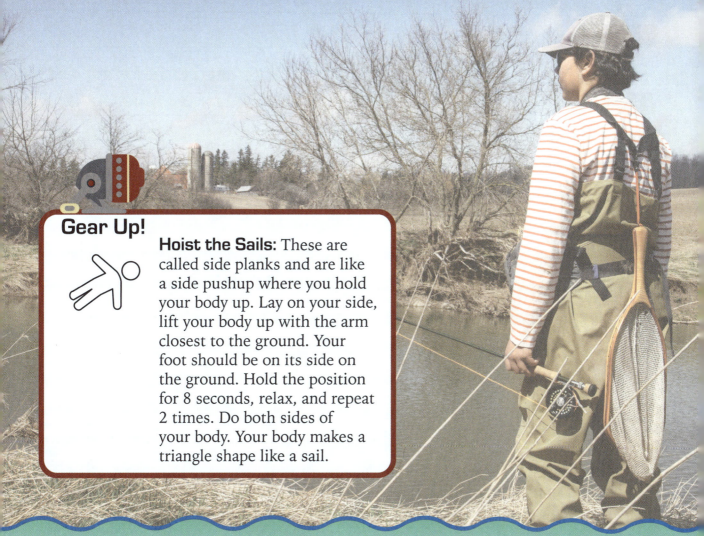

Gear Up!

Hoist the Sails: These are called side planks and are like a side pushup where you hold your body up. Lay on your side, lift your body up with the arm closest to the ground. Your foot should be on its side on the ground. Hold the position for 8 seconds, relax, and repeat 2 times. Do both sides of your body. Your body makes a triangle shape like a sail.

Capital H: Start the capital H like you do the capital N. Begin below the pole line, curve up and bump the pole line as you swim down to the waterline. Lift your pencil as you move over to the right. Make a line down from the pole line to the waterline and without stopping, slant up and back toward the boat line and the first line you drew as you loop around and out at the boat line.

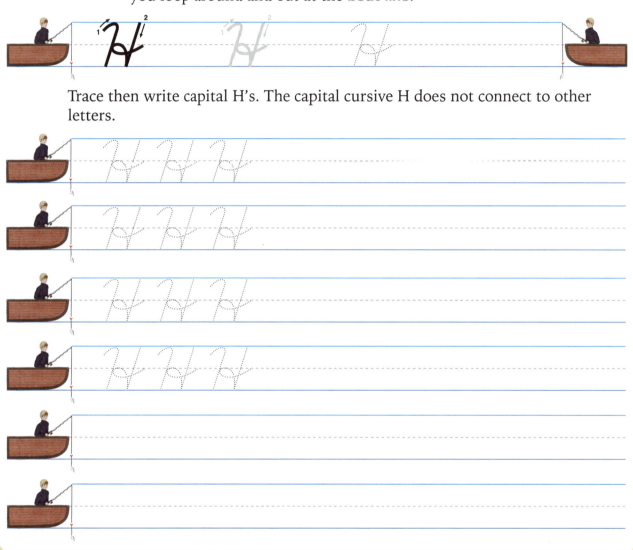

Trace then write capital H's. The capital cursive H does not connect to other letters.

☐ **REMINDER:** Take some time to work on your weigh-in challenge.

Name: _____

Bait & Tackle 28.2

> The first story or parable we will read is found in Luke 14:15–24. Read that or have a parent read it in your Bible. This story is about a man who is having a dinner party and invited many. The problem was that those invited began finding other things to do or giving excuses as to why they couldn't come to the party. Then the master in this story had his servant invite all those in the streets to come. The poor, hurt, those who couldn't walk, and the blind were now all invited. Then, he told his servant to go out and compel them or plead with them to come in so his house would be full. This parable is like the kingdom of heaven. Heaven is being prepared for us much like this man prepared a large dinner for everyone. The problem is that many find excuses and other things to do rather than come to Jesus and gain an eternal life in heaven. We are like the servant and should be urging people to come.

Gear Up!

Crawdad Crawl: You will use a tennis ball or a ball that size. You have two "pinchers" like the crawdad, which are your thumb and pointing finger. Start with the ball beside your foot, using only your two pinchers (thumb and pointer finger), and roll the ball up the side of your leg to your hip, across your tummy, and back down the side of the other leg. This may be difficult at first, but it will get easier with practice. Do this three to four times.

If you cannot do this with only two pinchers, you may add in one more to use your middle finger as well.

Capital H: Begin below the pole line, curve up and bump the pole line as you swim down to the waterline. Lift your pencil as you move over to the right. Make a line down from the pole line to the waterline and without stopping, slant up and back toward the boat line and the first line you drew as you loop around and out at the boat line.

Trace then write two capital H's and Isaiah 43:19. Remember the cursive capital H does not connect to other letters so you will lift your pencil after writing it.

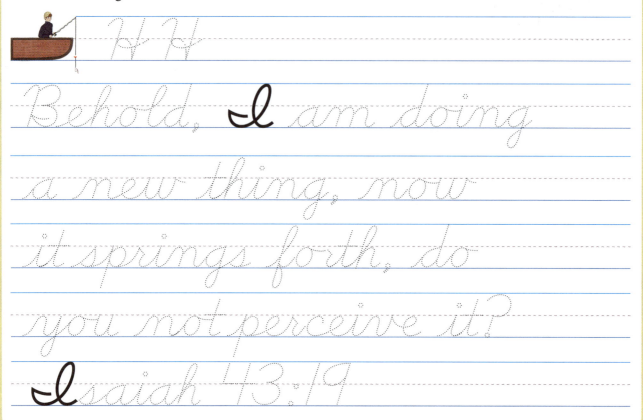

☐ **REMINDER:** Take some time to work on your weigh-in challenge.

Name _____

Bait & Tackle 28.3

"I know if I have found a good fishing hole, I want my friends to come join me, just like I want my friends to join me in heaven. Can you think of a way to be like the servant in the parable and urge people to come to Jesus? Compel, or urge, them to come so the house, or heaven, is full? Oh, what a joyous day that will be! It will be better than any fishing adventures I've had. Talk with a parent about ways you can compel others to come to know Jesus and accept His free gift of eternal life."

Gear Up!

Changing Shells: You will need 2 plastic cups for "shells," a marble, and your parent/sibling. Each of you sits across from one another at a table. Place the cup upside down over the marble. Gently push your cup toward the other person and lift it so it rolls the marble toward the other person. Both of you should remain seated during the game. They should capture the marble under their shell (cup) before it rolls off the table. Try not to roll it too hard. Then they gently push their cup forward and lift it to roll the marble toward you. You remain seated and place your shell (cup) over the marble before it rolls off the table. Each of you should do this at least 10 times.

Capital H: Begin below the pole line, curve up and bump the pole line as you swim down to the waterline. Lift your pencil as you move over to the right. Make a line down from the pole line to the waterline, and without stopping, slant up and back toward the boat line and the first line you drew as you loop around and out at the boat line.

Trace then write two capital H's and the rest of Isaiah 43:19. Remember the cursive capital H does not connect to other letters. Be sure to lift your pencil after writing it.

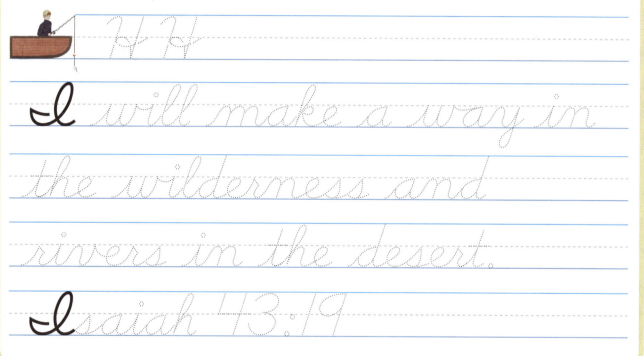

" Did you complete your shoulder workout weigh-in challenge? If you did, you may color in the shoulder badge below then add it to your achievement board.

Your next challenge is to do another writing warm-up activity called Gator Chomps. You will extend your arms straight out in front of you, place your palms together, and open and close like an alligator chomps his jaws. Make sure you start with the hand you write with on top, then after doing 3, swap to your other hand on top. Do 3 with this hand on top also. "

Name _____

Bait & Tackle 28.4

"There is one part of this parable that we haven't discussed. I want you to look at Luke 14:24. Notice that the master, which represents Jesus in this story, says, "none of those men who were invited shall taste my banquet." This is also telling us that those who reject Jesus will not have eternal life in heaven. This is another reason it is important for our families to share Jesus with others. We don't want anyone to be lost without God."

Gear Up!

Make Weights: Using approximately 2-inch by 2-inch squares of foil, place one hand behind your back as you use the other hand to make the foil into balls like these round weights. After you have made 3, swap hands and make 3 with your other hand. (See lesson 25 on day 4 if you need further instructions/graphics.)

Capital T: Start at the pole line as you go down and curve back like the manuscript J, but then make a straight line right. Lift your pencil and go back up near the pole line as you make a wavy line below the pole line.

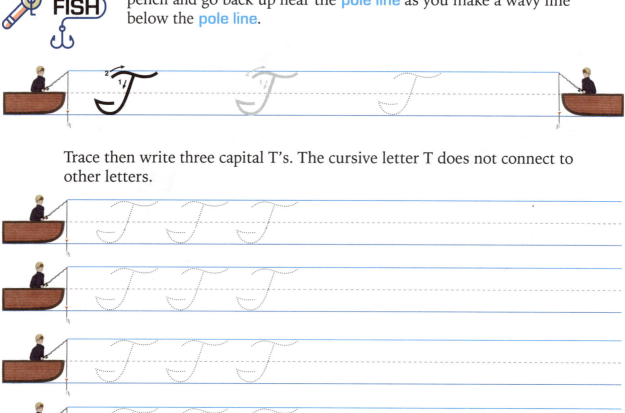

Trace then write three capital T's. The cursive letter T does not connect to other letters.

☐ **REMINDER:** Take some time to work on your weigh-in challenge.

Name _____

Bait & Tackle 28.5

> "Did you notice the master wasn't satisfied with a few visitors; He wanted his house to be full more than I want my live well to be full. Jesus suffered and died so we could live in heaven with Him. He wants heaven to be full. I want heaven to be full. We have to compel, or urge, people to come to Jesus."

Gear Up!

Walk the Plank: Use painter's tape, a rope, or sidewalk chalk to make a long line. Walk the Plank by balancing on the line with one foot in front of the other. Don't fall in! There might be gators in that water! Do this 3 times. How fast can you do this? Try to beat your time each time you do it.

(You can also use a 2x4 or balance beam.)

Capital T: Start the pole line as you go down and curve back like the manuscript J, but then make a straight line right. Lift your pencil and go back up near the pole line as you make a wavy line below the pole line.

Trace then write two capital T's without connecting them, and Isaiah 43:19. Remember you do not connect the capital T's to the next, so you will lift your pencil.

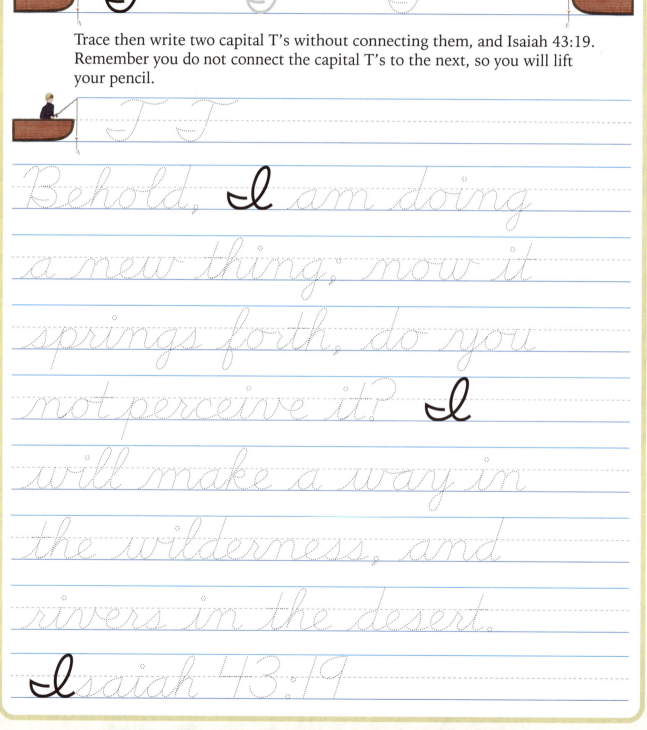

☐ **REMINDER:** Take some time to work on your weigh-in challenge.

Name _____

TACKLE BOX 29

"Hey, club buddy, are you enjoying Club Skeeter as you earn all these badges? I sure am! I'll be sending more challenges your way, so keep an eye out."

"We've got more fun activities for you to complete, but don't get too excited and forget your gear."

Gather Your Gear

Day 1:
☐ Toothpicks
☐ Play-Doh

Day 2:
☐ Tweezers and yarn worms from previous lessons

Day 4:
☐ Play-Doh

Tackle Box 29 355

I've got some fun new words that may come in handy when you're fishing.

Read the definition for each word, then find the word in the word search.

BRACKISH: water that has a mixture of saltwater and freshwater.
ANAL FIN: this single fin is found at the rear of the fish.
CAUDAL FIN: the tail fin.
DORSAL FIN: one or more fins that are along the back of the fish.
ESTUARY: the place where a river or stream flows into the sea.

V	G	D	O	R	S	A	L	F	I	N	P	V	E	D	U	D	I
K	E	S	T	U	A	R	Y	Z	A	S	B	A	Z	J	E	C	X
I	V	C	A	U	D	A	L	F	I	N	P	N	B	J	V	N	L
Y	Q	F	H	P	L	J	E	P	C	J	Q	A	Q	S	Z	L	U
S	Q	E	R	K	X	Y	A	H	M	T	U	L	K	D	J	H	J
W	V	P	U	C	R	X	G	K	U	R	W	F	W	I	X	O	L
K	S	A	X	D	K	D	W	T	P	D	Y	I	K	Q	L	M	F
P	T	M	F	S	S	N	Z	W	H	B	K	N	T	F	B	Z	D
M	Z	B	D	M	I	M	Z	G	F	L	T	T	Y	J	D	S	S
B	R	A	C	K	I	S	H	X	T	Q	M	E	T	N	M	J	O
H	N	Q	J	Q	I	R	B	I	E	E	E	S	O	T	C	X	R
B	K	H	L	I	K	N	H	P	O	M	X	U	D	W	T	Z	X

(resource for terms: *Marvels of Creation: Sensational Sea Creatures*)

Name

Bait & Tackle 29.1

"Today I want you to read, or have a parent read to you, Luke 15:4–7."

Gear Up!

Complete the maze to help the shepherd find the lost sheep.

Capital T: Start the pole line as you go down and curve back like the manuscript J, but then make a straight line right. Lift your pencil and go back up near the pole line as you make a wavy line below the pole line.

Trace then write two capital T's without connecting them, and our verse. Remember you do not connect the capital T's to other letters.

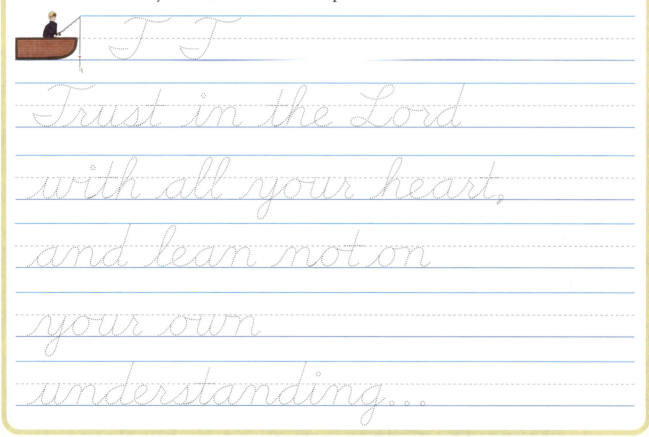

> I told you I would have another challenge for you and here it is, but first things first. Did you complete your gator chomps weigh-in challenge? If so, check out this gator badge you earned. Color in the gator if you completed the challenge and remember to add this gator to your achievement board. Your next challenge is to make a porcupine fish.
>
> Use Play-Doh, roll it into a ball, and poke toothpicks in it to make a porcupine fish. Do this each day using 15 toothpicks a day. You can save the toothpicks in a plastic bag or bowl and re-use them each day.

Name _____

Bait & Tackle 29.2

> "Yesterday you read the parable about the lost sheep. Remember that parables tell us a spiritual message in a way we can understand. In this parable, the shepherd had one sheep that was missing out of his flock. He left his entire flock to go find the one sheep, and then he rejoiced when he found it. Then he called everyone together to rejoice with him. This is what happens when one sinner comes to Jesus. All of heaven rejoices."

Gear Up!

Worm Squeezes: Use tweezers to pick up worms (pieces of yarn). Make sure you get 5–10 worms.

Capital F: The only difference in a cursive capital T and a capital F is there is a line across at the boat line for a capital F. Start at the pole line as you go down and curve back like the manuscript J, but then make a straight line right. Lift your pencil and go back up near the pole line as you make a wavy line below the pole line. Then go back and cross the F at the boat line.

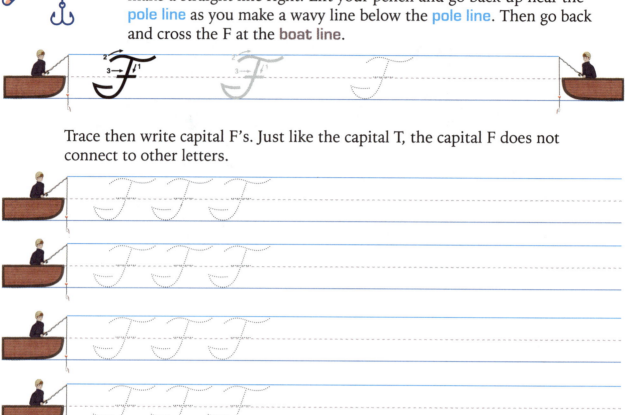

Trace then write capital F's. Just like the capital T, the capital F does not connect to other letters.

☐ **REMINDER:** Take some time to work on your weigh-in challenge.

Name _____

Bait & Tackle 29.3

" Remember when the shepherd found the sheep and the Bible said he rejoiced over the lost sheep? This means that Christ rejoices over someone who is in need of the Savior. Are you in need of saving, like this lost sheep? If so, find your parent and talk with them about being saved. "

Gear Up!

Anchor Up: Stand with your feet about shoulder width apart. Bend over and pretend to pull up a heavy anchor. Give the anchor 10 good pulls all the way up. Remember, that anchor is heavy!

Capital F: Start the pole line as you go down and curve back like the manuscript J, but then make a straight line right. Lift your pencil and go back up near the pole line as you make a wavy line below the pole line. Then, go back and cross the F at the boat line.

Trace then write two capital F's without connecting them, and the first part of Proverbs 3:5 (NKJV). Remember, you do not connect the cursive capital F to other letters, so lift your pencil after writing it.

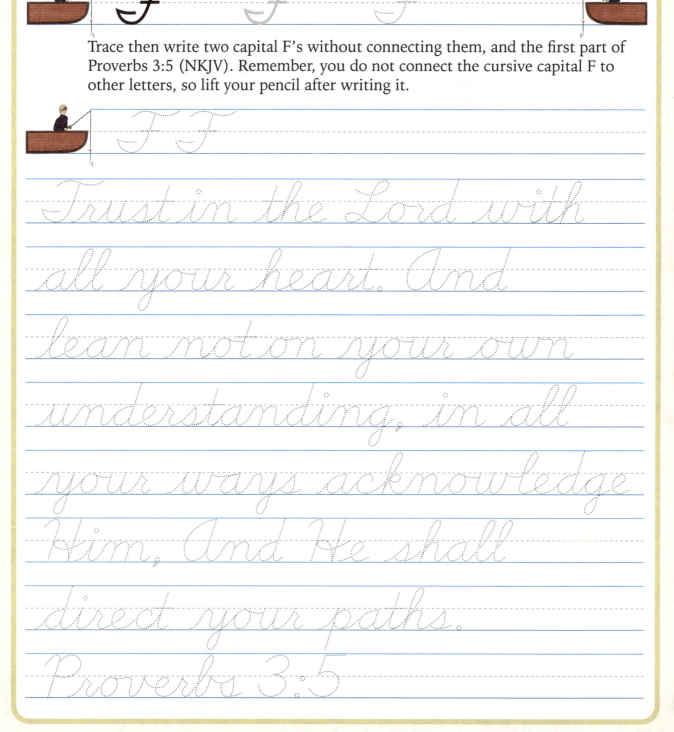

☐ **REMINDER:** Take some time to work on your weigh-in challenge.

Name _____

Bait & Tackle 29.4

"Just like our parable last week, God has a plan for those who will come to Him. The way to salvation is through Jesus Christ. There is rejoicing for those who choose to come to Him. We make the decision to become a follower of Christ and receive eternal life in heaven."

Gear Up!

Complete the dot-to-dot. Remember to first complete it with your eyes.

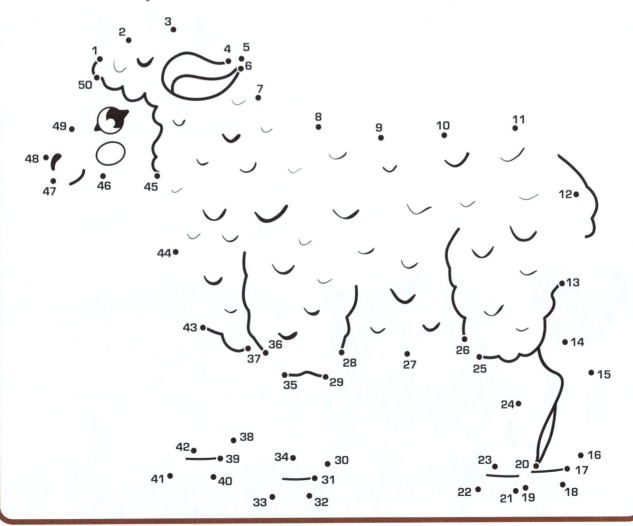

Capital F: Start the pole line as you go down and curve back like the manuscript J, but then make a straight line right. Lift your pencil and go back up near the pole line as you make a wavy line below the pole line. Then, go back and cross the F at the boat line.

Trace then write two capital F's without connecting them, and the rest of Proverbs 3:5 (NKJV). Remember, you do not connect the capital F to other letters.

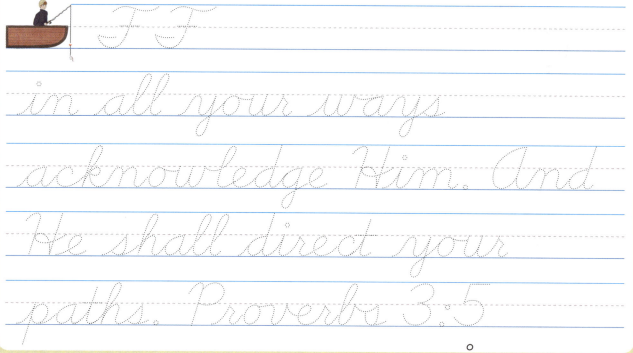

"I bet you made a great porcupine fish. If you completed the weigh-in challenge, go ahead and complete the porcupine fish dot-to-dot."

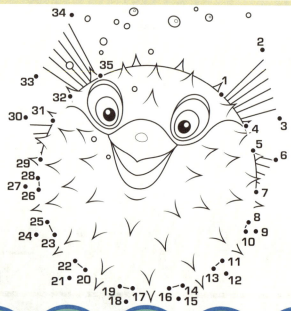

Name _____

Bait & Tackle 29.5

"Standing up for Christ and our beliefs may bring persecution sometimes, but we have the hope of eternal life with Christ Jesus. Praise the Lord! What a fabulous hope!"

Gear Up!

Under & Over: You will help the fish swim over the obstacles. On the top row, begin by going under the first obstacle and back up between the next obstacles. You want to try to stay in the middle of the two obstacles you are going under and over. See the example to help you recall how to do this.

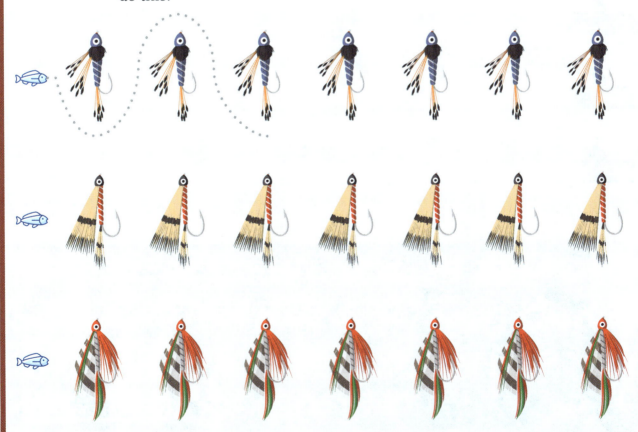

Review your letters: letters H, T, and F

Capital H: Begin below the pole line, curve up and bump the pole line as you swim down to the waterline. Lift your pencil as you move over to the right. Make a line down from the pole line to the waterline, and without stopping, slant up and back toward the boat line and the first line you drew as you loop around and out at the boat line.

Capital T: Start the pole line as you go down and curve back like the manuscript J, but then make a straight line right. Lift your pencil and go back up near the pole line as you make a wavy line below the pole line.

Capital F: Start the pole line as you go down and curve back like the manuscript J, but then make a straight line right. Lift your pencil and go back up near the pole line as you make a wavy line below the pole line. Then, go back and cross the F at the boat line.

Trace the letters H, T, and F. Trace them three times without connecting them, and then write them once on your own. Be sure to leave a pinky space between each set.

> This is your time to showcase your best catch again. Use the section in the back of the book labeled "Fishing Derby: Showcasing My Best Catch." Find lesson 29 and complete the page. Remember, this is your "best" work. Ask your parents if they want to keep these in the book or remove them to showcase them.

CATCH ON TO CURSIVE
FISHING Derby
SHOWCASING MY BEST CATCH
BAIT & TACKLE 29

366 Hooked on Cursive

Name

" We've got a new Gear Up Activity for you this week, so be sure to pay attention on day 4 this week. Now, let's get to your weigh-in challenge. Your challenge is a one-handed worm challenge. Make Play-Doh worms using one hand. Roll Play-Doh into a ball, then roll it back and forth on the table to make it into worms. Each day of this challenge make 2 worms with each hand. "

" Be sure to check out the gear you'll need. I see you'll be labeling a fish today. Who knew a fish had so many parts! "

Gather Your Gear

Day 1:
☐ Cotton swabs and sidewalk chalk

Day 3:
☐ Marble
☐ 2 plastic cups

Day 5:
☐ Pencil with eraser or pencil with pushpin in the eraser

Tackle Box 30　367

Trace the words in cursive to label the fish diagram.

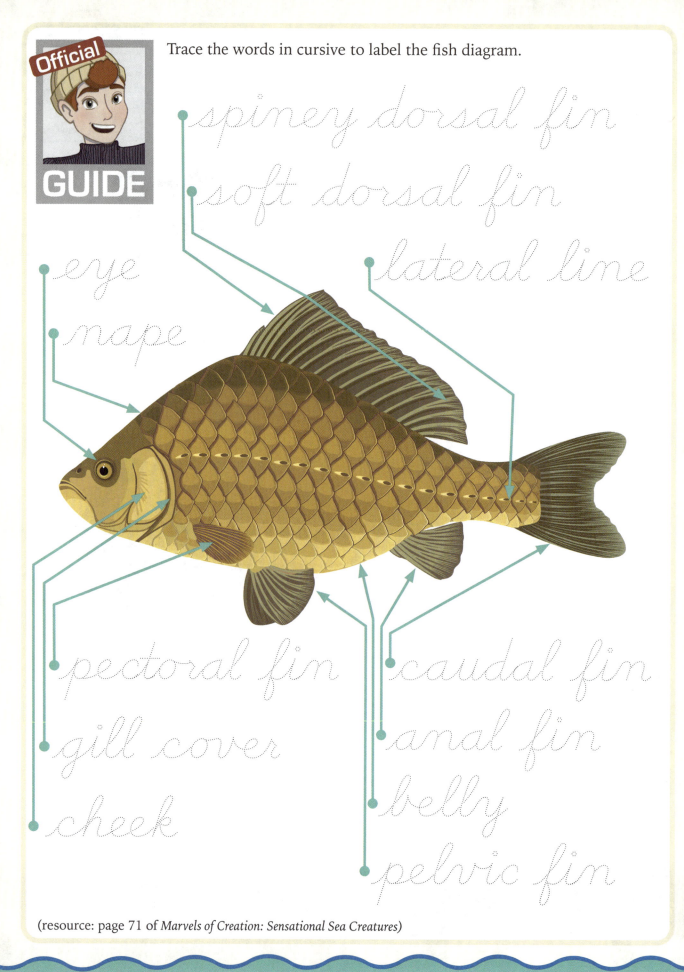

368 Hooked on Cursive

Name _____

Bait & Tackle 30.1

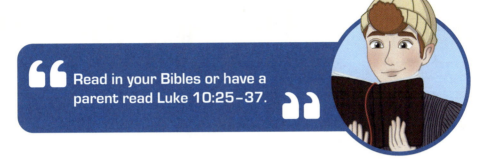
"Read in your Bibles or have a parent read Luke 10:25–37."

Gear Up!

Let's make these worms all different colors using your cotton swabs and sidewalk chalk.

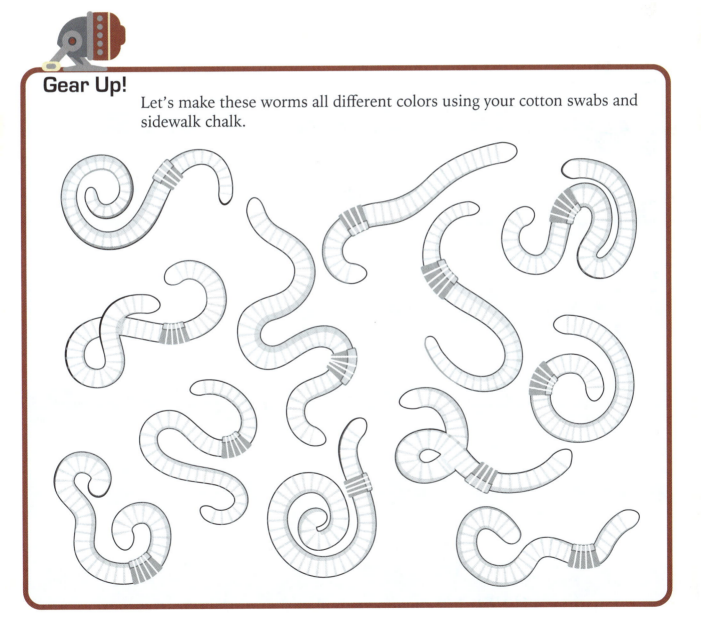

Capital K: Begin the capital cursive K like a capital H. Begin below the pole line, curve up and bump the pole line as you swim down to the waterline. Lift your pencil as you move over to the right. Slant inward toward the boat line and tap your first line. Then, slant down to the waterline to swim out.

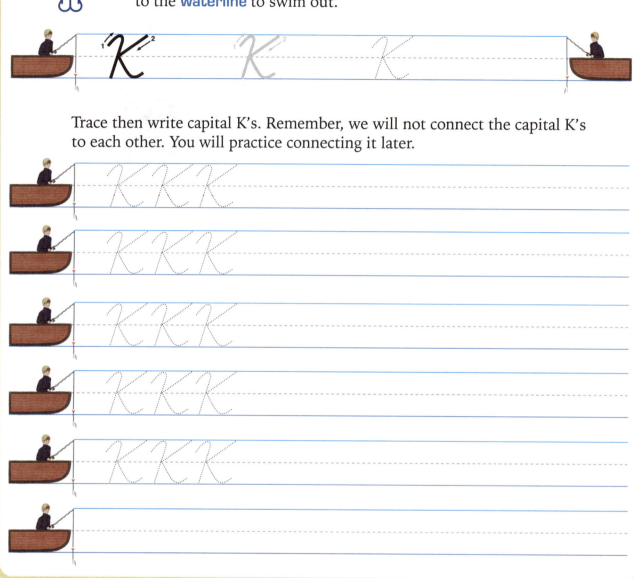

Trace then write capital K's. Remember, we will not connect the capital K's to each other. You will practice connecting it later.

REMINDER: Take some time to work on your weigh-in challenge.

Name _____

Bait & Tackle 30.2

> "Yesterday you read about the parable of the Good Samaritan. This story wasn't simply about different people passing by the hurt man. The lawyer questioning Jesus wanted to know who his neighbor was. Jesus uses this story to teach him an important lesson. The type of people who passed by the man and the one who did stop to help all have a big meaning. Notice, Jesus tells him first a priest passed by and didn't help him. The priest is known to be a man of God or one who obeyed and applied the laws of God. We'll keep discussing this point each day, but would you expect your pastor or minister to pass by if you needed help? This definitely wasn't something the lawyer expected either. How would you feel if this did happen to you?"

Gear Up!

Lighthouse Taps: Lighthouses flash their lights, so we are going to tap for lighthouse flashes. Bring your pinky and thumb together to tap and open, tap and open, like a lighthouse flash. Do this 12 times with both hands.

Capital K: Begin below the pole line, curve up and bump the pole line as you swim down to the waterline. Lift your pencil as you move over to the right. Slant inward toward the boat line and tap your first line. Then, slant down to the waterline to swim out.

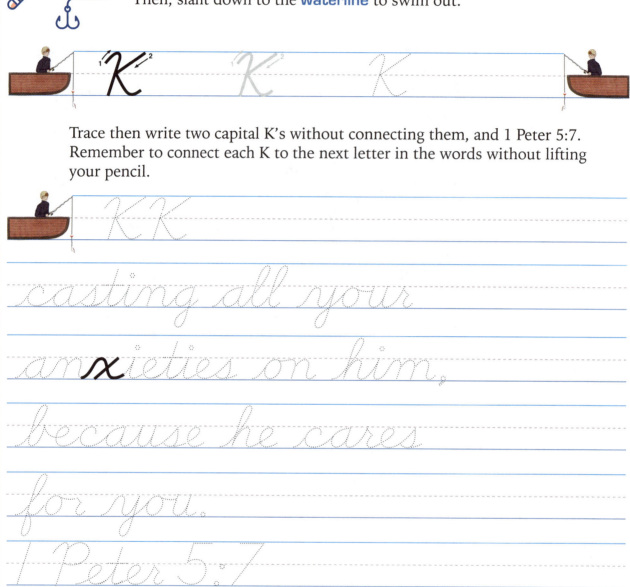

Trace then write two capital K's without connecting them, and 1 Peter 5:7. Remember to connect each K to the next letter in the words without lifting your pencil.

☐ **REMINDER:** Take some time to work on your weigh-in challenge.

Name _____

Bait & Tackle 30.3

"Who is your neighbor? Hmm . . . let's look again at what else Jesus says. After the priest, the one who obeys biblical laws, passed the hurt man, then Jesus tells us a Levite passed by. There is some deeper meaning here, but a Levite was an expert on the biblical laws. So first, we have the one who obeys the laws, then we have the one who has all the knowledge of the laws, but both pass by this hurt man. Both men knew the biblical laws, yet both men passed by the man in need. Why? We'll find out more tomorrow. This is kind of a mystery to us. We're slowly unwrapping the story to figure out what Jesus really wants us to know about our neighbors."

Gear Up!

Changing Shells: You will need 2 plastic cups for "shells," a marble, and your parent/sibling. Each of you sits across from one another at a table. Gently roll the marble toward the other person. They need to stay seated but capture the marble under their shell (cup) before it rolls off the table. Try not to roll it too hard. Then they gently push their cup forward and lift it to roll the marble toward you. You remain seated and place your shell (cup) over the marble before it rolls off the table. Each of you should do this at least 10 times.

Capital K: Begin below the pole line, curve up and bump the pole line as you swim down to the waterline. Lift your pencil as you move over to the right. Slant inward toward the boat line and tap your first line. Then, slant down to the waterline to swim out.

Trace then write two capital K's and 1 Peter 5:7. Remember to connect each K to the next letter in the words without lifting your pencil.

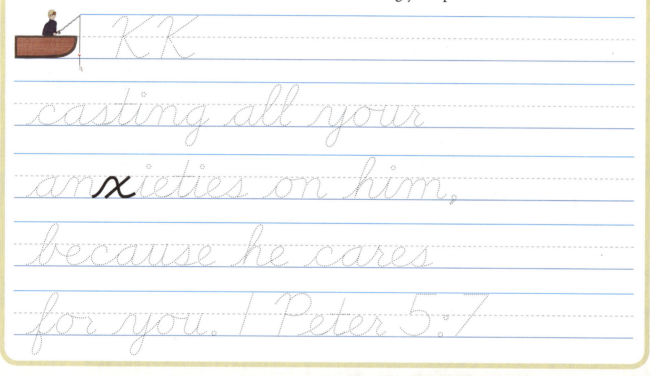

KK casting all your anxieties on him, because he cares for you. 1 Peter 5:7

> Did you complete the one-handed worm weigh-in challenge using Play-Doh? If so, help the worm find its way through the tunnel without getting caught.
>
> Your next challenge is to get some scissors and cut out a bucket and worm each day from the weigh-in section in the back of the book. You'll earn the scissors badge for completing this challenge.

Name _____

Bait & Tackle 30.4

> "Lastly, the third man to come by on the road was a Samaritan. Now, so far, we've had a priest and a Levite pass by the hurt man. These two men obey and know the laws well. This last man, a Samaritan, is not a Jew. In fact, Samaritans were outcasts and enemies of the Jewish people. Why would Jesus have an outcast, one known to be an enemy, be the hero in this story?
>
> Jesus was trying to tell us that our neighbor isn't the person who lives next door or attends our Sunday school class. The answer to who is my neighbor is greater than what we understand. It is the sinner person in need of Jesus. It is the one who needs mercy. It is the person who doesn't look like you. Jesus asked the lawyer, "Which of these three . . . proved to be a neighbor. . . ?" The answer is the one who showed mercy, or compassion. Jesus told him to "go and do likewise," or go and show mercy to others.
>
> So, who is our neighbor? The one who is in need of mercy or compassion. Who can you show compassion to? "Love our neighbor as ourselves." Love those who need compassion and mercy."

Gear Up!

You have been strengthening your body, and now it's time to focus on spacing between your words. Did you know the *best* way to get better at something is to practice? Yep, so the more you practice something, the better you will be. Let's practice using your pinky finger (the little one) between you making circles. Begin in between these two lines making circles but keep a pinky space between each one. This will help you know how much space should be between your words.

Bait & Tackle 30.4 375

Capital G: The bottom of a G reminds me of a little boat. Beginning at the waterline, slant up toward the pole line. Loop back, dip down and curve up, then swim down and slightly back toward the waterline as you make a curved line up. Last, slant a line to the right.

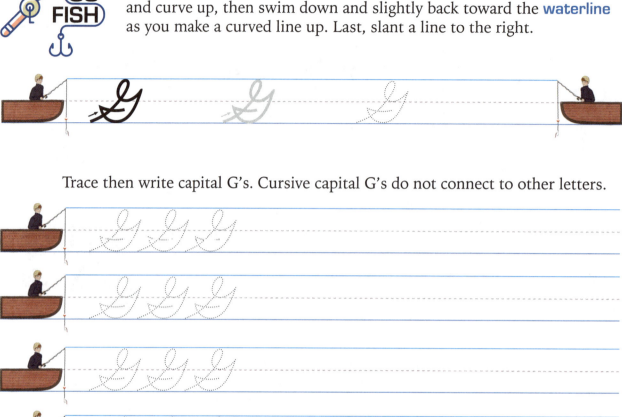

Trace then write capital G's. Cursive capital G's do not connect to other letters.

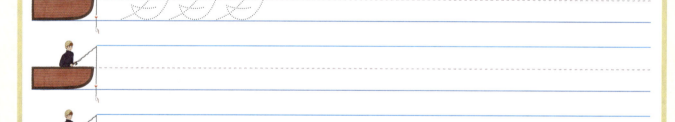

☐ **REMINDER:** Take some time to work on your weigh-in challenge.

Name _____

Bait & Tackle 30.5

> "I want to make one more point about this parable. If we look at the three men Jesus chose for His story (priest, Levite, and Samaritan), we can see that He was trying to prove a point about who needs mercy and who shows mercy. Everyone needs mercy. Everyone should show mercy. It doesn't matter your background, the shade of your skin, or where your momma buys your clothes. What matters is who we are to others. What matters is how are we treating our neighbor. God has shown us mercy — go and do the same."

Gear Up!

The Eye of the Hook: If you can, use a pushpin in the tip of an eraser or just a pencil with an eraser. Hold the pencil straight up and down in front of your nose. Bring it in slowly as you keep your eyes on the pin or eraser. Keep your focus. See how close you can bring it in before you see two of it.

Capital G: Beginning at the **waterline**, slant up toward the **pole line**. Loop back, dip down and curve up, then swim down and slightly back toward the **waterline** as you make a curved line up. Last, slant a line to the right.

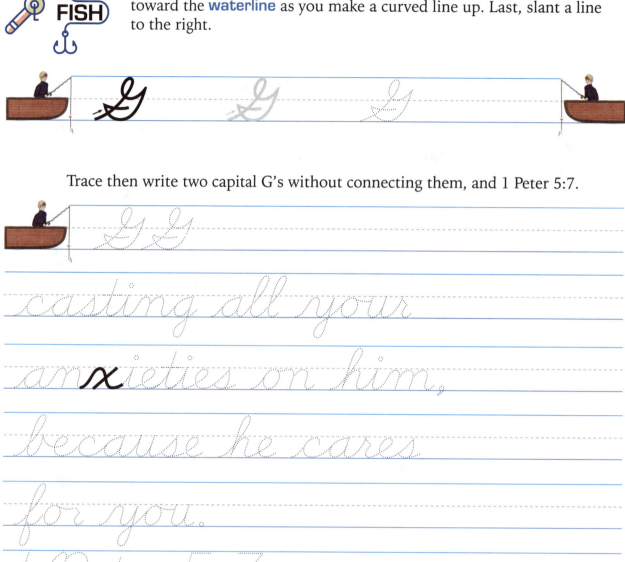

Trace then write two capital G's without connecting them, and 1 Peter 5:7.

casting all your anxieties on him, because he cares for you. 1 Peter 5:7

☐ **REMINDER:** Take some time to work on your weigh-in challenge.

Name _____

"I'm so excited over your achievement board and how many badges you've earned in Club Skeeter! I can't wait for you to fill your board."

"We've got quite a list of gear this week. Be sure to gather it all."

Gather Your Gear

Day 1
☐ Hole punch
☐ Play-Doh or a squishy ball/stress ball

Day 2:
☐ Paper clips

Day 3:
☐ Sticky notes or paper
☐ Ball (tennis or approx. size)

Day 4:
☐ 6 2-inch x 2-inch foil squares.

Tackle Box 31　379

Foolish: one who makes bad choices

Wise: one who makes good choices

Name _____

Bait & Tackle 31.1

> "Today, read Matthew 7:24–27 in your Bibles, or have your parents read it to you. Then, think about sand and rocks. Have you stood on sand before? What happens when you walk in sand? Have you stood on a rock before? What happens when you walk on rocks?"

Gear Up!

We're going to use the hole punch that you used in one of your weigh-in challenges. Use the hole punch to punch holes in the bubbles from the fish at the bottom of the page.

Capital G: Beginning at the waterline, slant up toward the pole line. Loop back, dip down and curve up, then swim down and slightly back toward the waterline as you make a curved line up. Last, slant a line to the right.

Trace then write two capital G's without connecting them, and Psalm 62:8 (NKJV). Remember to connect each G to the next letters in the words without lifting your pencil.

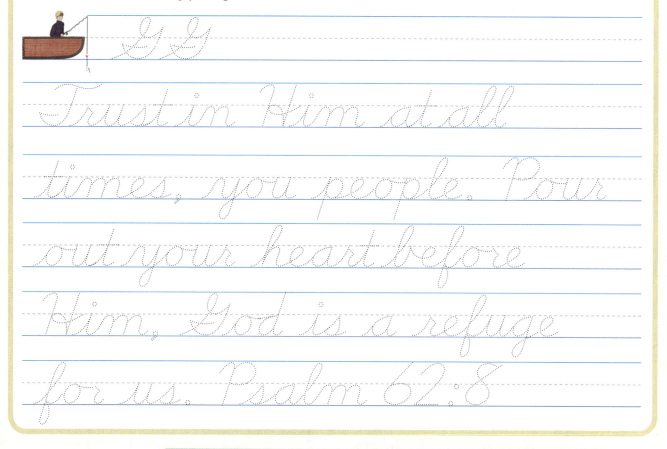

" Did you do the scissors challenge? If you did, color your scissors badge and add it to your achievement board.

Here is another weigh-in challenge. I'm sure you'll complete the challenge and earn another badge. Make a ball using Play-Doh and then squeeze the ball 3 times as if you're squeezing a lemon. Do this in each hand each day. You may need to reshape the ball after you squeeze it a bit. You can use stress balls or a squishy ball if you have that. "

Name: _____

Bait & Tackle 31.2

> "Yesterday I had you think about sand and rock. If you've ever built a sandcastle on the beach or played in sand, you know that sand isn't firm. If water comes over sand, it washes away, and the sandcastle goes flat after the waves hit it. Now, think about a rock. When the waters come over a rock, it doesn't wash away, and it stays firmly solid. The wise person built his house on the rock. A wise person is one who makes good choices. A foolish person does not make good choices. Would you rather your house be built on sand or rock? Are you making a wise decision or a foolish decision in your choice?"

Gear Up!

Hook the Fly: Clip the fly fishing lures at the bottom of the page with paper clips.

Capital I: Begin just below the boat line. Swing back and slightly up toward the boat line, and back down as you bump the waterline and swim up to bump the pole line. Loop back down to the waterline and swim out to connect to the next letter.

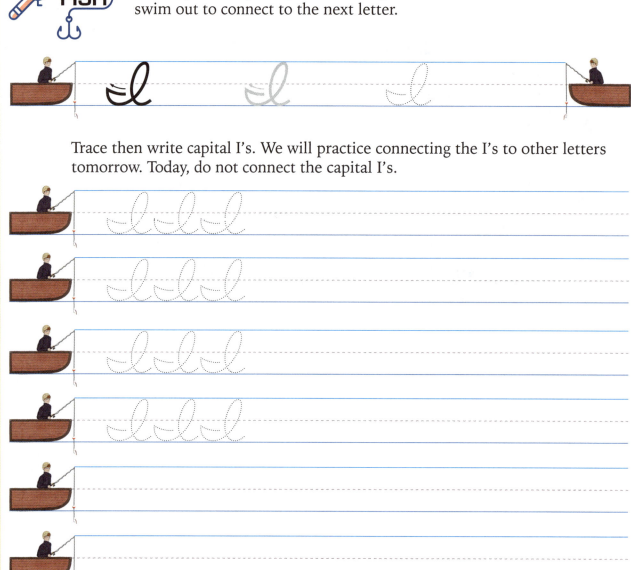

Trace then write capital I's. We will practice connecting the I's to other letters tomorrow. Today, do not connect the capital I's.

☐ **REMINDER:** Take some time to work on your weigh-in challenge.

Name _____

Bait & Tackle 31.3

"Remember, the reason for a parable was to help us understand spiritual or Kingdom things by using stories we can understand. Jesus says that the house on the rock stood. It lasted through the storms. We know the Bible tells us that Jesus is the Rock. He should be our foundation or what we build our lives on. Not a physical body built on a rock, but a spiritual body built on the Rock, Jesus."

Gear Up!

Aim and Cast: Place a piece of paper or sticky note on a door or wall about eye level. You can make a target on it if you'd like. Take about 10 steps back and try to AIM and CAST the ball to hit the target. If you miss 3 times, you can step forward 1 step. Try to hit the paper/target in the middle at least 3 times in a row.

Capital I: Begin just below the boat line. Swing back and slightly up toward the boat line, and back down as you bump the waterline and swim up to bump the pole line. Loop back down to the waterline and swim out to connect to the next letter.

Trace then write two capital I's and Psalm 62:8 (NKJV). Remember to connect each I to the next letter in the words without lifting your pencil.

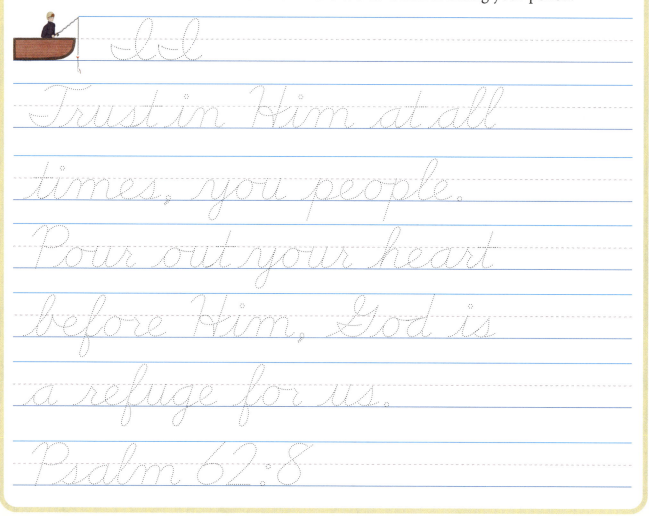

☐ **REMINDER:** Take some time to work on your weigh-in challenge.

Name _____

Bait & Tackle 31.4

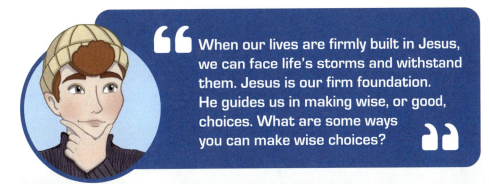

"When our lives are firmly built in Jesus, we can face life's storms and withstand them. Jesus is our firm foundation. He guides us in making wise, or good, choices. What are some ways you can make wise choices?"

Gear Up!

Make Weights: Using approximately 2-inch by 2-inch squares of foil, place one hand behind your back as you use the other hand to make the foil into balls like these round weights. After you have made 3, swap hands and make 3 with your other hand. (See lesson 25 day 4 if you need further instructions/graphics.)

Capital I: Begin just below the boat line. Swing back and slightly up toward the boat line, and back down as you bump the waterline and swim up to bump the pole line. Loop back down to the waterline and swim out to connect to the next letter.

Trace then write two capital I's and Psalm 62:8 (NKJV). Remember to connect each I to the next letter in the words without lifting your pencil.

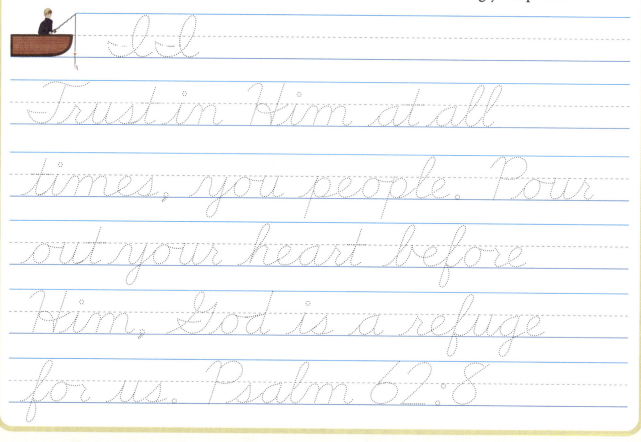

Trust in Him at all times, you people. Pour out your heart before Him. God is a refuge for us. Psalm 62:8

" If you completed the Squeeze the Lemon weigh-in challenge you've earned a lemon badge. Be sure to add it to your achievement board. "

Hooked on Cursive

Name _____

Bait & Tackle 31.5

" Jesus tells us in verse 26 that if we hear His words, His instructions in the Word, and do not follow His instructions, we will be like the foolish man. In order to be wise, we must follow God's instructions to us in His Word. Hebrews 4:12 tell us His Word is living and active, and sharper than any 2-edged sword. His Word is what we can use to fight the enemy. Let's closely follow God's Word so we can be wise. "

Gear Up!

Let's practice using your pinky finger between your drawing worms. Begin in between these two lines drawing worms but keep a pinky space between each one. This will help you know how much space should be between your words.

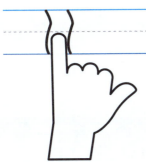

Review your letters: letters K, G, and I.

Capital K: Begin below the pole line, curve up and bump the pole line as you swim down to the waterline. Lift your pencil as you move over to the right. Slant inward toward the boat line and tap your first line. Then, slant down to the waterline to swim out.

Capital G: Beginning at the waterline, slant up toward the pole line. Loop back, dip down and curve up, then swim down and slightly back toward the waterline as you make a curved line up. Last, slant a line to the right.

Capital I: Begin just below the boat line. Swing back and slightly up toward the boat line, and back down as you bump the waterline and swim up to bump the pole line. Loop back down to the waterline and swim out to connect to the next letter.

Trace the letters K, G, and I. Trace them three times without connecting them, and then write them once on your own. Be sure to leave a pinky space between each set.

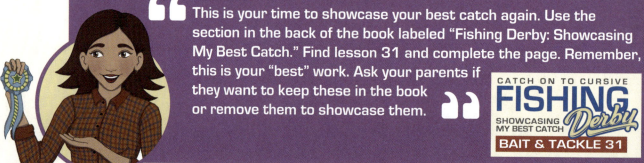

"This is your time to showcase your best catch again. Use the section in the back of the book labeled "Fishing Derby: Showcasing My Best Catch." Find lesson 31 and complete the page. Remember, this is your "best" work. Ask your parents if they want to keep these in the book or remove them to showcase them."

CATCH ON TO CURSIVE
FISHING Derby
SHOWCASING MY BEST CATCH
BAIT & TACKLE 31

390 Hooked on Cursive

Name _____

TACKLE BOX 32

" I bet you are up for another weigh-in challenge! Fishermen wear vests that may have buttons, zippers, or fasteners. Ask a parent to let you borrow a button-up shirt, a jacket with a zipper, and a belt. To earn another badge, button each button on the shirt, zip the zipper up and down, and fasten and unfasten the belt each day until your weigh-in. This also helps build up hand strength. "

" What a fun week of activities you have! Check out the gear you'll need so you can be prepared. "

Gather Your Gear

Day 1:
☐ Button-up shirt
☐ Jacket with zipper
☐ Belt

Day 1:
☐ Sheet of foam
☐ Sheet of plain paper

Day 2:
☐ Ball (tennis or approx. size)

Day 3:
☐ Plastic knife (1 for course)
☐ Plastic fork (1 for course)
☐ Play-Doh

Day 4:
☐ Plastic lid with a lip or a round cake pan
☐ Marble

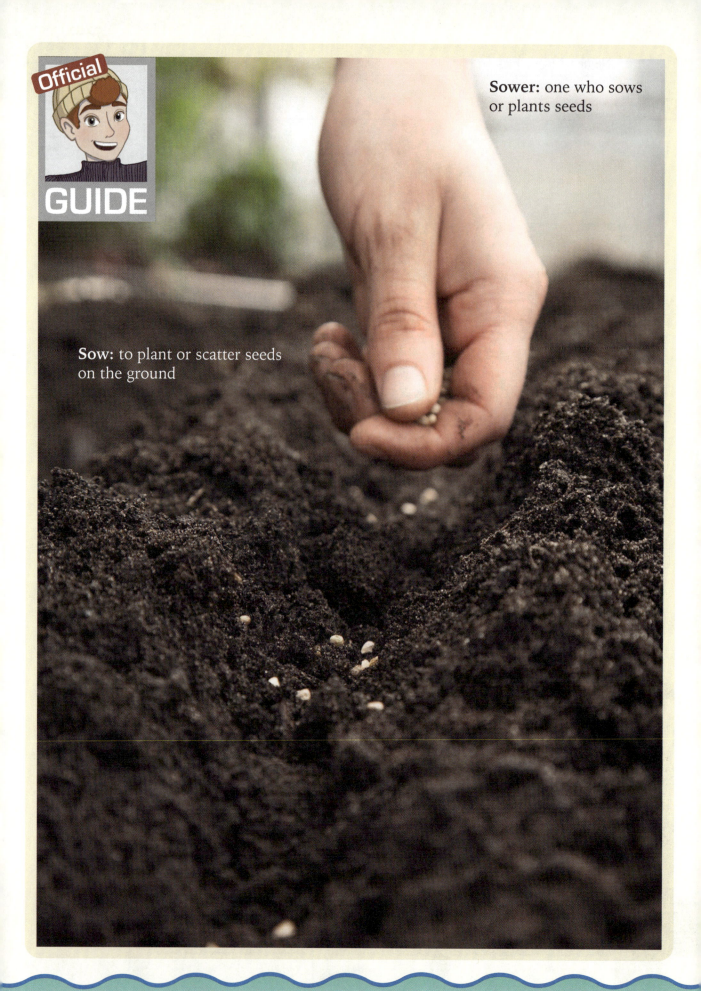

Sower: one who sows or plants seeds

Sow: to plant or scatter seeds on the ground

Name _____

Bait & Tackle 32.1

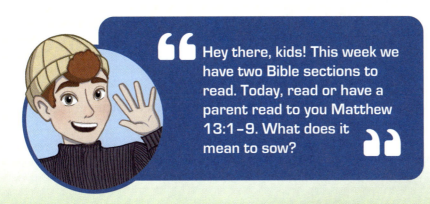

"Hey there, kids! This week we have two Bible sections to read. Today, read or have a parent read to you Matthew 13:1–9. What does it mean to sow?"

Gear Up!

The Right Conditions: Place a plain piece of paper on a piece of foam. When you write, if you apply too little pressure, it is difficult to see your writing and it can even look shaky. If you apply too much pressure, it will cause you pain. You need the right pressure to see your words, but not too much or you'll push through the paper to the foam. Draw 5 fish on the paper.

Capital S: The capital S is similar to the capital G. Beginning at the waterline, slant up toward the pole line. Loop back and down to bump the waterline as you swim back and up to make a curved line. Stopping before the boat line, make a slanted line to the right. The bottom reminds me of the bottom of a boat!

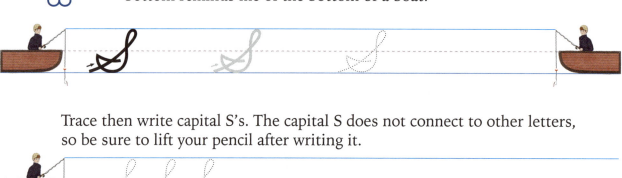

Trace then write capital S's. The capital S does not connect to other letters, so be sure to lift your pencil after writing it.

☐ **REMINDER:** Take some time to work on your weigh-in challenge.

Name _____

Bait & Tackle 32.2

 "Today, read or have a parent read to you Matthew 13:18–23."

Gear Up!

Crawdad Crawl: You will use a tennis ball or a ball that size. You have two "pinchers" like the crawdad, which are your thumb and pointing finger. Start with the ball beside your foot, using only your two pinchers (thumb and pointer finger), roll the ball up the side of your leg to your hip, across your tummy, and back down the side of the other leg. This may be difficult at first, but it will get easier with practice. Do this three times.

If you cannot do this with only two pinchers, you may add in one more to use your middle finger as well. Please try to do it with two only.

Capital S: Beginning at the **waterline**, slant up toward the **pole line**. Loop back and down to bump the **waterline** as you swim back and up to make a curved line. Stopping before the **boat line**, make a slanted line to the right.

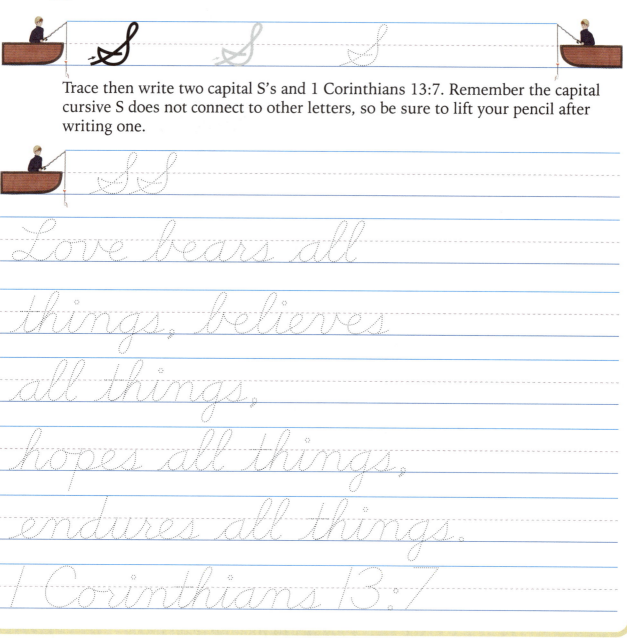

Trace then write two capital S's and 1 Corinthians 13:7. Remember the capital cursive S does not connect to other letters, so be sure to lift your pencil after writing one.

S S

Love bears all things, believes all things, hopes all things, endures all things.
1 Corinthians 13:7

☐ **REMINDER:** Take some time to work on your weigh-in challenge.

Name

Bait & Tackle 32.3

"Let's break down what happened to the seed in the parable of the sower. First, we see that the seeds that were sown on the path, which was packed-down soil, were devoured by birds. The seeds sown on the rocks didn't have good roots and although they grew at first, the sun scorched or burned them up because they couldn't get the water or nutrition they needed. Third, the seeds that fell among the thorns were choked or robbed by the thorns of their nutrition. Last, the seeds that fell on good soil produced good grain."

 Gear Up! Help the fish find the right path to the worm. Be sure to try to follow through the maze with your eyes first, then trace it.

 **Capital S:** Beginning at the waterline, slant up toward the pole line. Loop back and down to bump the waterline as you swim back and up to make a curved line. Stopping before the boat line, make a slanted line to the right.

Trace then write two capital S's and then 1 Corinthians 13:7. Remember the capital cursive S does not connect to other letters.

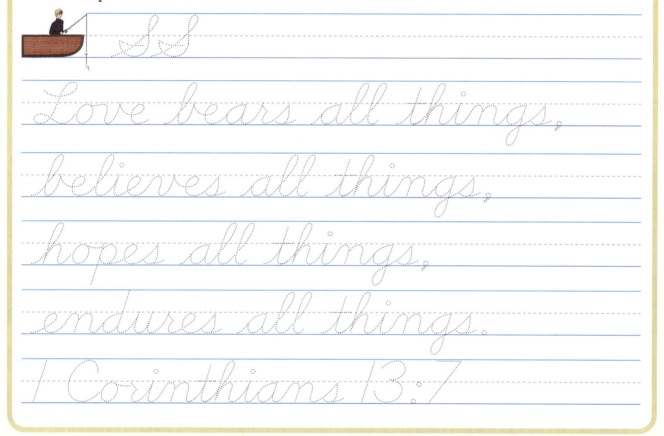

" Did you complete the fishing vest buttons, zippers, and fasterners weigh-in challenge? If you did, you have earned another badge for your achievement board! Look at all the badges you've earned. Add this one to your achievement board after you color in the fishing vest.

Sometimes when you're out camping you have to eat with plastic silverware. Use a plastic fork and knife to cut Play-Doh like you'd cut a large piece of fish or steak. Cut the piece of Play-Doh into at least 6 pieces each day. "

Name _____

Bait & Tackle 32.4

> "If we look at verses 18–23, Jesus explains this parable to us. Remember, parables are to help us understand spiritual or Kingdom things. Here, each type of soil is an example of our heart's condition. If the Word of God falls on a heart that is hardened like the path was, then we cannot produce fruits of the Spirit. If our hearts are excited at first, but lack strength and roots to grow, then we are like the seeds on the rocks. If our hearts are not fully committed to Christ and we allow the world to affect us, then we are like the seeds that fell into the thorns. Last, if we are dedicated to Christ and have a good support system, then we are like the seeds that fell on good soil."

Gear Up!

Marble in the Whirlpool: Using a plastic lid with a lip or a round cake pan, place a marble inside. Have someone move the lid/pan so the marble rolls in the inside edge back and forth and eventually all the way around in a circle. Follow the marble with your eyes, but do not move your head. Move only your eyes as you follow the marble back and forth for one minute.

Bait & Tackle 32.4 399

Capital J: Start at the waterline, curve back and up to the pole line, then swim back down to and into the hook space as you loop back and up to the waterline and swim out.

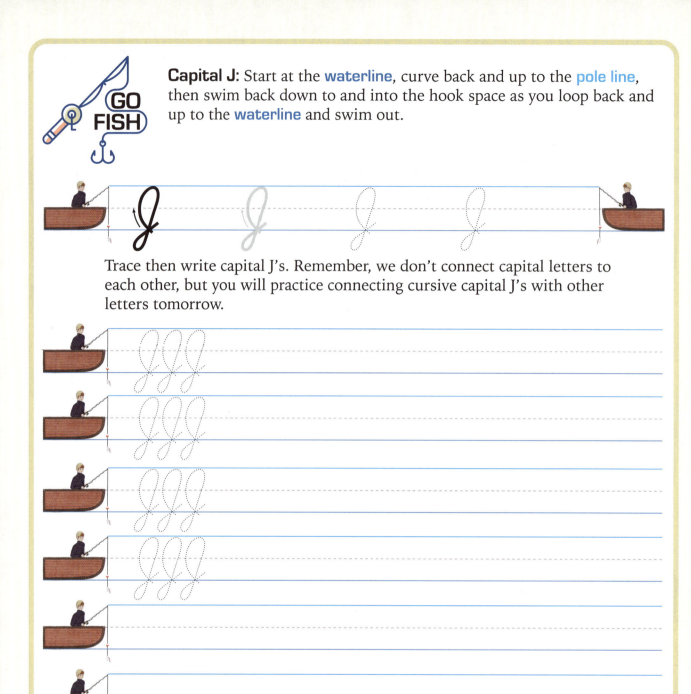

Trace then write capital J's. Remember, we don't connect capital letters to each other, but you will practice connecting cursive capital J's with other letters tomorrow.

☐ **REMINDER:** Take some time to work on your weigh-in challenge.

Name _____

Bait & Tackle 32.5

"Which heart are you? This parable helps us to take a good look at our own hearts so we can see how to become a strong Christian. We want to be sure we have good soil in order to grow and produce fruits of the Spirit."

Pathway:
• trampled on
• birds ate it up
= Destroyed

Rocky:
• not rooted
• sun scorched
= Withered

Thorny:
• choked
• suffocated
= Died

Good Soil:
• grew up
• increased
= Fruitful

Gear Up!

Under & Over: You will help the crawdad climb over and under the obstacles. On the top row, begin by going under the first obstacle and back up between the next obstacles. You want to try to stay in the middle of the two obstacles you are going under and over. See the example to help you recall how to do this.

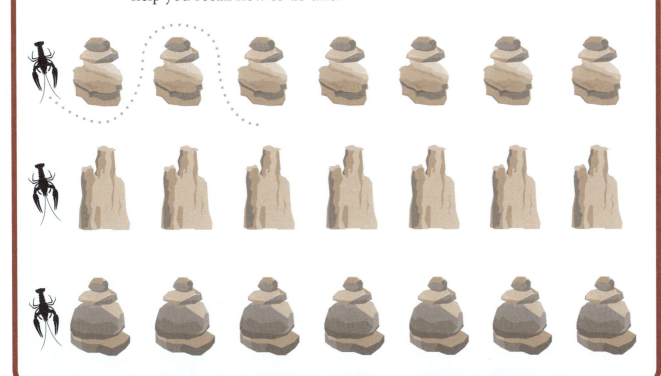

Bait & Tackle 32.5   401

Capital J: Start at the waterline, curve back and up to the pole line, then swim back down to and into the hook space as you loop back and up to the waterline and swim out.

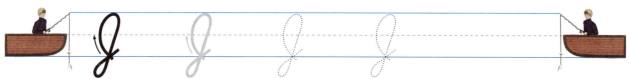

Trace then write two capital J's without connecting them, and 1 Corinthians 13:7. Remember to connect each J to the next without lifting your pencil.

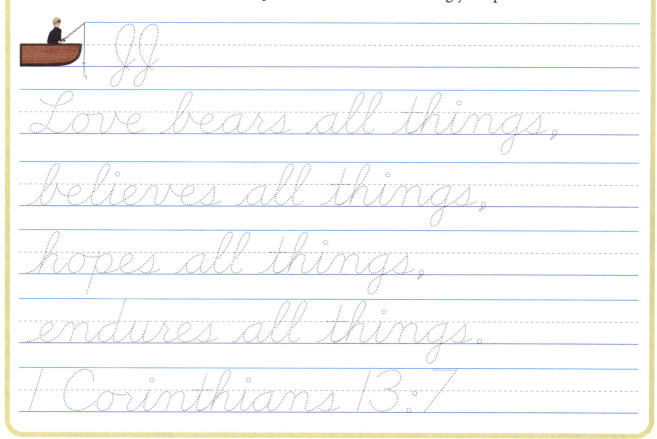

☐ **REMINDER:** Take some time to work on your weigh-in challenge.

Name

> " Oh, I'm so excited about how full your achievement board is! You will have it completely full in no time. Be sure to complete the challenges and weigh-in to earn more. "

> " My grandpa always ran trot lines when I was younger. It's a way to catch a lot of fish at once. He loved catching catfish for his food. On his trot lines, he used milk jugs as floats. Check out the picture on the next page. You'll have a challenge this week to make your own trot lines. Once, he caught an alligator gar, and it pulled his trot lines way out into the lake! "

Gather Your Gear

Day 1:
- ☐ 1 plastic straw (cut into 1-in. pieces)
- ☐ 1 foot of yarn or 1 chenille wire

Day 2:
- ☐ Hole punch

Optional:
- ☐ 1 paper plate (any size)
- ☐ Approx. 2 ft. of yarn
- ☐ 2 strips of tape (any kind)

Day 4:
- ☐ 6 2-inch x 2-inch foil squares

Tackle Box 33   403

Official GUIDE

Fishing net: fibers woven together in a grid pattern to make a net used to catch or scoop up fish.

Trot lines: fishing lines with several lures with bait, and floats at the end. You set them and leave them in the water, usually not too far off the banks of the lake. Usually, you check your lines twice a day to see what you caught.

Alligator gar: one of the largest freshwater fish in North America and can be found in lakes with bass and crappie.

Name _____

Bait & Tackle 33.1

> "We're talking about another parable this week. This week our parable is called the Parable of the Net. Read, or have a parent read, Matthew 13:47–50 in your Bible."

Gear Up!

We've got another challenge for you today. Have you ever made a fish outline without lifting your pencil as you drew it? Well, check out these steps to make 4 outlines of fish without lifting your pencil. This also helps you use both sides of your brain when you draw this! Super cool, huh? You can add in a mouth, eyes, bubbles, and more to give it more details.

1   2   3   4

Capital J: Start at the waterline, curve back and up to the pole line, then swim back down to and into the hook space as you loop back and up to the waterline and swim out.

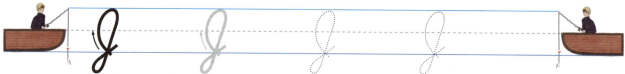

Trace then write two capital J's without connecting them, and part of Joshua 1:9. Remember to connect each J and letters to the next without lifting your pencil.

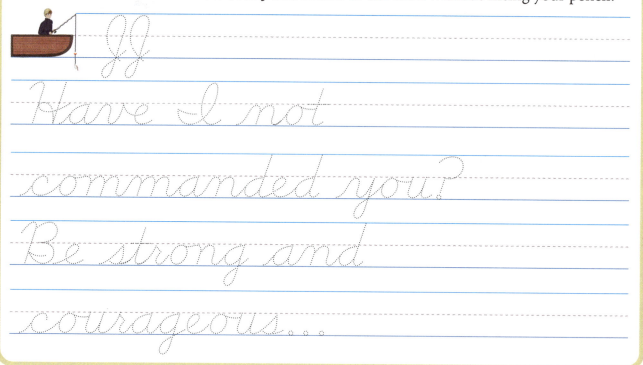

> Did you complete the fork and knife weigh-in challenge? If you did, check out the badge you earned! Color in the fork and knife on the badge, and remember to add it to your achievement board.
>
> Your next challenge is to make trot lines. Cut apart a plastic straw into approximately 1-inch pieces and thread yarn or a chenille wire through it to make floats for your line. Look back at the diagram on Bait & Tackle 33. Add two floats each day to your trot line. Make a great trot line to earn your badge.

Name _____

Bait & Tackle 33.2

> "This parable is difficult for us because we don't always like the consequences of sin. We know that the fishermen in the parable separated the good fish from the bad fish. The bad fish were thrown away. Do you know what separates us from God? Sin separates us from God."

Gear Up!

I've got a fun project for you! Using a paper plate and your hole punch, punch around the edges of the paper plate to make 1/2 circles about 2 inches apart. Then, get about 2 feet of yarn and tape one end to the back of the plate. Draw fish on the front side of the plate (at least 4). Then, using the 1/2 circle notches you made, wrap the yarn to make a "net" over the fish.

*This is a fun, but optional activity. If you do not like crafts, please just make holes on the edge of this paper with your hole punch.

Lowercase x: This time you will lift your pencil to make the letter. First, begin at the waterline, swim up to the boat line and curve down to the waterline. Then, lift your pencil, and at the boat line right above where you just stopped your line, make a slanted line that crosses your first line and goes back to the waterline. This slanted line is similar to the t or i. You complete the word you are writing first, then come back to finish the slanted line.

Trace then write lowercase x's. Remember to connect each x together before finishing with the slanted line.

☐ **REMINDER:** Take some time to work on your weigh-in challenge.

Name

Bait & Tackle 33.3

"In this parable, we are told that in the end times, angels will come and separate the evil people from the righteous people. Evil people are those who live in sin and try to destroy others. Righteous people are like Noah. They are blameless and walk with God. I want to be found blameless before the Lord like Noah was. (See Genesis 6:9.)"

Gear Up!

Complete the dot-to-dot.

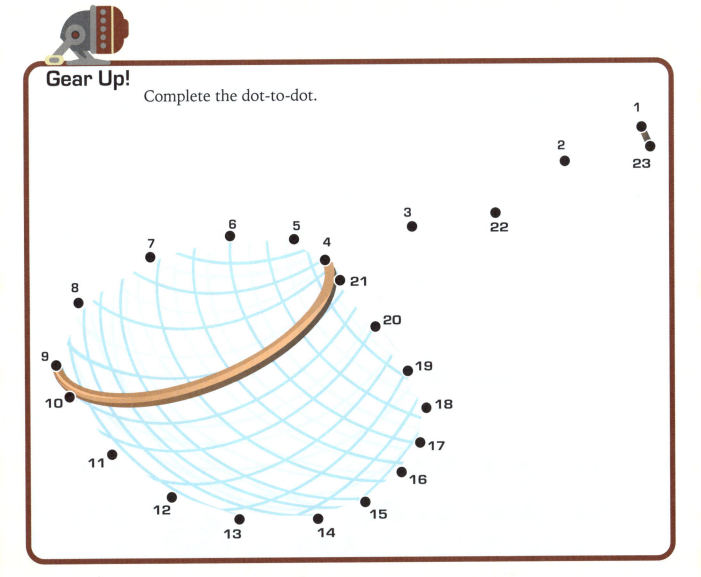

Lowercase x: To write a lowercase x, begin at the **waterline**, swim up to the **boat line** and curve down to the **waterline**. Then, lift your pencil, and at the **boat line** right above where you just stopped your line, make a slanted line that crosses your first line and goes back to the **waterline**. Remember to complete the word you are writing first, then come back to finish the slanted line.

Trace then write two lowercase x's and Joshua 1:9. Remember to connect each x and letters to the next without lifting your pencil, then come back and finish the slanted line of the x.

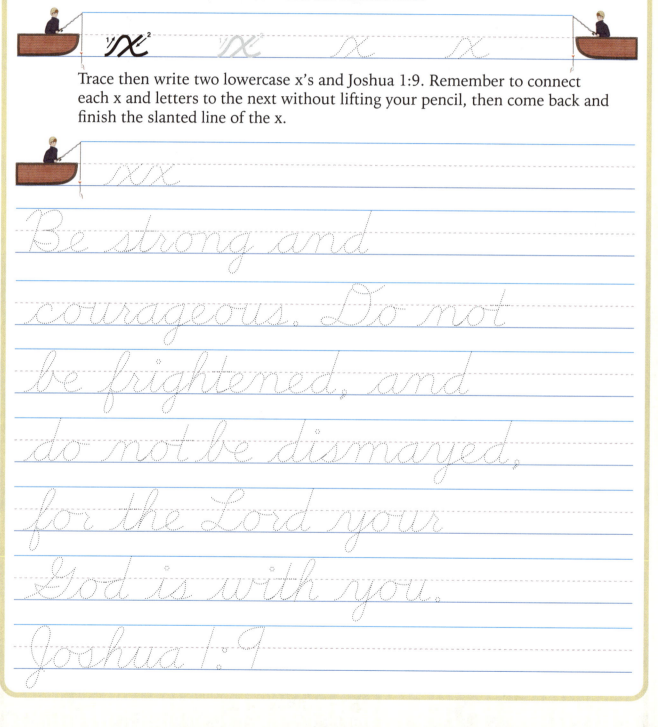

☐ **REMINDER:** Take some time to work on your weigh-in challenge.

Name _____

Bait & Tackle 33.4

> "Just as in Noah's day, when God separated Noah and his family from the evil people, God will do this again. We will be separated from God forever if we are found to be evil. If we are found to be righteous, then we will receive our eternal home in heaven with God. And we become righteous by putting our trust and faith in Jesus, who has become righteousness for us (1 Corinthians 1:30)."

Gear Up!

Make Weights: Using approximately 2-inch by 2-inch squares of foil, place one hand behind your back as you use the other hand to make the foil into balls like these round weights. After you have made 3, swap hands and make 3 with your other hand. (See lesson 25 day 4 if you need further instructions/graphics.)

Bait & Tackle 33.4   411

Lowercase x: To write a lowercase x, begin at the waterline, swim up to the boat line and curve down to the waterline. Then, lift your pencil, and at the boat line right above where you just stopped your line, make a slanted line that crosses your first line and goes back to the waterline. Remember to complete the word you are writing first, then come back to finish the slanted line.

Trace then write two lowercase x's and part of Joshua 1:9. Remember to connect each x and words to the next without lifting your pencil, then come back and finish the slanted line of the x.

Do not be frightened, and do not be dismayed, for the Lord your God is with you. Joshua 1:9

> Did you complete the trot line weigh-in challenge? If so, you can color in your float on the trot line on the badge. I wonder how many more badges you'll add to your achievement board.
>
> Sometimes when you're out camping you have to eat with plastic silverware. Use a plastic fork and knife to cut Play-Doh like you'd cut a large piece of fish or steak. Cut the piece of Play-Doh into at least 6 pieces each day.

412 Hooked on Cursive

Name _____

Bait & Tackle 33.5

"What are some ways we can live a righteous life? Discuss this with your parents. I encourage you to memorize the Word of God and pray. Those are two great ways to walk with the Lord."

Gear Up!

Complete the maze first by tracking through it with your eyes, then complete it with your pencil.

Review your letters: letters S, J, and x

Capital S: Beginning at the waterline, slant up toward the pole line. Loop back and down to bump the waterline as you swim back and up to make a curved line. Stopping before the boat line, make a slanted line to the right.

Capital J: Start at the waterline, curve back and up to the pole line, then swim back down to and into the hook space as you loop back and up to the waterline and swim out.

Lowercase x: To write a lowercase x, begin at the waterline, swim up to the boat line and curve down to the waterline. Then, lift your pencil, and at the boat line right above where you just stopped your line, make a slanted line that crosses your first line and goes back to the waterline. Remember to complete the word you are writing first, then come back to finish the slanted line.

Trace the letters S, J, and x. Trace them three times, and then write them once on your own. Be sure to leave a pinky space between each set.

> This is your time to showcase your best catch again. Use the section in the back of the book labeled "Fishing Derby: Showcasing My Best Catch." Find lesson 33 and complete the page. Remember, this is your "best" work and a great way to review what you have learned. Ask your parents if they want to keep these in the book or remove them to showcase them.

CATCH ON TO CURSIVE
FISHING Derby
SHOWCASING MY BEST CATCH
BAIT & TACKLE 33

Hooked on Cursive

Name _____

TACKLE BOX 34

"I've got another weigh-in challenge that I know you're going to do so well with! You're going to squish worms in between your fingers. Make 2 worms from Play-Doh. Then, place it between your index (pointing) finger and your middle finger on the same hand and squeeze the worms by squeezing your two fingers together. Then, move the worm between your middle and ring finger and squeeze the worm. Again, move it between your ring finger and pinky finger and squeeze. Do this with both hands squeezing between each space 5 times."

"You have done so well on your Fishing Derbies! Check out the fun word search on the next page."

Gather Your Gear

Day 1:
☐ Play-Doh

Day 2:
☐ Marble
☐ 2 plastic cups

Day 3:
☐ Optional: 1 rubber band

Day 4:
☐ Ball (tennis or approx. size)

Tackle Box 34   415

Pace yourself and find 3 words each day this week.

BASS	DERBY	LIVE WELL
CATFISH	DOCK	LURE
COELACANTH	FISHING POLE	SALMON
CRAWDAD	TACKLE BOX	SAIL
CREATION	LIGHTHOUSE	TROUT

S	A	I	L	B	N	T	A	C	K	L	E	B	O	X	G	L	K
H	L	I	G	H	T	H	O	U	S	E	I	S	B	X	A	K	Q
P	N	C	L	M	E	I	M	E	Z	V	N	D	S	M	X	S	W
R	C	R	A	W	D	A	D	M	L	B	N	B	Y	F	D	A	Q
L	M	K	F	I	S	H	I	N	G	P	O	L	E	A	O	L	A
W	V	R	O	J	C	O	E	L	A	C	A	N	T	H	C	M	P
E	I	Y	P	S	M	N	U	L	X	G	X	W	U	C	K	O	G
C	K	V	D	E	R	B	Y	X	U	B	A	S	S	J	K	N	I
V	O	K	T	R	O	U	T	B	G	R	U	I	O	S	I	E	I
M	U	L	I	V	E	W	E	L	L	S	E	M	Y	I	X	X	K
V	K	C	A	T	F	I	S	H	J	J	Y	U	X	G	W	A	M
Q	C	R	E	A	T	I	O	N	I	J	T	K	O	N	F	I	A

Name _____

Bait & Tackle 34.1

"Read, or have your parent read, Luke 13:1–20 for the parable of the Mustard Seed and Yeast (Leaven)."

Gear Up!

Let's practice using your pinky finger between your fishing hooks. Begin in between these two lines drawing hooks but keep a pinky space between each one. This will help you know how much space should be between your words.

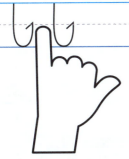

Bait & Tackle 34.1   417

Capital X: The capital X makes the same movement as the lowercase x, except it is larger. Start just below the pole line, curve up and down to the waterline. Then, go straight up to the pole line and slant back and down to the waterline.

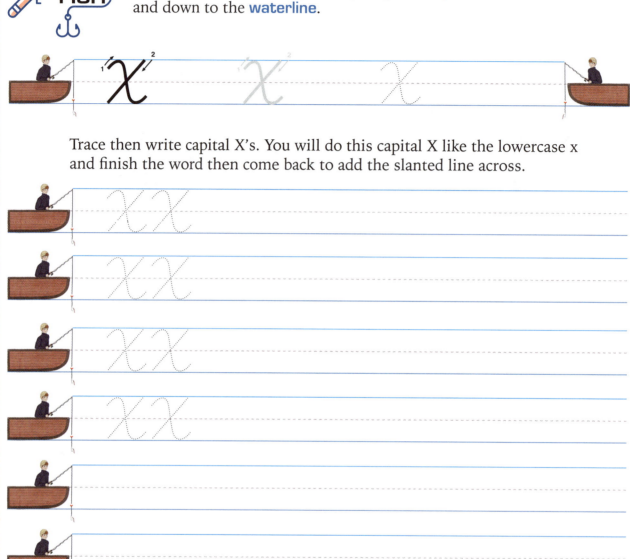

Trace then write capital X's. You will do this capital X like the lowercase x and finish the word then come back to add the slanted line across.

☐ **REMINDER:** Take some time to work on your weigh-in challenge.

Name _____

Bait & Tackle 34.2

" Yesterday you read in your Bibles about the mustard seed and yeast (leaven). Let's talk about these items. Have you ever seen a mustard seed? It is a very small round seed. One cell of yeast, or leaven, is tiny. Now, I know we've talked a lot about fishing in this course and I think we all would prefer a larger fish, so why did Jesus use two tiny things to explain what the Kingdom of Heaven is like? Come back tomorrow as we dig in to find out. "

Mustard seeds

Yeast

" I wonder if you're getting better at this game. "

Gear Up!

Changing Shells: You will need 2 plastic cups for "shells," a marble, and your parent/sibling. Each of you sits across from one another at a table. Gently roll the marble toward the other person. They need to stay seated but capture the marble under their shell (cup) before it rolls off the table. Try not to roll it too hard. Then, they gently push their cup forward and lift it to roll the marble toward you. You remain seated and place your shell (cup) over the marble before it rolls off the table. Each of you should do this at least 10 times.

Capital X: Start just below the pole line, curve up and down to the waterline. Then, go straight up to the pole line and slant back and down to the waterline.

Trace then write two capital X's without connecting them, and Psalm 99:5. Remember to connect each X and letters to the next without lifting your pencil. Once the word is finished, you will come back and add the slanted line for the X.

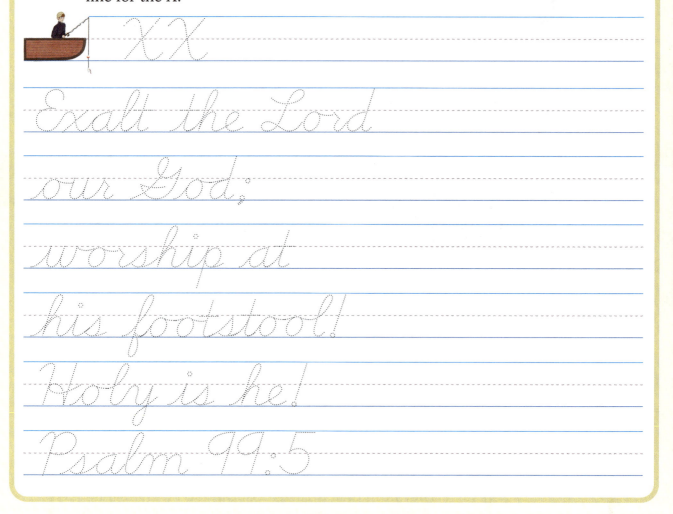

X X

Exalt the Lord

our God;

worship at

his footstool!

Holy is he!

Psalm 99:5

☐ **REMINDER:** Take some time to work on your weigh-in challenge.

Name

Bait & Tackle 34.3

> " I told you we would dig in to why Jesus used a mustard seed to explain what the Kingdom of Heaven is like. Let's look at a mustard seed, then look at the tree it produces.
>
> You see, this tiny seed can produce a plant as large as a tree, which then provides for the birds. I think this explains that the Kingdom of Heaven grows from our smallest efforts just as the small mustard seed grows into something so large. The small mustard seed also shows us no one is too young to be used by God. Then, the mustard seed provides for the needs of the birds just like the Kingdom of Heaven provides for all we need. I think it's amazing how Jesus used stories to help us understand big Kingdom ideas. "

Gear Up!

We're doing more **Lighthouse Taps**, and if you have a rubber band, you can put it over your thumb and pinky finger as you do them to really build up those muscles!

Bring your pinky and thumb together to tap and open, tap and open, like a lighthouse flash. Do this 12 times with both hands.

Capital X: Start just below the pole line, curve up and down to the waterline. Then, go straight up to the pole line and slant back and down to the waterline.

Trace then write two capital X's without connecting them, and Psalm 99:5. Remember to connect each X and letters to the next without lifting your pencil.

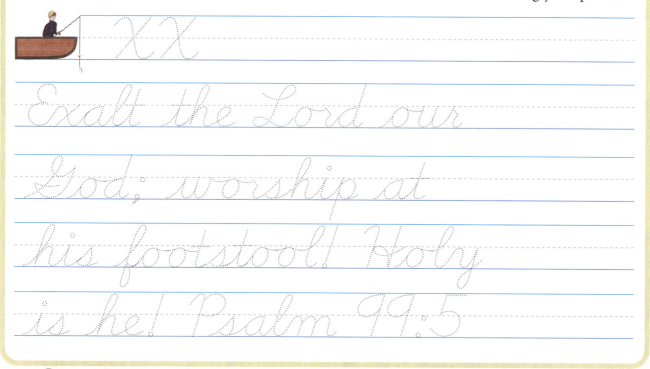

XX

Exalt the Lord our God; worship at his footstool! Holy is he! Psalm 99:5

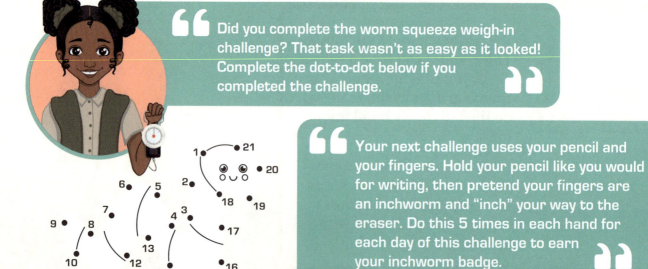

"Did you complete the worm squeeze weigh-in challenge? That task wasn't as easy as it looked! Complete the dot-to-dot below if you completed the challenge."

"Your next challenge uses your pencil and your fingers. Hold your pencil like you would for writing, then pretend your fingers are an inchworm and "inch" your way to the eraser. Do this 5 times in each hand for each day of this challenge to earn your inchworm badge."

Name _____

Bait & Tackle 34.4

> "So how does yeast show us what the Kingdom of Heaven is like? Well, if you use water, flour, salt, and sugar mixed with a tiny bit of yeast, the yeast will spread into the mixture and cause it to rise into dough to make bread. What if we didn't add the yeast to that mixture? Well, the dough wouldn't rise. Those ingredients depend on the effect of the yeast. This shows us that one small piece of yeast is like the Christians' impact on the world. Without us spreading the Gospel like the yeast spreads through the doughy mix, we wouldn't be fulfilling God's command in Mark 16:15 for us to "Go into all the world and proclaim the gospel to the whole creation." The Gospel message changes lives just as yeast changes the dough. One act from a Christian to witness to one person will spread to another and another. Wow! What an impact we can have by sharing the message of Christ."

Gear Up!

Crawdad Crawl: You will use a tennis ball or a ball that size. You have two "pinchers" like the crawdad, which are your thumb and pointing finger. Start with the ball beside your foot, using only your two pinchers (thumb and pointer finger), roll the ball up the side of your leg to your hip, across your tummy, and back down the side of the other leg. This may be difficult at first, but it will get easier with practice. Do this three times.

*If you cannot do this with only two pinchers, you may add in one more to use your middle finger as well. Please try to do it with two only.

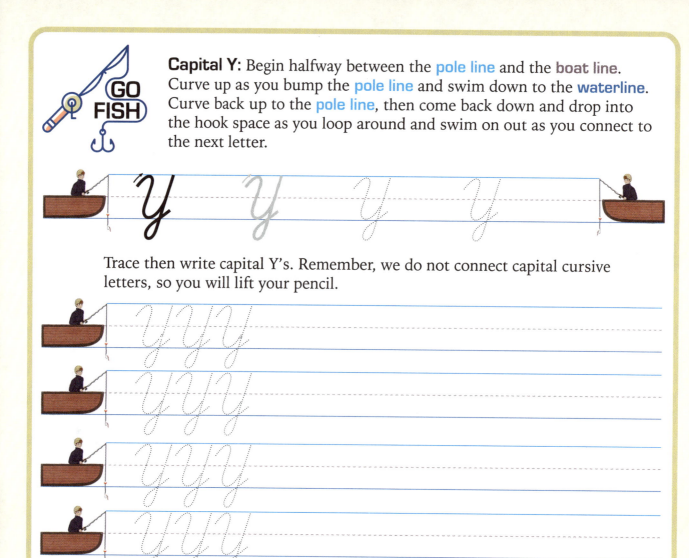

Capital Y: Begin halfway between the pole line and the boat line. Curve up as you bump the pole line and swim down to the waterline. Curve back up to the pole line, then come back down and drop into the hook space as you loop around and swim on out as you connect to the next letter.

Trace then write capital Y's. Remember, we do not connect capital cursive letters, so you will lift your pencil.

☐ **REMINDER:** Take some time to work on your weigh-in challenge.

Name: _____

Bait & Tackle 34.5

> "Are you ready to be like a mustard seed and grow into a mighty man or woman of God? Are you ready to learn how to witness and help change the world like yeast changes the dough? Who can your family witness to? How can your family help grow the Kingdom? Discuss with your parent the ways you can be like a mustard seed or yeast and share the Gospel of Jesus Christ. An example is to take food to a widow or someone sick and pray with them."

Gear Up!

Paddle the Boat: Sit in a chair or on the side of a bathtub with your feet flat on the ground. Pretend to paddle the boat. Make sure you swap sides so your boat doesn't get off course! Give a good 15 total strokes of the paddle for each side.

Capital Y: Begin halfway between the pole line and the boat line. Curve up as you bump the pole line and swim down to the waterline. Curve back up to the pole line, then come back down and drop into the hook space as you loop around and swim on out as you connect to the next letter.

Trace then write two capital Y's without connecting them, and Psalm 99:5. Remember to connect to the next letter without lifting your pencil.

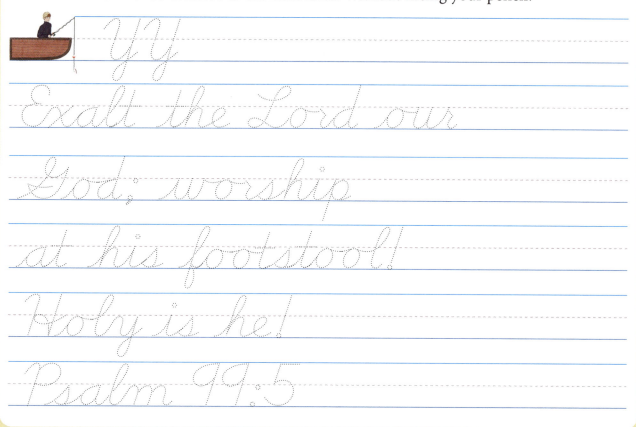

Y Y
Exalt the Lord our God; worship at his footstool! Holy is he! Psalm 99:5

☐ **REMINDER:** Take some time to work on your weigh-in challenge.

Name

 TACKLE BOX 35

"Wow! Check out the achievement board! Only a few more weigh-in challenges left. Who knew you would earn this many badges when we started Club Skeeter?"

"We're completing our last Fishing Derby for the course. I know you'll do your very best! I know you're an experienced fisherman by now, but sometimes experienced fishermen forget their gear! Be sure to gather yours."

Gather Your Gear

Day 2:
☐ Hole punch
☐ Paper (any kind or color, 1 sheet)

Day 3:
☐ 6 2-inch x 2-inch foil squares

Day 5:
☐ Small objects such as beads, small buttons, or sunflower seeds,
☐ Play-Doh or other dough

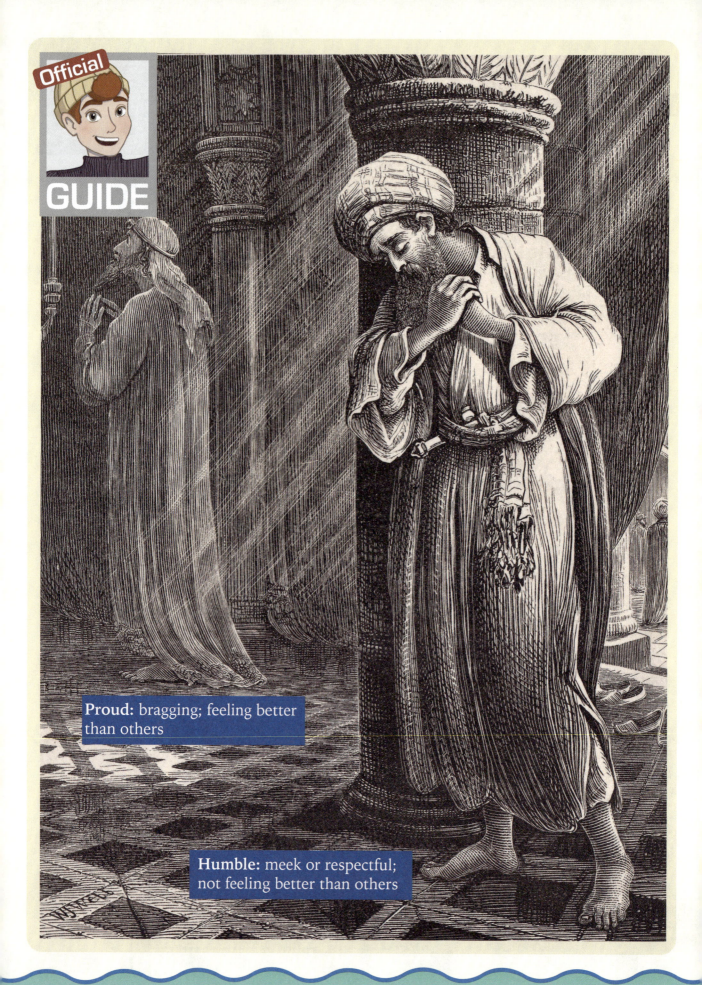

Name

Bait & Tackle 35.1

"This week we're talking about the parable of the Pharisee and Tax Collector. Read, or have your parent read, Luke 18:9–14."

Gear Up!

We're trying something new today to see how sharp your eyes are. Find and color 6 fish in the picture.

Capital Y: Begin halfway between the pole line and the boat line. Curve up as you bump the pole line and swim down to the waterline. Curve back up to the pole line, then come back down and drop into the hook space as you loop around and swim on out as you connect to the next letter.

Trace then write two capital Y's without connecting them, and the first part of Jeremiah 29:11 (NIV). Remember to connect to the next letter without lifting your pencil.

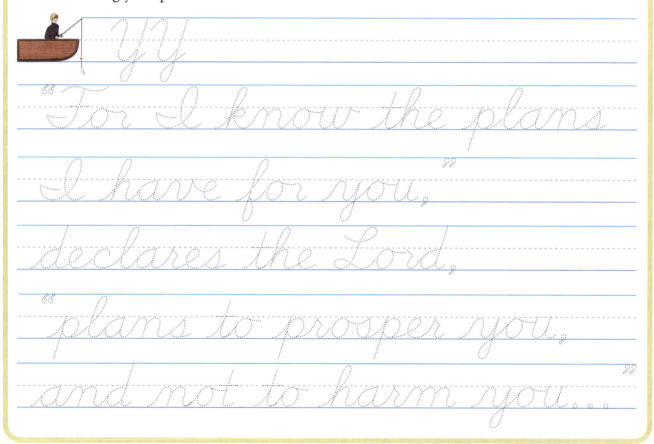

"For I know the plans
I have for you,"
declares the Lord,
"plans to prosper you,
and not to harm you…"

" Did you earn your inchworm badge? If so, be sure to color the inchworm on the badge and add it to your achievement board.

Let's keep testing your eyes. Find the Seek & Find page in the Weigh-In Challenges section in the back of the book. Complete one activity each day. "

Name

Bait & Tackle 35.2

> "When I think about the Pharisee, the man who was following the rules of religion, I often think that he missed the fact that he was speaking to Jesus. I mean, Jesus knows our hearts and this man was listing everyone else's sins instead of seeing his own. His heart was one of pride, not a humble heart. Have you ever gotten in trouble for something, and you said, "But Mom, he did ____ to me first?" The issue with this is that we are trying to justify or make an excuse for our actions. We just need to recognize how much we need forgiveness for what we did."

Gear Up!

Grab your hole punch and a piece of paper (any kind or color). Punch several holes in the paper you chose, then use a small amount of glue from a glue stick to place the dots from the hole punch to decorate the fish below.

Bait & Tackle 35.2 431

This week we will learn the lowercase and capital Z.

Lowercase z: Begin at the waterline and swim up to bump the boat line as you curve back down to the waterline. Then, make a little hop up above the waterline as you swim down to the hook space and loop back up to the waterline and swim on out.

Capital Z: The capital Z is like the lowercase z. Begin slightly above the boat line, curve up as you bump the pole line and down the waterline. Then, hop back up and curve down into the hook space and loop back up to the waterline and swim on out.

Trace then write capital Z's without connecting them, as well as lowercase z's. Remember to connect to the next lowercase letter without lifting your pencil.

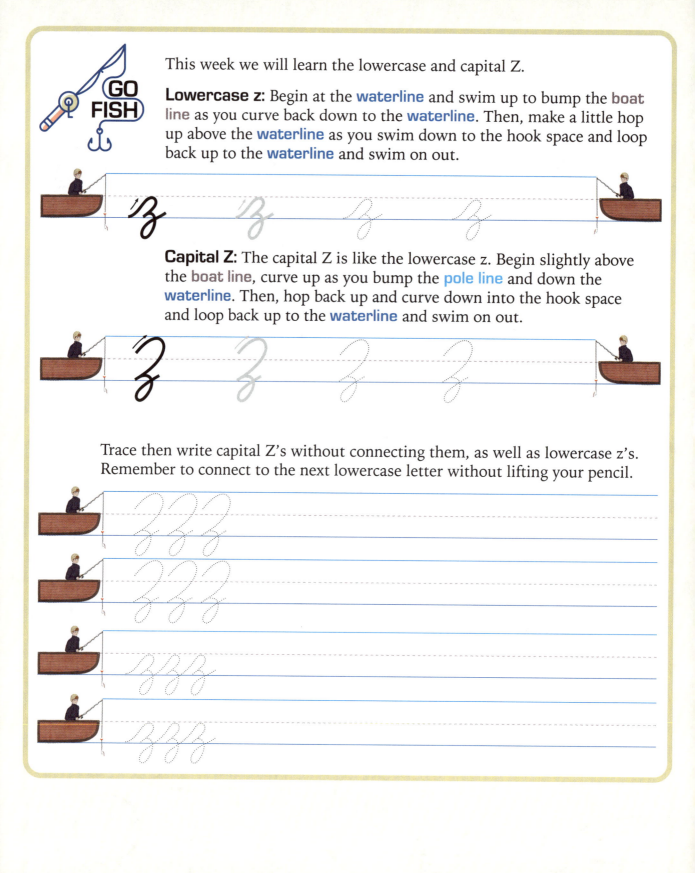

Name

Bait & Tackle 35.3

> "The tax collector was known to be one who cheated people. Notice the tax collector wouldn't even come close to the temple nor would he lift his eyes up. He showed humility and deep respect for the temple and God. He knew he was a sinner, and he sincerely prayed for God to show him mercy. This is the attitude we should have when we get into trouble. Admit we are sinners and ask for mercy and forgiveness."

Gear Up!

Make Weights: Using approximately 2-inch by 2-inch squares of foil, place one hand behind your back as you use the other hand to make the foil into balls like these round weights. After you have made 3, swap hands and make 3 with your other hand. (See lesson 25 day 4 if you need further instructions/graphics.)

Lowercase z: Begin at the waterline and swim up to bump the boat line as you curve back down to the waterline. Then, make a little hop up above the waterline as you swim down to the hook space and loop back up to the waterline and swim on out.

Capital z: Begin slightly above the boat line, curve up as you bump the pole line and down the waterline. Then, hop back up and curve down into the hook space and loop back up to the waterline and swim on out.

Trace then write two capital and two lowercase Z's and the first part of Jeremiah 29:11 (NIV). Remember to connect to the next letter without lifting your pencil. Remember, the capital Z's do not connect to each other, but they do connect to other letters.

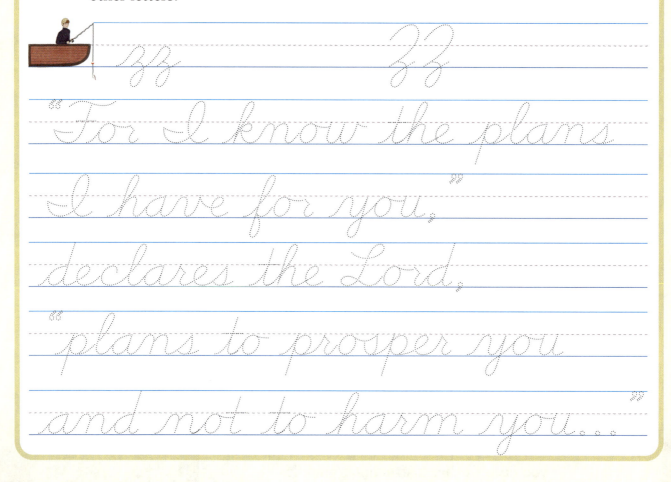

☐ **REMINDER:** Take some time to work on your weigh-in challenge.

Name _____

Bait & Tackle 35.4

> "What is something you have gotten in trouble for that you tried to prove why it was okay that you did wrong? Do you think it would be better to just say, "I lost my temper when I hit my sister? I'm sorry," or "Mom, she was singing loudly and got on my nerves, so she deserved to be hit"? I think the apology is the better choice, don't you? Sometimes we don't want to apologize for what we did, we would rather point our finger and justify, or make an excuse, for what we did. That type of attitude is like the Pharisee, which is a proud attitude to have."

Gear Up!

Hoist the Sails: These are called side planks and are like a side pushup where you hold your body up. Lay on your side, lift your body up with the arm closest to the ground. Your foot should be on its side on the ground. Hold the position for 8 seconds, relax, and repeat 2 times. Do both sides of your body. Your body makes a triangle shape like a sail.

Lowercase z: Begin at the waterline and swim up to bump the boat line as you curve back down to the waterline. Then, make a little hop up above the waterline as you swim down to the hook space and loop back up to the waterline and swim on out.

Capital z: Begin slightly above the boat line, curve up as you bump the pole line and down the waterline. Then, hop back up and curve down into the hook space and loop back up to the waterline and swim on out.

Trace then write two capital and two lowercase Z's and the rest of Jeremiah 29:11 (NIV). Remember to connect to the next letter without lifting your pencil.

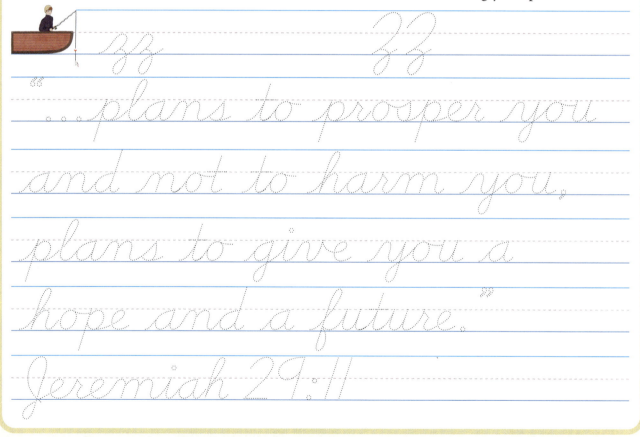

> " I bet you found a lot of things in your Seek & Find weigh-in challenge. If you completed the challenge, color in the binoculars on the badge and add it to your achievement board. "

Name

Bait & Tackle 35.5

> It's better to take ownership of our actions instead of blaming someone else. You control you. If someone is doing something that isn't right, please let an adult know. I'm not talking about that. I'm talking about looking around for an excuse to make your wrong behavior right instead of showing self-control in the first place. We need to keep a humble attitude and recognize that we all sin and we all fall short (Romans 3:23). The Word tells us in James 4:6, "But he gives more grace." Therefore it says, "God opposes the proud but gives grace to the humble." I know I need grace, so I'm going to work on keeping a humble attitude.

Gear Up!

Lures in Mud: Push at least 5 small objects with each hand into dough. Be sure to use your fingers to get them started and your thumb to get them all the way in. Clean up when you're done.

Review your letters: letters X, Y, z, and Z.

Capital X: Start just below the pole line, curve up and down to the waterline. Then, go straight up to the pole line and slant back and down to the waterline.

Capital Y: Begin halfway between the pole line and the boat line. Curve up as you bump the pole line and swim down to the waterline. Curve back up to the pole line, then come back down and drop into the hook space as you loop around and swim on out as you connect to the next letter.

Lowercase z: Begin at the waterline and swim up to bump the boat line as you curve back down to the waterline. Then, make a little hop up above the waterline as you swim down to the hook space and loop back up to the waterline and swim on out.

Capital Z: Begin slightly above the boat line, curve up as you bump the pole line and down the waterline. Then, hop back up and curve down into the hook space and loop back up to the waterline and swim on out.

Trace the letters X, Y, z, and Z. Trace them three times without connecting them, and then write them once on your own. Be sure to leave a pinky space between each set.

> "This is your time to showcase your best catch again. Use the section in the back of the book labeled "Fishing Derby: Showcasing My Best Catch." Find lesson 35 and complete the page. Remember, this is your "best" work and a great way to review what you have learned. Ask your parents if they want to keep these in the book or remove them to showcase them."

CATCH ON TO CURSIVE
FISHING Derby
SHOWCASING MY BEST CATCH
BAIT & TACKLE 35

Hooked on Cursive

Name

> "Club Skeeter is honored that you joined us for the adventures in *Catch on to Cursive*. Our club has enjoyed watching you do your best as you faced each challenge. Way to go! Your last weigh-in challenge is for this whole week. I'm asking you to do your best in your copy work, make sure you use capital letters where needed, and use spacing between your words. If you do this, then I will give you your last badge on day 5."

> "I am so proud of how far you have come. You have persevered and put in the effort in all of the challenges and derbies. This week you will be copying Scripture as you review everything you have learned in Club Skeeter."

Gather Your Gear

Day 1:
☐ Painter's tape or rope or sidewalk chalk

Day 2:
☐ Sticky notes or paper
☐ Ball (tennis or approx. size)

Day 4:
☐ Paper clips (all the ones from the course)

Day 5:
☐ Ball (tennis or approx. size)

Name _____

Bait & Tackle 36.1

> "Read Matthew 18:21–35, or have a parent read it to find out about the Parable of the Unforgiving Servant."

Gear Up!

Walk the Plank: Use painter's tape, a rope, or sidewalk chalk to make a long line. Walk the Plank by balancing on the line with one foot in front of the other. Don't fall in! There might be gators in that water! Do this 3 times.

(You can also use a 2x4 or balance beam.)

 Trace Joel 3:16 below.

The Lord roars from
Zion, and utters his
voice from Jerusalem,
and the heavens
and the earth quake.
But the Lord is a
refuge to his people,
a stronghold to the
people of Israel.
Joel 3:16

☐ **REMINDER:** Take some time to work on your weigh-in challenge.

Name _____

Bait & Tackle 36.2

> "Forgiveness is huge. Let's break this parable down. Peter asks Jesus how many times he should forgive his brother. Jesus tells him a large amount. Don't just forgive him 7 times, no that's not good enough. Forgive him 70 times 7. I think you understand that 70 times 7 is a large number. This was so that Peter would know we are to forgive them however many times needed. We shouldn't hold on to unforgiveness, because if we do, it only hurts us."

Gear Up!

Aim and Cast: Place a piece of paper or sticky note on a door or wall about eye level. You can make a target on it if you'd like. Take about 10 steps back and try to AIM and CAST the ball to hit the target. If you miss 3 times, you can step forward 1 step. Try to hit the paper/target in the middle at least 3 times in a row.

GO FISH

Trace the Scripture, then copy the Scripture in cursive on the lines provided.

Your challenge checklist:

☐ Do your best.
☐ Use a capital letter when needed.
☐ Use a pinky space between words.

Do not be overcome by evil, but overcome evil with good. Romans 12:21

☐ **REMINDER:** Take some time to work on your weigh-in challenge.

Name

 Bait & Tackle 36.3

"In the next verses, we see a servant who owed money to a king. The servant begged for more time to pay him. The master of the servant showed mercy and allowed the servant more time. But then the same servant that was just given mercy went out to his fellow servant that owed him money. Did he react the same way and show mercy to his fellow servant? No. Instead, he was mean to the fellow servant and threw him in jail. This doesn't seem like this servant followed the "treat others how you want to be treated" rule."

 Gear Up!

Find out who caught what by completing the maze of fishing lines.

GO FISH

Trace the verse from 1 Chronicles 16:11, then copy the verse in cursive.

Your challenge checklist:

☐ Do your best.
☐ Use a capital letter when needed.
☐ Use a pinky space between words.

Seek the Lord and his strength; seek His presence continually!
1 Chronicles 16:11

☐ **REMINDER:** Take some time to work on your weigh-in challenge.

Name

Bait & Tackle 36.4

> "Well, word got back to the king about the servant he had shown mercy to, but in return was mean to his fellow servant. Now, his actions of unforgiveness or not showing mercy to his fellow servant cost him the mercy he had received from the king. The king placed him in jail. You see, when we don't forgive or show mercy to others, then we cannot receive mercy and forgiveness ourselves. The last Scripture we read from this parable tells us that if we do not forgive from our hearts, then we are like this servant."

Gear Up!

Just for fun, connect your paper clips together to make a fish shape.

Trace the verse from Galatians 6:9, then copy the verse in cursive.

Your challenge checklist:

☐ Do your best.
☐ Use a capital letter when needed.
☐ Use a pinky space between words.

And let us not grow weary of doing good, for in due season we will reap, if we do not give up. Galatians 6:9

☐ **REMINDER:** Take some time to work on your weigh-in challenge.

Name _____

Bait & Tackle 36.5

> "Not forgiving others, even when they don't ask for your forgiveness, only hurts you. I know from experience that it leads to bitterness and anger. That isn't something you want in your hearts. Just like the Scripture says, if we don't forgive from our hearts, we are like the servant in the parable. Always show forgiveness and mercy just like Christ shows it to us. I know sometimes it is difficult to forgive, but if you pray and ask God to help you, He will."

> "Challenge yourself here today. If you haven't been only using two fingers, do it with only two today."

Gear Up!

Crawdad Crawl: You will use a tennis ball or a ball that size. You have two "pinchers" like the crawdad which are your thumb and pointing finger. Start with the ball beside your foot, using only your two pinchers (thumb and pointer finger), roll the ball up the side of your leg to your hip, across your tummy, and back down the side of the other leg. This may be difficult at first, but it will get easier with practice. Do this three times.

Trace the verse from James 1:12.

Blessed is the man who remains steadfast under trial, for when he has stood the test he will receive the crown of life, which God has promised to those who love Him.
James 1:12

" Did you complete the weigh-in checklist for your copy work this week? I bet your cursive is fabulous! You've earned your last badge for Club Skeeter. Remember to display it on your achievement board. "

Activities for Older Students:

These Older Student Activities are for those following the alternate schedule. Students will need a notebook of ruled paper that has at least 80 pages.

Activity 1:

In your notebook or ruled paper, write three rows of the letters a and c. Make sure to connect the letters in the row. Keep the strokes as your lesson stated and don't lift your pencil/pen between letters.

Activity 2:

In your notebook or ruled paper, write the nonsense word "cad" in cursive as you connect each letter to the next without lifting your pencil. Leave a space between each nonsense word. Fill three lines with the word "cad."

Activity 3:

In your notebook or ruled paper, write the words "dog" and "cod" in cursive. Don't forget to leave a space between your words and connect the letters in each word without lifting your pencil. Fill four lines with the two words.

Activity 4:

In your notebook or ruled paper, write the following words and nonsense words in cursive. Fill 6 lines with the words.

    doc, coda, cad, qoa, go, do, ad

Remember:

- Connect each letter within each word without lifting your pencil
- Leave about a pencil eraser space between each word

Activity 5:

In your notebook or ruled paper, write the following words in cursive. Write each word three times.

    Ado, Ad, Coda, Cod, dog

Remember:

- Connect each letter within each word without lifting your pencil
- Leave about a pencil eraser space between each word

Activity 6:

In your notebook or ruled paper, write the following words and nonsense words in cursive. Fill 6 lines with the words.

    Odd, Cag, dad, go, Add

Remember to connect the letters in words and leave a space between each word.

Activity 7:

In your notebook or ruled paper, write the following words and nonsense words in cursive. Fill 6 lines with the words.

    Ego, Egg, Qad, Ago, Codaq

Remember to connect the letters in words and leave a space between each word.

Activity 8:

Write the following words in cursive in your notebook. Remember to leave spaces between words, but not the letters in a word. Write each word three times.

    Eat, toga, toad, dot, tad, data, coat, taco, Eco, Oat, Cat

Activity 9:

Write the following words in cursive in your notebook. Remember to leave spaces between words, but not the letters in a word. Write each word four times. If you do not know the meaning of any of these words, look them up and write or draw a picture for their meaning. BONUS: Can you make up any more words with the cursive letters you have learned?

    jag, jot, jag, taj, coat, Octad, jato, dicot, Qadi

Activity 10:
Write the following words in cursive in your notebook. Remember to leave spaces between words, but not the letters in a word. Write each word four times. If you do not know the meaning of any of these words, look them up and write or draw a picture for their meaning. BONUS: Can you make up any more words with the cursive letters you have learned?

pact, Epact, Ectopia, iodide, pico, pot, adopt, topic, paid

Activity 11:
Reading cursive is important so you can read cards or letters sent to you or historical documents, and it improves brain function! Yes, you read that right! Reading and writing in cursive engages more neural pathways (meaning it uses both sides of your brain—your right and left hemispheres). Read the following words aloud to your teacher.

dog, epic, pig, too, top, data, coat, ago, Ego, Oat, Aged

Now write these words in cursive in your notebook in alphabetical order:

Quit, acquit, squid, staged, cupid, spades, ages, paces

Activity 12:
Read the following words aloud to your teacher.

just, quits, adapts, jagged, depicts, judges, jaws, was

Write these words in your notebook in an artsy design. Gently sketch an outline of any object on your paper and write your words along the outline until it is covered with your words. You may write the words more than once to fill the edge.

Activity 13:
Write the following words in cursive in your notebook. Remember to leave spaces between words, but not the letters in a word. Write each word three times. If you do not know the meaning of any of these words, look them up and write or draw a picture for their meaning.

discourage, waited, guidepost, produces, raises, grasses, dress, stewed, progress

Activity 14:
Write these words in your notebook in an artsy design. Gently sketch an outline of any object on your paper and write your words along the outline until it is covered with your words.
*BONUS: Can you make more words in cursive?

Eagle, league, quills, steal, litter, delta, palace, Quilted, leader, jester

Activity 15:
Write these words in your notebook in cursive in alphabetical order, then use the words to fill in the missing words from the Scripture below (ESV version). (You will need a Bible for the rest of these assignments. ESV is preferred as the translation aligns with the letter scope and sequence.)

peace, the, all, at, be, with

Now may _____ Lord of _____ himself give you _____ ____ _____ times ____ every way. The Lord _____ _____ you _____.

2 Thessalonians 3:16

Activity 16:
Write each word three times in your notebook. Then, fill in the missing words to complete the scripture from Romans 3:23 (ESV).

Words to use:

all, and, for, sinned, fall, of

_____ _____ have _____ _____ _____ short ____ the glory ____ God.

Activity 17:

Write these words in your notebook from shortest word to longest word, then fill in the words from Ephesians 4:32 (ESV) to complete the verse. (*Hint:* you may have more than one word with the same number of letters.)

forgiving, in, one, kind, to, another, tenderhearted, as

Be _____ ___ _____
_____, _____,
forgiving _____ _____ , ___
God ____ Christ forgave you.

Activity 18:

Complete the verses below in cursive (ESV):

1 John 1:9: If _____

John 1:4: In _____

Proverbs 10:12: Hatred _____

Activity 19:

Look up these verses in your Bible and copy them in cursive in your notebook (ESV).

Proverbs 13:1; Proverbs 13:7; Proverbs 15:1

Activity 20:

Write this quote from Dr. Henry Morris in cursive in your notebook.

"Other human institutions — government, the school, the church — all find their pattern and purpose originally in the basic family unit." (Dr. Henry Morris)

Write this quote from Ken Ham in cursive in your notebook:

"Only Christianity and its teachings can explain the purpose and meaning of this world — and also gives the basis for right and wrong, good and evil, etc." (Ken Ham)

Activity 21:

Using your Bible (ESV), write the following verses in cursive in your notebook.

Luke 6:31; Matthew 5:2–6

Activity 22:

Using your Bible (ESV), write the following verses in cursive in your notebook.

Matthew 5:7–11

Activity 23:

Using your Bible (ESV), write James 3:17 in cursive in your notebook. Next copy the quote from a poem by John Greenleaf Whittier titled "One of the Signers."

"Amidst those picked and chosen men, than his, who here first drew his breath, no firmer fingers held the pen that wrote for liberty or death."

Activity 24:

In your notebook, write in cursive Proverbs 16:18 and then copy the quote from George Washington from the Fight for Freedom on page 8.

"Nothing can be more hurtful to the service than the neglect of discipline; for that discipline, more than numbers, gives one army the superiority over another."

Activity 25:

Using your Bible (ESV), write the following verses in cursive in your notebook.

Proverbs 20:11; Proverbs 21:2; Proverbs 22:24–25

Activity 26:

Using your Bible (ESV), write the following verses in cursive in your notebook.

Proverbs 24:3–7

Activity 27:

Using your Bible (ESV), write the following verses in cursive in your notebook.

Numbers 6:24–26

Activity 28:

Using your Bible (ESV), write the following verses in cursive in your notebook.

James 4:7; Psalm 118:24; Proverbs 15:22

Activity 29:

Write the quotes from Dr. Henry Morris' book, *Many Infallible Proofs*[1], in your notebook in cursive.

> "The God of the Bible is claimed to be the only true God."

> "The Bible is claimed as the only true revelation from God."

> "Our purpose in using the evidences is not to win arguments but to win souls, and also to win a more favorable intellectual environment for the presentation of the gospel."

Activity 30:

Write this quote from Dr. Henry Morris' book, *The Revelation Record*[2], in your notebook in cursive.

> "It is foundational to know Him as Maker; it is salvational to know Him as Redeemer, Friend and Lord; it is motivational to know Him as coming King."

Now write this quote in cursive in your notebook. This quote is from Dr. Henry Morris' book, *The Genesis Record: A Scientific and Devotional Commentary on the Book of Beginnings*[3].

> "It has often been pointed out that if a person really believes Genesis 1:1, he will not find it difficult to believe anything else recorded in the Bible."

Activity 31:

Find two of your favorite quotes or Scriptures and copy them in your notebook in cursive.

Activity 32:

Copy the quotes by Lester Sumrall in cursive in your notebook.

> "You are what you are because that is what you really want to be! We make decisions and those decisions make us who we are! You can judge anything in the world by this. God builds up and the Devil tears down."

> "Champions are a rare breed. They see beyond the dangers, the risks, the obstacles, and the hardships."

Activity 33:

Write these verses from your lessons in your notebook in cursive. Try this on your own without looking at how any letters are formed.

Isaiah 40:31; Galatians 6:9; Psalm 118:29; Psalm 118:14; Isaiah 43:19

Activity 34:

Read this passage aloud to your teacher, then copy it in your notebook.

I pledge allegiance to the Flag of the United States of America, and to the Republic for which it stands, one Nation under God, indivisible, with liberty and justice for all.

Activity 35:

Write the title to your favorite book in cursive in your notebook.

Activity 36:

Write your full name in your notebook in cursive.

---

[1] Henry M. Morris and Henry M. Morris, *Many Infallible Proofs: Evidences for the Christian Faith* (Green Forest, AR: Master Books, 2002).

[2] Morris, Henry M. *The Revelation Record: A Scientific and Devotional Commentary on the Book of Revelation.* Wheaton, IL: Tyndale House Publishers, 1983.

[3] Morris, Henry M. *The Genesis Record: A Scientific and Devotional Commentary on the Book of Beginnings.* Grand Rapids, MI: Baker Book House, 2009.

Activity 37:
Copy a paragraph from something you are reading. Be sure to use good cursive penmanship and write it in your notebook.

Activity 38:
Read the following aloud to your teacher:

"Congress shall make no law respecting an establishment of religion, or prohibiting the free exercise thereof; or abridging the freedom of speech, or of the press, or the right of the people peaceably to assemble, and to petition the Government for a redress of grievances."
—The 1st Amendment of the Bill of Rights.

Activity 39:
Write the First Amendment to the Bill of Rights in your notebook in cursive.

Activity 40:
Write the title of your favorite movie or favorite subject in school in cursive in your notebook.

Activity 41:
Write a paragraph (topic sentence + two detail sentences + concluding sentence) in cursive in your notebook to complete this sentence starter:

*Note — your paragraph may be humorous and fiction (made up).

In the days when buffalos roamed the prairies...

Activity 42:
Look around the room and write 10 nouns you can see from where you are in cursive in your notebook.

Activity 43:
Write the 10 Commandments in cursive in your notebook (see Exodus 20).

Activity 44:
Write Proverbs 3:1–4 in cursive in your notebook.

Activity 45:
Write Proverbs 3:5–8 in cursive in your notebook.

Activity 46:
Write Proverbs 3:9–12 in cursive in your notebook.

Activity 47:
Write Proverbs 3:13–18 in cursive in your notebook.

Activity 48:
Write Proverbs 3:19–23 in cursive in your notebook.

Activity 49:
Write Proverbs 3:24–27 in cursive in your notebook.

Activity 50:
Write Proverbs 3:28–32 in cursive in your notebook.

Activity 51:
Write Proverbs 3:33–35 in cursive in your notebook.

Activity 52:
Read your writing of Proverbs three aloud to your teacher (see activities 44–51).

Activity 53:
Write the Beatitudes in cursive in your notebook. (see Matthew 5:3–11).

Activity 54:
Write a paragraph about your favorite place to visit.

Activity 55:
If you were stranded on a deserted island, what five items would you want to bring along? Write your answer in complete sentences in cursive in your notebook.

Activity 56:
Copy these verses in cursive in your notebook:

> Galatians 5:13–17
>
> Galatians 5:22–26

Activity 57:
Write a paragraph you read today in cursive in your notebook.

Activity 58:
Write five adjectives in cursive (description words) to describe something in the room with you. Write them in your notebook.

Activity 59:
Write a description of yourself in cursive in your notebook.

Activity 60:
Read this to your teacher.

> Galatians 6:7–10

"Do not be deceived: God cannot be mocked. A man reaps what he sows. Whoever sows to please their flesh, from the flesh will reap destruction; whoever sows to please the Spirit, from the Spirit will reap eternal life. Let us not become weary in doing good, for at the proper time we will reap a harvest if we do not give up. Therefore, as we have opportunity, let us do good to all people, especially to those who belong to the family of believers."

Activity 61:
Copy this quote by Lester Sumrall in cursive in your notebook.

> "I know success or failure in my life or ministry does not depend on my own skill or even on external circumstances, it depends only on my faithfulness. God will give me the gifts necessary to do whatever He calls me to do, and He will not be hindered in His work by circumstances."

Activity 62:
Use this sentence starter to write a paragraph in cursive in your notebook.

> "I don't think we should go in there…"

Activity 63:
Copy five verses from your Bible in cursive in your notebook.

Activity 64:
Read this aloud to your parents, then copy it into your notebook.

Psalm 23:

The Lord is my shepherd; I shall not want. He makes me lie down in green pastures. He leads me beside still waters. He restores my soul. He leads me in paths of righteousness for his name's sake. Even though I walk through the valley of the shadow of death, I will fear no evil, for you are with me; your rod and your staff, they comfort me. You prepare a table before me in the presence of my enemies; you anoint my head with oil; my cup overflows. Surely goodness and mercy shall follow me all the days of my life, and I shall dwell in the house of the Lord forever.

Activity 65:
Copy a paragraph from one of your subjects, such as history, in cursive into your notebook.

Activity 66:
Use this story starter to complete the story in cursive in your notebook.

> WHAM! The loud sound startled me from my sleep as I searched the room to see what had happened. Then, I saw…

Activities 67–69:
Use these three days to copy seven verses in cursive from Obadiah into your notebooks. Obadiah is 1 chapter long with 21 verses, so you will have copied the entire book of Obadiah.

Activity 70:
Copy 1 Corinthians 13 in your notebook in cursive.

Activity 71:
Copy Hebrews 11:1 and 13:5 in cursive in your notebook.

Activity 72:
Copy Psalm 139:13–14 and Proverbs 15:1 in cursive in your notebook.

Activity 73:
Copy Matthew 5:23–24 and Jeremiah 31:3 in cursive your notebook.

Activity 74:
Copy Deuteronomy 6:5–9 and Deuteronomy 4:9–10 in cursive in your notebook.

Activity 75:
Use this story starter to complete the story in cursive in your notebook.

> The rain had been pouring down for days. The river was flowing swiftly and appeared to be rising every second. Suddenly, I see ….

Activities for Older Students

Activity 76:
Copy 1 Timothy 4:10–11 in cursive in your notebook.

Activity 77:
Pretend you are making a Get Well Soon card. Write what the inscription would be in your notebook. Include more than "Get Well Soon."

Activity 78:
Write your family members' names in cursive in your notebook.

Activity 79:
If you were to be challenged to eat the most disgusting sandwich in the world, what would be on your sandwich? Write your response in your notebook in cursive.

Activity 80:
Tall Tales are known for their embellishment and not quite believable. Write your own Tall Tale in cursive in your notebook.

Activity 81:
Write a poem about creation in your notebook. Remember, not all poems rhyme. Make it at least three lines.

Activity 82:
Play the "What if game" with a friend or family member. How to play: Make up what if statements such as "What if cows gave soda instead of milk?" or "What if pigs really could fly?" Make up five "What if" statements and write them in cursive in your notebook, then, write the answers from your friend/family member.

Activity 83:
Write 10 adjectives (description words) and five verbs in cursive in your notebook.

Activity 84:
Use the adjectives and verbs from Activity 83 to make a story.

Activity 85:
In your notebook write 6 nouns and 6 adjectives to describe those nouns in cursive. Then, write four verbs in cursive in your notebook.

Activity 86:
Use the nouns, adjectives, and verbs from Activity 85 to write a story.

Activity 87:
Create your own character (for a book or game) and describe him/her in cursive in your notebook.

Activity 88:
If you needed to survive on a deserted island, what would you want to have with you? Why? Write in your notebook in complete sentences to explain. Be sure to write in cursive.

Activity 89:

Read this aloud to your teacher, then copy it in your notebook.

Proverbs 4:1–9

"Hear, O sons, a father's instruction, and be attentive, that you may gain insight, for I give you good precepts; do not forsake my teaching. When I was a son with my father, tender, the only one in the sight of my mother, he taught me and said to me, 'Let your heart hold fast my words; keep my commandments, and live. Get wisdom; get insight; do not forget, and do not turn away from the words of my mouth. Do not forsake her, and she will keep you; love her, and she will guard you. The beginning of wisdom is this: Get wisdom, and whatever you get, get insight. Prize her highly, and she will exalt you; she will honor you if you embrace her. She will place on your head a graceful garland; she will bestow on you a beautiful crown.'"

Activity 90:

After following their map, the pirate and his crew came ashore. His crew dug for hours but only found an old shoe. What could have happened? Write your response in cursive in your notebook.

Activity 91:

Hours after arriving at the airport, Sam was still waiting to board his plane. The flight crew was preparing to board the passengers, but then his flight was cancelled. What could have happened? Write your response in cursive in your notebook.

Activity 92:

Write five facts about your favorite animal in cursive in your notebook.

Activity 93:

Describe your house with as many details as possible. Write the description in cursive in your notebook. Have your teacher read your description and see if they agree with your description.

Activity 94:

Find 6 different food products in your kitchen (fridge, pantry, etc.) and write the name of the product or brand/logo in cursive in your notebook.

Activity 95:

Write 10 color words in cursive in your notebook.

Activity 96:
List 10 things you can't imagine living without. Be sure to write in cursive in your notebook.

Activity 97:
What do you think the world needs the most? Write your response in cursive using complete sentences in your notebook.

Activity 98:
If you could invent anything to help others, what would you invent? Why? Write your response in cursive using complete sentences in your notebook.

Activity 99:
Read this passage aloud to your teacher, then copy it into your notebook.

Proverbs 4:10–15

Hear, my son, and accept my words, that the years of your life may be many. I have taught you the way of wisdom; I have led you in the paths of uprightness. When you walk, your step will not be hampered, and if you run, you will not stumble. Keep hold of instruction; do not let go; guard her, for she is your life. Do not enter the path of the wicked, and do not walk in the way of the evil. Avoid it; do not go on it; turn away from it and pass on.

Activity 100:
If you could live anywhere in the world, where would you live? Why? Write your response in cursive in complete sentences in your notebook.

Activity 101:
Read Genesis 1 and list the days of Creation with what was created for each day. Be sure to write in cursive in your notebook.

Activity 102:
If you had an invisible helper, what would you have him/her do? Why? Write your response in cursive in complete sentences in your notebook.

Activity 103:
Make a list comparing two animals. List everything you can think of that describes or gives information about the animal. An example would be how a dog wags its tail when it is happy or excited or toads have poison glands behind their eyes. Write the lists in cursive in your notebook.

Activity 104:
What is your favorite season or holiday? Why? Write your response in cursive in complete sentences in your notebook.

Activity 105:

Write the similes for these in cursive in your notebook. Be sure to write the beginning section given here as well as your ending.

Example: Ice cream is as <u>cold as a snowball.</u>

Her smile is as _____.

He runs as fast as _____.

She was as busy as _____.

Her eyes sparkle like _____.

That tire is as flat as _____.

This biscuit is as hard as _____.

Activity 106:

Write down six facts you have learned about fish or fishing from this course. Be sure to put this in your notebook in cursive.

Activity 107:

Personification gives human action or feelings to non-human things. Here are two examples:

The sky is angry and throwing lightning.

The aroma of the freshly baked apple pie was calling my name.

Write a sentence for each of the following adding personification. Write these in cursive in your notebook.

Car, moon, leaves, cat, stars, boat

Activity 108:

What is your favorite hobby or sport? Explain how you play or do it in complete sentences. Remember, your response should be in cursive in your notebook.

Activity 109:

Alliteration repeats the same sound at the beginning of each word. Here is an example:

Silly Sally sold seashells at the seashore. Notice the 'S' is at the beginning of each word. This is usually used in poetry. Pick any letter of the alphabet to write a silly sentence using alliteration. Remember, this assignment should be in cursive in your notebook.

Activity 110:

In these verses you will find some valuable advice the Apostle Paul gave to Timothy. Copy these verses in cursive in your notebook. I suggest you memorize these verses as they will be valuable to you also.

2 Timothy 1:14; 2:3; 2:23; 3:1–5; 4:5

Intentionally left blank.

CATCH ON TO CURSIVE
FISHING Derby
SHOWCASING MY BEST CATCH
BAIT & TACKLE 3

Name

Date

I can write the word ad in cursive.

I can trace wavy lines.

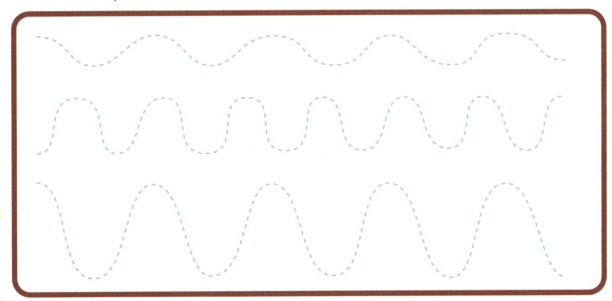

I can complete a maze.

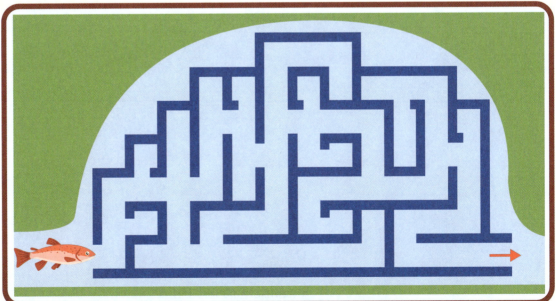

Fishing Derby Bait & Tackle 3 463

Intentionally left blank.

CATCH ON TO CURSIVE
FISHING Derby
SHOWCASING MY BEST CATCH
BAIT & TACKLE 5

Name

Date

I can write the word dog in cursive.

I can trace curved and looped lines.

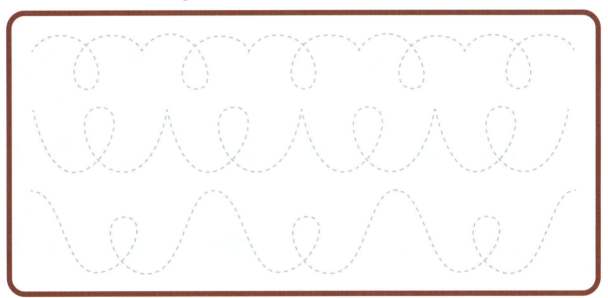

I can complete the dot-to-dot.

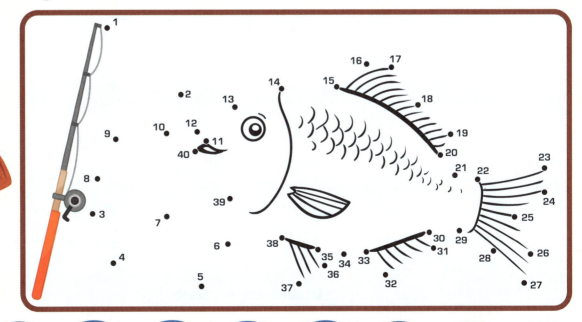

Fishing Derby Bait & Tackle 5   465

Intentionally left blank.

CATCH ON TO CURSIVE
FISHING DERBY
SHOWCASING MY BEST CATCH
BAIT & TACKLE 7

Name

Date

I can write the word coda and doc in cursive.

I can write the letters C, A, O, d, o, g, a, and q in cursive.

I can paint the fish with cotton swabs and chalk.

Intentionally left blank.

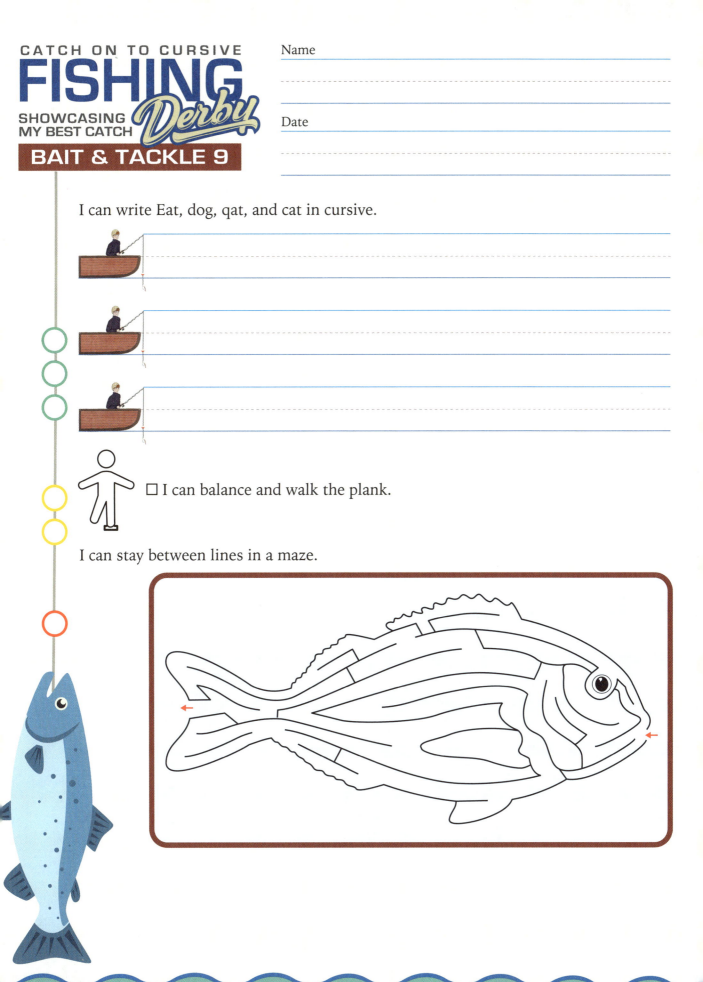

Intentionally left blank.

Intentionally left blank.

CATCH ON TO CURSIVE
FISHING DERBY
SHOWCASING MY BEST CATCH
BAIT & TACKLE 13

Name

Date

I can write the words Quit, pods, wags, jots, Eats, peace, and squats in cursive.

I can sting like a sting ray and poke the fish with pushpins to build my strength.

Intentionally left blank.

CATCH ON TO CURSIVE
FISHING DERBY
SHOWCASING MY BEST CATCH
BAIT & TACKLE 15

Name

Date

I can write the words Equips, just, leak, quiet, pigs, pages, dodges, jars, was, and stoop in cursive.

I can complete 1 John 4:19 (NIV).

We love because he first loved us.
1 John 4:19

Intentionally left blank.

CATCH ON TO CURSIVE
FISHING DERBY
SHOWCASING MY BEST CATCH
BAIT & TACKLE 17

Name

Date

I can write the words face, skip, write, wrote, logs, slows, facets, walls, walker, slower.

I can complete Philippians 4:13 (BSB).

I can do all things through Christ who gives me strength.

Philippians 4:13

Fishing Derby Bait & Tackle 17 477

Intentionally left blank.

CATCH ON TO CURSIVE
FISHING DERBY
SHOWCASING MY BEST CATCH
BAIT & TACKLE 19

Name

Date

I can write the words flow, ham, work, saw, trace, blog.

I can complete Proverbs 4:23 (NIV).

Above all else, guard your heart, for everything you do flows from it.

Proverbs 4:23

Intentionally left blank.

CATCH ON TO CURSIVE
FISHING Derby
SHOWCASING MY BEST CATCH
BAIT & TACKLE 21

Name

Date

I can write the words quality, backs, blank, banker, helper.

I can write the Scripture in cursive:

like newborn infants, long for the pure spiritual milk, that by it you may grow up into salvation.

1 Peter 2:2

Intentionally left blank.

CATCH ON TO CURSIVE
FISHING Derby
SHOWCASING MY BEST CATCH

BAIT & TACKLE 23

Name

Date

I can write the words Basil, balm, cashew, pecan, fish, flute, sky, cloud, water.

I can write the Scripture in cursive:

In the beginning, God created the heavens and the earth.

Genesis 1:1

Intentionally left blank.

CATCH ON TO CURSIVE
FISHING Derby
SHOWCASING MY BEST CATCH
BAIT & TACKLE 25

Name

Date

I can write the following quote in cursive from *Marvels of Creation: Sensational Sea Creatures* (page 19):

The coelacanth is the only living animal that can lift and move the front part of its head when feeding.

I can copy and write this Scripture in cursive:

Again, the kingdom of heaven is like a net that was thrown into the sea and gathered fish of every kind. Matthew 13:47

CATCH ON TO CURSIVE
FISHING DERBY
SHOWCASING MY BEST CATCH
BAIT & TACKLE 27

Name

Date

I can write the following quote in cursive from *Marvels of Creation: Sensational Sea Creatures* (page 21):

Cowfish have two spines in front that look like horns.

I can complete the Scripture in cursive:

"Behold, I am sending for many fishers, declares the Lord, and they shall catch them. And afterward I will send for many hunters, and they shall hunt them from every mountain and every hill, and out of the clefts of the rocks."
Jeremiah 16:16

CATCH ON TO CURSIVE
FISHING DERBY
SHOWCASING MY BEST CATCH
BAIT & TACKLE 29

Name

Date

I can write the following quote in cursive from *Marvels of Creation: Sensational Sea Creatures* (page 63):

The sturgeon is well-known as a supplier of caviar.

I can write the Scripture in cursive:

"When they got out on land, they saw a charcoal fire in place, with fish laid out on it and bread." John 21:9

Intentionally left blank.

CATCH ON TO CURSIVE
FISHING DERBY
SHOWCASING MY BEST CATCH
BAIT & TACKLE 31

Name

Date

I can write the following quote in cursive from *Marvels of Creation: Sensational Sea Creatures* (page 69):

The snapper is named because of its many teeth and large jaws which snap open and shut when the fish is caught and pulled on land.

I can copy and write this Scripture in cursive:

"And he said to them,
"Follow me, and I
will make you fishers
of men.""
Matthew 4:19

CATCH ON TO CURSIVE

FISHING DERBY

SHOWCASING MY BEST CATCH

BAIT & TACKLE 33

Name

Date

I can write the following quote in cursive from *Marvels of Creation: Sensational Sea Creatures* (page 73):

The great variety of sea life clearly shows the creative genius of God.

I can write the Scripture in cursive:

"He said to them, "Cast the net on the right side of the boat, and you will find some." So they cast it and now they were not able to haul it in, because of the quantity of fish." John 21:6

CATCH ON TO CURSIVE
FISHING DERBY
SHOWCASING MY BEST CATCH
BAIT & TACKLE 35

Name

Date

I can write the following quote in cursive from *Marvels of Creation: Sensational Sea Creatures* (page 74):

The fossil record is clear. The first time you find a fish in the fossil record, it is 100 percent fish.

I can copy and write this Scripture in cursive:

"All things were made through him, and without him was not any thing made that was made."
John 1:3

Live Well Badge:
You can earn the live well badge by completing the challenge of 2 extra days of live well reaches.

Challenge Issued
Bait & Tackle 3.1

Challenge Earned
Bait & Tackle 3.4

Balance Badge
You can earn the balance badge by completing the challenge of doing the Don't Tip the Boat exercise.

Challenge Issued
Tackle Box 6

Challenge Earned
Bait & Tackle 6.3

Guide Badge
You can earn the guide badge by completing the challenge of placing your letters on the line correctly.

Challenge Issued
Bait & Tackle 7.1

Challenge Earned
Bait & Tackle 7.4

Capital Letter Badge
Complete the challenge of using a capital letter at the beginning of sentences.

Challenge Issued
Bait & Tackle 9.1

Challenge Earned
Bait & Tackle 9.4

Right Conditions Badge
Complete the challenge of doing the Right Conditions exercise to learn the correct pressure as you write.

Challenge Issued
Tackle Box 10

Challenge Earned
Bait & Tackle 10.3

Whirlpool Badge
Earn the whirlpool badge by completing the challenge of doing the Marble in the Whirlpool exercise.

Challenge Issued
Bait & Tackle 10.3

Challenge Earned
Bait & Tackle 11.1

Worm Badge
You can earn the worm badge by completing the challenge of doing the Worm Squeezes exercise.

Challenge Issued
Bait & Tackle 11.1

Challenge Earned
Bait & Tackle 11.4

Artist Badge
You can earn the artist badge by completing the challenge of making artwork.

Challenge Issued
Tackle Box 12

Challenge Earned
Bait & Tackle 12.3

Bridge Badge
You can earn the bridge badge by holding bridges for 15 seconds 3 times each.

Challenge Issued
Bait & Tackle 12.3

Challenge Earned
Bait & Tackle 13.1

Intentionally left blank.

Bullseye Badge
You can earn the bullseye badge by hitting the bullseye during Aim & Cast exercises.

Challenge Issued
Bait & Tackle 13.1

Challenge Earned
Bait & Tackle 13.4

Cursive Word Badge
You can earn the cursive word badge by making words from the letters you have learned.

Challenge Issued
Tackle Box 14.3

Challenge Earned
Bait & Tackle 15.1

Dot-to-Dot Badge
You can earn the dot-to-dot badge by completing three dot-to-dots.

Challenge Issued
Bait & Tackle 15.1

Challenge Earned
Bait & Tackle 15.4

Eye Tracking Badge
You can earn the eye tracking badge by completing the tracking practice in the back of the book.

Challenge Issued
Tackle Box 16

Challenge Earned
Bait & Tackle 16.3

Hook Badge
You can earn the hook badge by hooking crawdads.

Challenge Issued
Bait & Tackle 16.3

Challenge Earned
Bait & Tackle 17.1

Paddle Badge
You can earn the paddle badge by completing the Paddle the Boat challenge.

Challenge Issued
Bait & Tackle 17.1

Challenge Earned
Bait & Tackle 17.4

Maze Badge
You can earn the maze badge by completing three mazes from the A-MAZE-ing Mazes section.

Challenge Issued
Tackle Box 18

Challenge Earned
Bait & Tackle 18.3

Sail Badge
You can earn the sail badge by completing the Hoist the Sails activity challenge.

Challenge Issued
Bait & Tackle 18.3

Challenge Earned
Bait & Tackle 19.1

Anchor Badge
You can earn the anchor badge by completing the Anchor Up activity challenge.

Challenge Issued
Tackle Box 20

Challenge Earned
Bait & Tackle 20.3

Intentionally left blank.

Crawdad Badge
You can earn the crawdad badge by completing the crawdad crawl activity challenge.

Challenge Issued
Bait & Tackle 20.3

Challenge Earned
Bait & Tackle 21.1

Under & Over Badge
Complete the under and over activity from the weigh-in section in the back of the book.

Challenge Issued
Tackle Box 22

Challenge Earned
Bait & Tackle 22.3

Pressure Test Badge
You can earn the pressure test badge by completing a pressure test with dough or clay.

Challenge Issued
Bait & Tackle 22.3

Challenge Earned
Bait & Tackle 23.1

Hole Punch Badge
You can earn the hand warm up badge by punching 10 holes a day with a hole punch before writing.

Challenge Issued
Bait & Tackle 23.1

Challenge Earned
Bait & Tackle 23.4

Fish Badge
You can earn the fish badge by coloring fish in each day to show pencil control.

Challenge Issued
Bait & Tackle 24.3

Challenge Earned
Bait & Tackle 25.1

Shell Badge
You can earn the shell badge by playing Changing Shells each day.

Challenge Issued
Bait & Tackle 25.1

Challenge Earned
Bait & Tackle 25.4

Weight Badge
You can earn the weight badge by making 5 weights per hand each day using foil.

Challenge Issued
Tackle Box 26

Challenge Earned
Bait & Tackle 26.3

Fly Lure Badge
You can earn the fly lure badge by threading a needle 5 times with each hand per day.

Challenge Issued
Bait & Tackle 26.3

Challenge Earned
Bait & Tackle 27.1

Shoulder Badge
You can earn the shoulder badge by completing the shoulder workout challenges for writing warm-ups.

Challenge Issued
Tackle Box 28

Challenge Earned
Bait & Tackle 28.3

Intentionally left blank.

Gator Badge
You can earn the gator badge by completing the Gator Chomp challenge.

Challenge Issued
Bait & Tackle 28.3

Challenge Earned
Bait & Tackle 29.1

Scissors Badge
Complete by cutting buckets and worms from the weigh-in section in the back of the book.

Challenge Issued
Tackle Box 30.3

Challenge Earned
Bait & Tackle 31.1

Lemon Badge
You can earn the lemon badge by squeezing a ball like squeezing a lemon.

Challenge Issued
Bait & Tackle 31.1

Challenge Earned
Bait & Tackle 31.4

Fishing Vest Badge
You can earn the fishing vest badge by buttoning, zipping, and fastening items.

Challenge Issued
Tackle Box 32

Challenge Earned
Bait & Tackle 32.3

Fork & Knife Badge
You can earn the fork & knife badge by cutting up Play-Doh.

Challenge Issued
Bait & Tackle 32.3

Challenge Earned
Bait & Tackle 33.1

Trot Line Badge
You can earn the trot line badge by making threading floats (straws) on a line.

Challenge Issued
Bait & Tackle 33.1

Challenge Earned
Bait & Tackle 33.4

Inch Worm Badge
You can earn the inchworm badge by inching your way to the top of the pencil.

Challenge Issued
Bait & Tackle 34.3

Challenge Earned
Bait & Tackle 35.1

Seek & Find Badge
You can earn the seek & find badge by completing the special activities at the back of the book.

Challenge Issued
Bait & Tackle 35.1

Challenge Earned
Bait & Tackle 35.4

Weigh-in Badge
Complete the checklist items as you complete your copy work.

Challenge Issued
Tackle Box 36

Challenge Earned
Bait & Tackle 36.5

Intentionally left blank.

Gather Your Gear: Complete Supply List

This is a supply list for the entire course. Several activities will repeat in the course to help build up strength and stamina over time. We have included how much of the supplies you will need for the entire course as well.

All Bait and Tackles:

- ☐ 1 foot of yarn or 1 chenille wire
- ☐ 1 paper plate (any size)
- ☐ 1 plastic straw (cut into 1 in. pieces)
- ☐ 2 plastic cups
- ☐ 2 strips of tape (any kind)
- ☐ 6 2-inch x 2-inch foil squares
- ☐ Approx. 2 ft. of yarn
- ☐ Ball (tennis or approx. size)
- ☐ Belt
- ☐ Bible
- ☐ Bicycle/scooter/skateboard items to help you balance
- ☐ Button-up shirt
- ☐ Cotton swabs (1 box for the whole course)
- ☐ Cutting board, cork board, or foam sheet (re-used throughout, but they will need 10 sheets of craft foam for the course)
- ☐ Hole punch, preferably single hole
- ☐ Jacket with zipper
- ☐ 1 marble
- ☐ Needle and thread (one needle and an 8–10-inch piece of thread for course)
- ☐ Paper (any kind or color, 1 sheet)
- ☐ Paper clips (approximately 10 to re-use for the course)
- ☐ Pencil
- ☐ Pencil (new, unsharpened; 1 per student for course)
- ☐ Pencil with eraser or pencil with pushpin in the eraser
- ☐ 1 plastic fork
- ☐ 1 plastic knife
- ☐ 1 plastic lid with a lip or a round cake pan
- ☐ Play-Doh or a squishy ball/stress ball
- ☐ Play-Doh or other dough (1 tub of Play-Doh for course)
- ☐ Pushpins (thumb tacks — they can re-use them. You will need 20 per student for the course.)
- ☐ Ribbon (approximately .5" or 1" wide, 18 in. long; 1 for course)
- ☐ 1 roll or 60 yards of painter's tape or 6-ft long piece of rope, or 1 stick of sidewalk chalk, or 2x4
- ☐ 1 rubber band (optional)
- ☐ Sheet of foam
- ☐ Sheet of plain paper
- ☐ Sidewalk chalk (4 or more colors for the whole course)
- ☐ Small objects such as beads, small buttons, or sunflower seeds (These will be re-used and you will need approximately 10 items.)
- ☐ Sticky notes or paper (If using sticky notes, you will need 20 for the course. If using paper, one piece of paper.)
- ☐ Toothpicks (45 toothpicks for course)
- ☐ Tweezers
- ☐ Wave wand from Bait and Tackle 1.1
- ☐ Yarn cut into 4 in. strips (approximately 64 inches of yarn per student for course [2 feet for week 33])

Gather Your Gear Weekly List:

This is a supply list for the entire course. Several activities will repeat in the course to help build up strength and stamina over time. We have included how much of the supplies you will need for the entire course as well.

All Bait and Tackles:
☐ Bible
☐ Pencil

Bait and Tackle 1:
Day 2:
☐ Pencil (new, unsharpened; 1 per student for course)
☐ Ribbon (approximately .5" or 1" wide, 18 in. long; 1 for course)

Day 5:
☐ Tweezers
☐ Yarn cut into 4 in. strips (approximately 64 inches of yarn per student for course [2 feet for week 33])

Bait and Tackle 2:
Day 1:
☐ Pushpins (thumb tacks — they can re-use them. You will need 20 per student for the course.)
☐ One of the following: cutting board, cork board, or foam sheet (re-used throughout, but they will need 10 sheets of craft foam for the course)

Bait and Tackle 3:
Day 3:
☐ Cotton swabs (1 box for the whole course)
☐ Sidewalk chalk (4 or more colors for the whole course)

Bait and Tackle 4:
Day 2:
☐ Paper clips (approximately 10 to re-use for the course)

Day 4:
☐ Pushpins
☐ One of the following: cutting board, cork board, or foam sheet

Day 5:
☐ Sticky notes or paper (If using sticky notes, you will need 20 for the course. If using paper, one piece of paper.)
☐ Ball (tennis or approx. size)

Bait and Tackle 5:
Day 1:
☐ Small objects such as beads, small buttons, or sunflower seeds (these will be re-used and you will need approximately 10 items.)
☐ Play-Doh or other dough (1 tub of Play-Doh for course)

Day 2:
☐ 1 roll or 60 yards of painter's tape or 6-ft long piece of rope, or 1 stick of sidewalk chalk, or 2x4

Day 3:
☐ Pushpins
☐ One of the following: cutting board, cork board, or foam sheet

Day 5:
☐ Wave wand from Bait and Tackle 1.1

Bait and Tackle 6:
Day 2:
☐ Tweezers and yarn from lesson 1

Day 3:
☐ Pushpins
☐ One of the following: cutting board, cork board, or foam sheet

Bait and Tackle 7:
Day 2:
☐ Cotton swabs
☐ Sidewalk chalk

Bait and Tackle 8:
Day 1:
☐ Pencil with eraser or pencil with pushpin in the eraser

Day 3:
☐ Paper clips

Day 4:
☐ Sticky notes or paper
☐ Ball (tennis or approx. size)

Day 5:
☐ Small objects such as beads, small buttons, or sunflower seeds
☐ Play-Doh or other dough

Bait and Tackle 9:

Day 1:
☐ Painter's tape or rope or sidewalk chalk (or 2x4)

Day 3:
☐ Bicycle/scooter/skateboard items to help you balance

Day 4:
☐ Sheet of foam
☐ Sheet of plain paper

Day 5:
☐ Plastic lid with a lip or a round cake pan (1 for course)
☐ Marble (1 for course)

Bait and Tackle 10:

Day 2:
☐ Wave wand from previous lessons

Day 4:
☐ Tweezers and yarn worms from previous lessons

Bait and Tackle 11:

Day 4:
☐ Cotton swabs and sidewalk chalk

Bait and Tackle 12:

Day 3:
☐ Paper clips

Day 5:
☐ Pushpins
☐ One of the following: cutting board, cork board, or foam sheet

Bait and Tackle 13:

Day 1:
☐ Sticky notes or paper
☐ Ball (tennis or approx. size)

Day 2:
☐ Small objects such as beads, small buttons, or sunflower seeds
☐ Play-Doh or other dough

Day 3:
☐ Painter's tape or rope or sidewalk chalk

Bait and Tackle 14:

Day 1:
☐ Wave wand from previous lessons

Day 3:
☐ Tweezers and yarn worms from previous lessons

Bait and Tackle 15:

Day 2:
☐ Cotton swabs and sidewalk chalk

Bait and Tackle 16:

Day 1:
☐ Pencil with eraser or pencil with pushpin in the eraser

Day 3:
☐ Paper clips

Day 4:
☐ Sticky notes or paper
☐ Ball (tennis or approx. size)

Bait and Tackle 17:

Day 1:
☐ Painter's tape or rope or sidewalk chalk

Day 2:
☐ Sheet of foam
☐ Sheet of plain paper

Day 5:
☐ Plastic lid with a lip or a round cake pan
☐ Marble

Bait and Tackle 18:

Day 2:
☐ Wave wands from previous lesson

Bait and Tackle 19:

Day 1:
☐ Cotton swabs and sidewalk chalk

Day 3:
☐ Pencil with eraser or pencil with pushpin in the eraser

Day 4:
☐ Tweezers and yarn worms from previous lessons

Bait and Tackle 21:

Day 1:
☐ Paper clips

Day 2:
☐ Sticky notes or paper
☐ Ball (tennis or approx. size)

Day 3:
☐ Pushpins (thumb tacks)
☐ One of the following: cutting board, cork board, or foam sheet

Bait and Tackle 22:

Day 1:
☐ Sheet of foam
☐ Sheet of plain paper

Day 2:
☐ Painter's tape or rope or sidewalk chalk

Day 3:
☐ Plastic lid with a lip or a round cake pan
☐ Marble

Day 4:
☐ Tennis ball or ball that size

Bait and Tackle 23:

Day 1:
☐ Hole punch, preferably single hole

Day 2:
☐ Wave wands from previous lesson

Day 4:
☐ Small objects such as beads, small buttons, or sunflower seeds
☐ Play-Doh or other dough

Bait and Tackle 24:

Day 1:
☐ Pencil with eraser or pencil with pushpin in the eraser

Day 4:
☐ Sheet of foam
☐ Sheet of plain paper

Day 5:
☐ Sticky notes or paper
☐ Ball (tennis or approx. size)

Bait and Tackle 25:

Day 1:
☐ Marble
☐ 2 plastic cups (2 for whole course)

Day 4:
☐ 6 2-inch x 2-inch foil squares

Bait and Tackle 26:

Day 1:
☐ Plastic lid with a lip or a round cake pan
☐ Marble

Day 3:
☐ Needle and thread (one needle and an 8–10-inch piece of thread for course)

Bait and Tackle 27:

Day 1:
☐ Tennis ball or ball that size

Day 5:
☐ Paper clips

Bait and Tackle 28:

Day 2:
☐ Tennis ball of ball that size

Day 3:
☐ Marble
☐ 2 plastic cups

Day 4:
☐ 6 2-inch x 2-inch foil squares

Day 5:
☐ Painter's tape or rope or sidewalk chalk

Bait and Tackle 29:

Day 1:
☐ Toothpicks (45 toothpicks for course)
☐ Play-Doh

Day 2:
☐ Tweezers and yarn worms from previous lessons

Bait and Tackle 30:

Day 1:
☐ Cotton swabs and sidewalk chalk

Day 3:
☐ Marble
☐ 2 plastic cups

Day 5:
☐ Pencil with eraser or pencil with pushpin in the eraser

Bait and Tackle 31:

Day 1:
☐ Hole punch
☐ Play-Doh or a squishy ball/stress ball

Day 2:
☐ Paper clips

Day 3:
☐ Sticky notes or paper
☐ Ball (tennis or approx. size)

Day 4:
☐ 6 2-inch x 2-inch foil squares

Bait and Tackle 32:

☐ Button-up shirt
☐ Jacket with zipper
☐ Belt

Day 1:
☐ Sheet of foam
☐ Sheet of plain paper

Day 2:
☐ Ball (tennis or approx. size)

Day 3:
☐ Plastic knife (1 for course)
☐ Plastic fork (1 for course)
☐ Play-Doh

Day4:
☐ Plastic lid with a lip or a round cake pan
☐ Marble

Bait and Tackle 33:

Day 1:
☐ 1 plastic straw (cut into 1 in. pieccess)
☐ 1 foot of yarn or 1 chenille wire

Day 2:
☐ Hole punch

Optional:
☐ 1 paper plate (any size)
☐ Approx. 2 ft. of yarn
☐ 2 strips of tape (any kind)

Day 4:
☐ 6 2-inch x 2-inch foil squares

Bait and Tackle 34:

Day 1:
☐ Play-Doh

Day 2:
☐ Marble
☐ 2 plastic cups

Day 3:
☐ Optional: 1 rubber band

Day 4:
☐ Ball (tennis or approx. size)

Bait and Tackle 35:

Day 2:
☐ Hole punch
☐ Paper (any kind or color, 1 sheet)

Day 3:
☐ 6 2-inch x 2-inch foil squares

Day 5:
☐ Small objects such as beads, small buttons, or sunflower seeds
☐ Play-Doh or other dough

Bait and Tackle 36:

Day 1:
☐ Painter's tape or rope or sidewalk chalk

Day 2:
☐ Sticky notes or paper
☐ Ball (tennis or approx. size)

Day 4:
☐ Paper clips (all the ones from the course)

Day 5:
☐ Ball (tennis or approx. size)

Intentionally left blank.

Dot-to-Dot Challenge from Bait & Tackle 15.1

Connect the dots and color in one picture a day. There are three total, one for each day of the challenge!

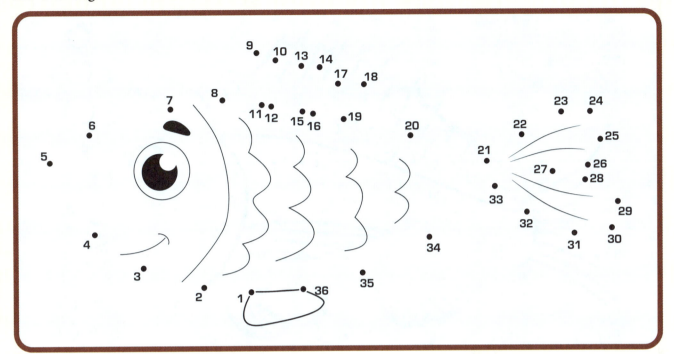

Dot-to-Dot Challenge 511

Tracking Practice Challenge from Tackle Box 16

Track and loop the letters to spell the word. There are three total, one for each day of the challenge!

Find the word TROUT.

L S K T G E R P J N O B W U Z H B T S J
K T F H W R S I E A H J O S U P O T E W
D F T G T I K L W R S O Z N U J T W F H
E W Q Z X T N H R I O R U C L T K H G E
P J T S B I Q Z R O K S U K T H G E P J

Find the word SALMON.

L S T A E R P L N O B M U O H N T W M
K T S A P R L I E A M J O S U N O T E W
D F T G S I K A J L S O Z M U J O N F H
E S Q Z A T N L R I M R U O L N K H J E
P J T S S I Q A R O L S B M O H G N I J

Tracking Practice Challenge 513

Find the word TURTLE.

L S T A E W U L R O B M T O L N E W M
K T S T P R U I E R C T O S L N O T E W
D F T G U I K R J L T O L M U E O N F H
E S Q Z A T N U E I M R U T L N K H J E
P T Q S U I Q A R O T S B L O H E N I J

A-MAZE-ing Mazes Challenge from Tackle Box 18

Complete one maze a day. There are three total, one for each day of the challenge!

Help the fish find the worm.

Help the fish make it through the maze.

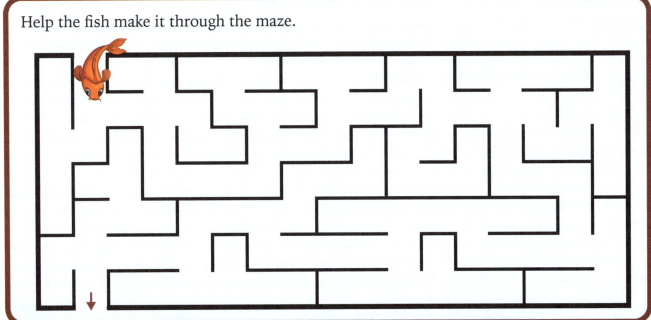

A-MAZE-ing Mazes Challenge 515

Circle the fisherman that catches the fish.

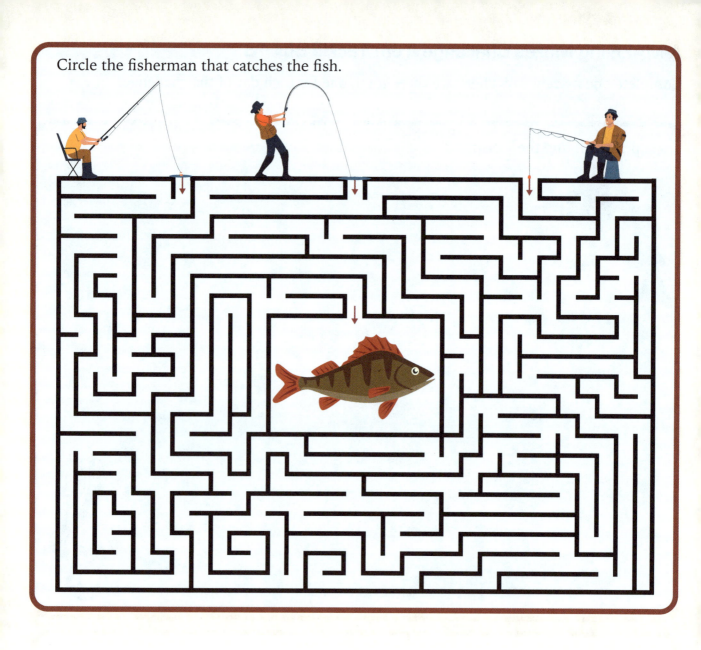

Under & Over Challenge from Tackle Box 22

Help the fish swim over the obstacles. On the top row, begin by going under the first obstacle and back up between the next obstacles. You want to try to stay in the middle of the two obstacles you are going under and over. Complete one set each day for three days.

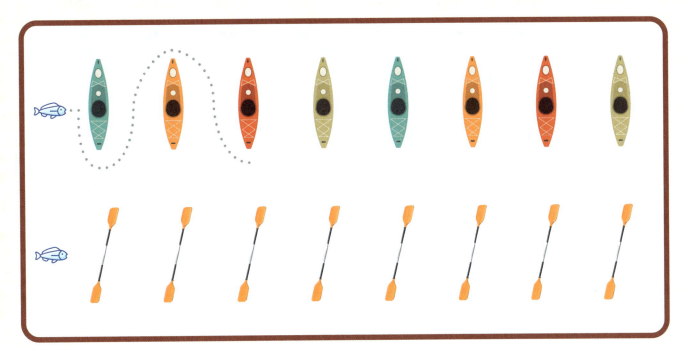

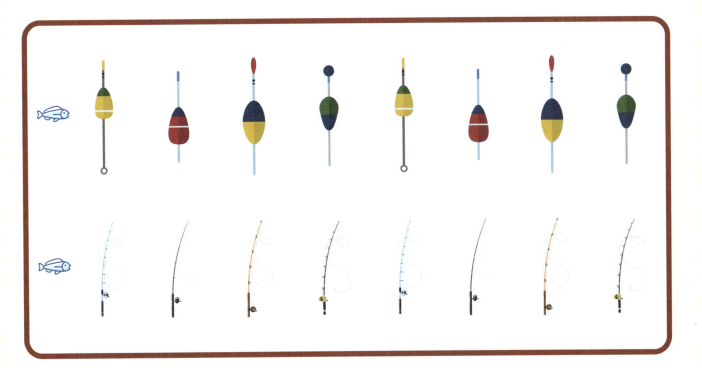

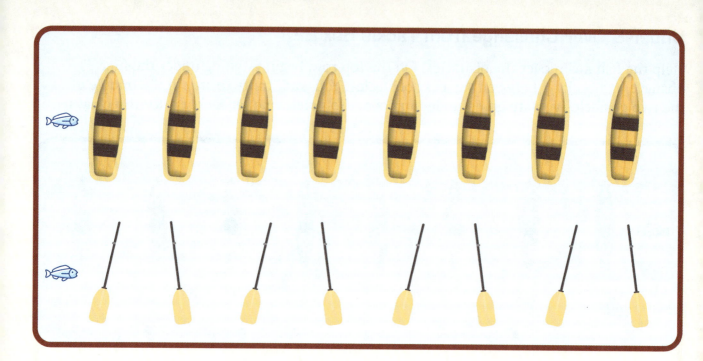

Warm-Ups Challenge from Bait & Tackle 27.1

Complete 2 lines each day, be sure to stay between the lines.

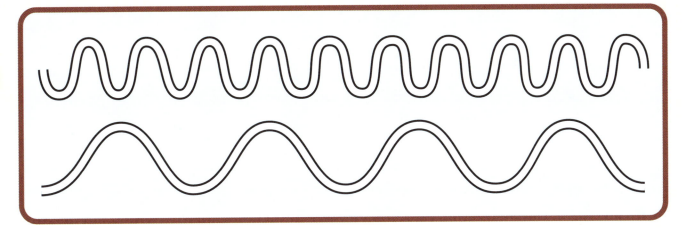

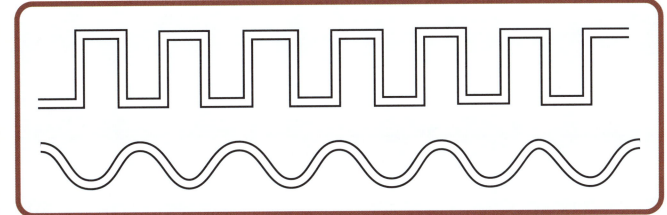

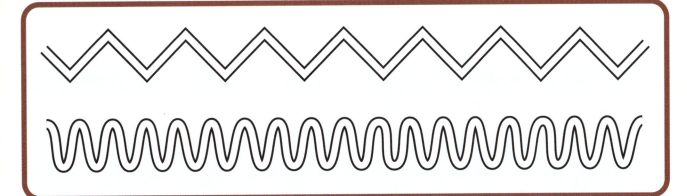

Warm-Ups Challenge 519

Intentionally left blank.

Warm-Ups Challenge from Bait & Tackle 30.3

Cutting helps build hand strength. Cut out a bucket and worm each day.

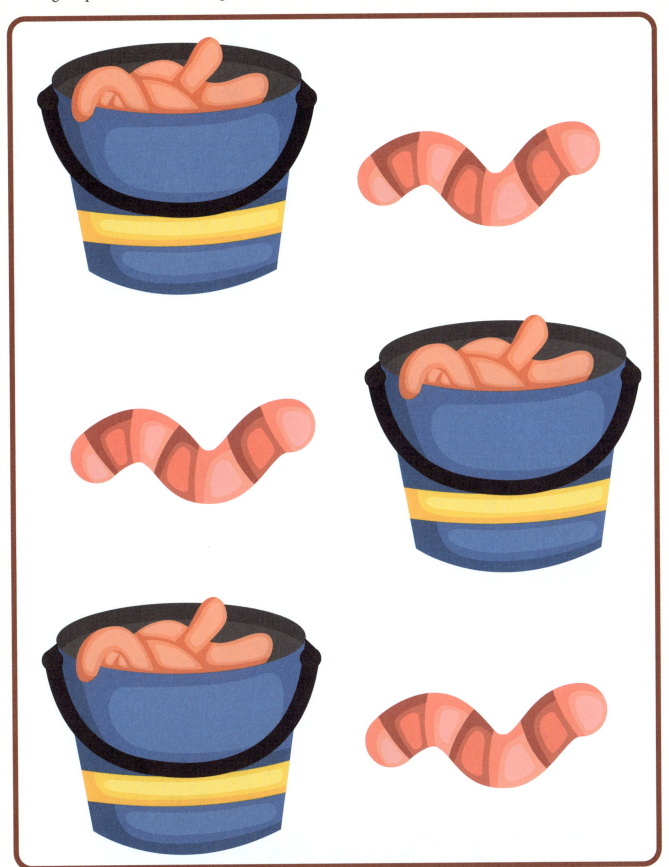

Warm-Ups Challenge 521

Intentionally left blank.

Seek & Find Challenge from Tackle Box 35

Find 7 differences.

Find 10 differences.

Seek & Find Challenge

Find nine differences.

Here's to Those Who Write with Their Left Hands!

Learning to write can be a difficult process for anyone. Learning to write left-handed when so many others write right-handed can be difficult, as well as frustrating. Many teachers simply say, "copy the letters," and give little or no special instruction for how the process works.

Here are some simple tips that can help students feel more joy in writing as a lefty!

- **The proper grasp:** There are many ways to hold a pen or pencil, but the best way for writing, by right or left-handed people, is to pinch the pen or pencil between your index finger and thumb and to let it rest on the middle finger. This can help reduce the hooked writing wrist that many left-handed writers have.

- **Where to grasp:** How to hold a pen or pencil is the first step. The second step is holding it a little more than an inch from the tip. Otherwise, when writing and moving your hand to the right, you won't be able to see the letters you've written. This also helps the writer avoid smudging the lead or ink.

- **The paper position:** Right-handed writers often angle their paper going up on the right-hand side. Left-handed writers should do the very opposite. Placing the left-hand side of the page higher than the right-hand side helps keep the hand in a normal writing position.

- **Holding the paper:** Just as right-handed writers will secure the paper they are writing on with their left hand, so left-handed writers should hold the paper with their right now. This will keep the paper from shifting around while they write.

Scope & Sequence — Semester 1

Week:	Day:	Focus:
1	1	movements & patterns
	2	movements & patterns
	3	movements & patterns
	4	movements & patterns
	5	movements & patterns
2	6	c
	7	c
	8	c
	9	a
	10	a
3	11	a
	12	d
	13	d
	14	d
	15	c–a–d
4	16	o
	17	o
	18	o
	19	g
	20	g
5	21	g
	22	q
	23	q
	24	q
	25	c–a–d–o–g–q
6	26	C
	27	C; c–a–d
	28	C; d–o–g
	29	A
	30	A; q–a–c
7	31	A; d–o–g
	32	O
	33	O; q–a–c
	34	O; d–a–c
	35	C–A–O
8	36	Q
	37	Q; C–A–O
	38	Q; a–c–d
	39	E
	40	E; o–g–q
9	41	E; C–A–O
	42	t
	43	t; d–o–g–q
	44	t; c–a–O–A
	45	Q–E–t

Week:	Day:	Focus:
10	46	i
	47	i; E–t–o–d–a
	48	i; O–c–t–q–E
	49	j
	50	j; t–o–a–d–g
11	51	j; C–A–E–c–a–q
	52	p
	53	p; c–a–d–o–g
	54	p; C–A–E–t
	55	i–j–p
12	56	s
	57	s; c–a–d–o–g
	58	s; i–C–A–O–t
	59	u
	60	u; Q–q–i–t–d
13	61	u; E–j–p–t
	62	w
	63	w; A–o–g–t–i
	64	w; j–a–p–o–d
	65	s–u–w
14	66	r
	67	r; c–a–d–o–g
	68	r; q–u–i–t–O–a
	69	e
	70	e; i–s–d–g–a
15	71	e; C–A–E–w
	72	l
	73	l; E–q–u–i–p
	74	l; j–u–s–t
	75	r–e–l
16	76	k
	77	k; w–r–o–t–e
	78	k; w–r–i–t–e
	79	b
	80	b; t–o–p–j–g
17	81	b; l–o–g–w–s
	82	f
	83	f; E–q–u–i–p
	84	f; A–C–a–e–c–t–w
	85	k–b–f
18	86	h
	87	h; h–e–l–p
	88	h; w–a–l–k
	89	n
	90	n; f–r–o–g

Scope & Sequence — Semester 2

Week:	Day:	Focus:
19	91	n; g–r–o–w
	92	m
	93	m; p–l–o–w–s
	94	m; g–u–a–r–d
	95	h–n–m
20	96	v
	97	v; s–u–r–e–j–t
	98	v; w–o–r–k–a–p
	99	y
	100	y; q–u–a–l–i–t
21	101	y; a–m–n–s–u–p
	102	D
	103	D; a–c–n–e–y–k
	104	D; a–d–g–e–c–b–n
	105	v–y–B
22	106	B
	107	B– B–a–s–e–d
	108	B; Ephesians 4:32
	109	P
	110	P; Matthew 24:13
23	111	P; E–q–u–i–p–e–d
	112	R
	113	R; Psalm 16:8
	114	R; h–o–r–n
	115	D–P–R
24	116	L
	117	L; Isaiah 40:31
	118	L; Isaiah 40:31
	119	M
	120	M; Isaiah 40:31
25	121	M; Galatians 6:9
	122	N
	123	N; Galatians 6:9
	124	N; Galatians 6:9
	125	L–M–N
26	126	U
	127	U; Psalm 118:29
	128	U; Psalm 118:29
	129	V
	130	V; Psalm 118:29
27	131	V; Psalm 118:14
	132	W
	133	W; Psalm 118:14
	134	W; Psalm 118:14
	135	U–V–W

Week:	Day:	Focus:
28	136	H
	137	H; Isaiah 43:19
	138	H; Isaiah 43:19
	139	T
	140	T; Isaiah 43:19
29	141	T; Proverbs 3:5
	142	F
	143	F; Proverbs 3:5
	144	F; Proverbs 3:5
	145	H–T–F
30	146	K
	147	K; 1 Peter 5:7
	148	K; 1 Peter 5:7
	149	G
	150	G; 1 Peter 5:7
31	151	G; Psalm 62:8
	152	I
	153	I; Psalm 62:8
	154	I; Psalm 62:8
	155	K–G–I
32	156	S
	157	S; 1 Corinthians 13:7
	158	S; 1 Corinthians 13:7
	159	J
	160	J; 1 Corinthians 13:7
33	161	J; Joshua 1:9
	162	x
	163	x; Joshua 1:9
	164	x; Joshua 1:9
	165	S–J–x
34	166	X
	167	X; Psalm 99:5
	168	X; Psalm 99:5
	169	Y
	170	Y; Psalm 99:5
35	171	Y; Jeremiah 29:11
	172	Z, z
	173	Z, z; Jeremiah 29:11
	174	Z, z Jeremiah 29:11
	175	X–Y–Z–z
36	176	Apply: Joel 3:16
	177	Apply: Romans 12:21
	178	Apply: 1 Chronicles 16:11
	179	Apply: Galatians 6:9
	180	Apply: James 1:12

Cursive Letter Practice Chart

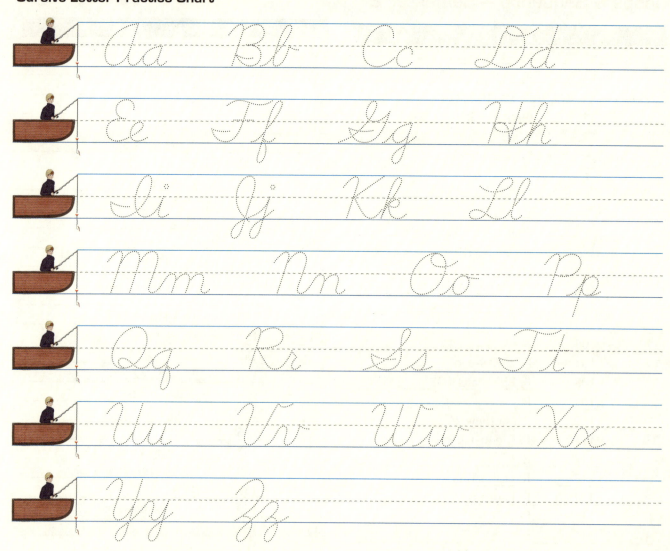

Photo Credits:

All Skeeter, Susie, and Anna illustrations by Katie O'Dell.
T-top, B-bottom, L-left, R-right, C-center
All images gettyimages.com unless stated.
CT.gov: p. 212 (Longnose Dace [both], Common Shiner [left facing], Ninespine Stickleback)
Public Domain: p. 212 (Emerald shiner, Common shiner [right facing], Pimephales promelas, Phoxinus eos, Pearl dace) p. 253, p. 308B (Michigan Department of Natural Resources), p. 404MR (Kansas City District U.S. Army Corps of Engineers),
Shutterstock.com: p. 140M, p. 152B (Grand-Duc), p. 169, p. 301 (maze), p. 413 (maze)
Wikimedia Commons: p. 47 (Chad Sparkes), p. 92B (Alus164), p 97 (Susan Bell), p. 205 (Reinhold MoÃàller), p. 321 (Shutinc), p. 329 (Nanamac47), p. 417 (Thamizhpparithi Maari), p. 421R (Forest & Kim Starr)
Images from Wikimedia Commons are used under the CC-BY-SA-2.0, CC-BY-SA-3.0 or the CC-BY-SA-4.0 license.